WITHDRAWN

Amer   Fiction

D1602848

Also available in this series:

Native American Literatures: An Introduction, by Suzanne Lundquist
Irish Fiction: An Introduction, by Kersti Tarien Powell

Forthcoming in this series:
Fantasy Fiction: An Introduction, by Lucie Armitt
Horror Fiction: An Introduction, by Gina Wisker
Crime Fiction: An Introduction, by Alistair Wisker
Science Fiction: An Introduction, by Pat Wheeler

American Gothic Fiction: An Introduction

ALLAN LLOYD-SMITH

continuum
NEW YORK • LONDON

2004

The Continuum International Publishing Group Inc
15 East 26 Street, New York, NY 10010

The Continuum International Publishing Group Ltd
The Tower Building, 11 York Road, London SE1 7NX

www.continuumbooks.com

Printed in the United States of America

Library of Congress Cataloging-in-Publication Data

Lloyd Smith, Allan, 1945–
   American gothic fiction : an introduction / Allan Lloyd-Smith.
      p. cm. — (Continuum studies in literary genre)
   Includes bibliographical references (p.) and index.
   ISBN 0-8264-1594-6 (alk paper) — ISBN 0-8264-1595-4 (pbk. : alk. paper)
      1. American fiction—History and criticism. 2. Gothic revival (Literature)—
United States. 3. Horror tales, American—History and criticism. I. Tile. II.
Series.
   PS374.G68L58 2004
   813'.0872909—dc22
                                                        2004013380

Contents

Dedication

To the students of my American Gothic seminars at the
University of East Anglia, Norwich.

Shadows present, foreshadowing deeper shadows to come.
Herman Melville, "Benito Cereno"

Acknowledgments

Thanks are due to the University of East Anglia for assistance through study leave and teaching remission, and to the University of East Anglia Library and Cambridge University Library for academic resources. A particular debt is owed to the International Gothic Association, whose regular biannual conferences have helped me to develop some of the following arguments.

Parts of Chapters Three and Four have appeared in somewhat different form in Blackwell's *A Companion to the Gothic*, edited by David Punter (London: Blackwell Publishers, 2000), and in *The Handbook of Gothic Literature*, edited by Marie Mulvey-Roberts (London: Macmillan Press, 1998). I am grateful to the publishers for permission to repeat my arguments in these contributions, and to Macmillan for permission to recapitulate some of the material in my earlier book on the Gothic uncanny, *Uncanny American Fiction* (London: Macmillan Press, 1989).

Introduction

"Can't repeat the past?" he cried incredulously. "Why of course you can!"[1]

The Great Gatsby

What Jay Gatsby refuses to see in his bright confidence is that the past is over: the message of Gothic on the other hand is that it isn't so much a matter of whether you can repeat the past as whether the past will repeat itself in you.

Gatsby winds up dead in his swimming pool, taking the rap for Daisy who has used and abandoned him again just as she had in their youth. *The Great Gatsby* is not a Gothic novel but, like many twentieth-century American fictions, it does employ Gothic tropes: the city as labyrinth; the imprisoned maiden/femme fatale motif; the wasteland wilderness "Valley of Ashes" presided over by the billboard of panoptican optician Dr. T. J. Eckleburgh, the mad-scientist god of the wasteland; the sadistic accident in which Myrtle Wilson's left breast is ripped off by Gatsby's speeding yellow Rolls, with Daisy at the wheel; the scene of Gatsby's death when a shadowy, ashen figure comes out of the trees to kill him.

Gatsby's mistake, and perhaps the honor in his failure, is to believe that the past can be superseded, transfigured, overcome by the valiant present—a very American assumption—the Gothic, however, is about the *return* of the past, of the repressed and denied, the buried secret that subverts and corrodes the present, whatever the culture does not want to know or admit, will not or dare not tell itself.

Any study of a genre is a study of repetitions, the patterns that constitute a tradition and the way that writers imitate, learn from, and modify the work of their predecessors: Poe from the German Gothicists and Brown from Godwin, Hawthorne from Brown and

1

Poe, James from Hawthorne, and so on. Repetition is a hallmark of the Gothic in another sense too, as Freud identified repetition as one of the central characteristics of the uncanny. So Gothic characters are often shown as struggling in a web of repetitions caused by their unawareness of their own unconscious drives and motives. And repetition figures in a Gothic understanding of trauma, and of Freud's *nachträglichkeit*, when an experience is fully felt only in its echoing repetition at another time, as we see in Tony Morrison's *Beloved*.

This book will offer repetitions of its own, looking sometimes at the same texts, usually those readily available, from different perspectives, in the understanding that its readers cannot be expected to bring to it any extensive previous knowledge of American Gothic. Gilman's story "The Yellow Wallpaper," or Melville's "Benito Cereno," for example, will appear in several places, with brief recapitulation so that it will make sense in each context, whether of "Key Texts," "Major Themes," or "Key Questions." In this way a deepening knowledge of such significant Gothic pieces should follow from reading through the book, while individual chapters may be read independently.

Notes

1. F. Scott Fitzgerald, *The Great Gatsby*, 1925 (Harmondsworth, England: Penguin Books, 1984) p. 102.

Chapter One

What Is American Gothic?

It is frequently assumed that Gothic fiction began as a lurid offshoot from a dominant tradition of largely realist and morally respectable fiction. Gothic's representations of extreme circumstances of terror, oppression and persecution, darkness and obscurity of setting, and innocence betrayed are considered to begin with Horace Walpole's *The Castle of Otranto* (1764), and to reach a crescendo in Ann Radcliffe's *Mysteries of Udolpho* (1794) and Matthew G. "Monk" Lewis's *The Monk* (1796). But genre-defining works such as these also retrospectively redefine their precursors, making it apparent that Gothic elements can also be seen even in the earlier works that began the English novel tradition: Samuel Richardson's epistolary tales of seduction and betrayal, *Pamela* (1740) and *Clarissa* (1747–1748), Defoe's *Moll Flanders* (1722); and even long before them in the romance tradition, or in Thomas Nashe's picaresque *The Unfortunate Traveller* (1594); along with parts of Shakespeare's plays and much Jacobean tragedy.

Similarly it has been assumed that early American writing should be considered an offshoot of the "Great Tradition," as F. R. Leavis called it, a "subaltern" we might now say, in post-colonialist terms, and largely imitative if eccentric version of the dominant culture. It is true that an imitative strain can be found in, for example, Charles Brockden Brown's novels, *Wieland* (1798), *Arthur Mervyn* (1799), or *Ormond* (1799). American writers were effectively still a part of the British culture, working in an English language domain and exposed, both intellectually and in terms of their market place, to British models. But on closer examination it is evident that their models were highly specific: Brown's principal model was William Godwin, author of *Caleb Williams* (1794) and also of *Political Justice*

(1796). Brown in turn influenced the British writers, among them, reciprocally, Godwin himself, and his daughter Mary Shelley, author of *Frankenstein* (1818). From the earliest period of American Gothicism—and some critics have seen almost the whole of American writing as a Gothic literature[1]—differences in American circumstances led American Gothicists in other directions: less toward Walpole and Radcliffe, perhaps, more toward Godwin and James Hogg's *Confessions of a Justified Sinner* (1824); or, in Poe's case, the extravagant sensationalism of *Blackwood's Edinburgh Monthly Magazine*.[2] Rather than a simple matter of imitation and adaptation, substituting the wilderness and the city for the subterranean rooms and corridors of the monastery, or the remote house for the castle, dark and dangerous woods for the bandit infested mountains of Italy, certain unique cultural pressures led Americans to the Gothic as an expression of their very different conditions.

Among these American pressures were the frontier experience, with its inherent solitude and potential violence; the Puritan inheritance; fear of European subversion and anxieties about popular democracy which was then a new experiment; the relative absence of developed "society"; and very significantly, racial issues concerning both slavery and the Native Americans. That these circumstances invited and even required a Gothic style is shown by the inclusion of "Gothic" elements within such clearly non-Gothic texts as James Fenimore Cooper's *The Spy* (1821), or *The Prairie* (1827). Such texts are not so much working to *adapt* the Gothic mode; instead the Gothic emerges from the conditions they seek to describe.

Strict interpreters of the Gothic as a genre would perhaps agree with Maurice Lévy's insistence that the true period of Gothic, and its cultural, aesthetic, religious, and political background, was from about 1764 to 1824, the period of the first Gothic Revival, and the culture of Georgian England.[3] Lévy acknowledges however that the term has now become of much broader application and popular understanding, and has been used to describe texts ranging from *Wuthering Heights* (1847) to William Gibson's *Neuromancer* or *Buffy the Vampire Slayer*. "Gothic," for Lévy, "conjures up images of female innocence engaged in labyrinthine pursuits and threatened by monarchal or baronial lubricity—in scenes which only Salvador

Rosa could have delineated" (2). There is truth in that description, but it is also not hard to see how Gothic might also describe, say, the situation of a runaway slave pursued by dogs, or the black man encountered by St. John de Crèvecoeur during his afternoon stroll to lunch at a plantation: a man suspended in a cage from a tree, without water, and assailed by insects and the birds who have pecked out his eyes.[4] After all, William Godwin's *Caleb Williams*, one of the originary Gothic texts, details the persecution throughout the land of a servant who has learned of his master's crimes. Most readers would now also think "Gothic" an appropriate description of Anne Rice's *Interview with the Vampire* or Poppy Z. Brite's *Lost Souls*.

Hallmarks of the Gothic include a pushing toward extremes and excess, and that, of course, implies an investigation of limits. In exploring extremes, whether of cruelty, rapacity and fear, or passion and sexual degradation, the Gothic tends to reinforce, if only in a novel's final pages, culturally prescribed doctrines of morality and propriety. The sensationalism of this at first almost universally deplored yet extremely popular form of writing allowed for a vicarious experience of forbidden excess, with punishment and retribution offered in the eventual return to psychic normality. The Gothic deals in transgressions and negativity, perhaps in reaction against the optimistic rationalism of its founding era, which allowed for a rethinking of the prohibitions and sanctions that had previously seemed divinely ordained but now appeared to be simply social agreements in the interest of progress and civic stability. Free-thinking characters appear frequently in the Gothic, and they are generally up to no good, disbelieving in the significance of virginity, for example (while obsessively eager to deflower those who maintain it), and proclaiming their own superiority and inherent freedom as rational beings above the shibboleths of convention and religious faith. Their prey are innocents who put their trust in the benevolence and right thinking of others, and it is not difficult to see in these contrasts that the Gothic is in essence a reactionary form, like the detective novel, one that explores chaos and wrongdoing in a movement toward the ultimate restitution of order and convention. As with the detective novel, the form allows the thrill of readerly experience of transgression within a safe and moralizing pattern of

closure. Because of the ongoing confrontation between these opposing forces, the Gothic situates itself in areas of liminality, of transition, at first staged literally in liminal spaces and between opposing
individuals, but subsequently appearing more and more as divisions
between opposing aspects within the self. Extreme polarities of
lightness and darkness, black and white ascriptions of evil and virtue
(and, in the American case, of racial assumptions and identifications), both outside and sometimes within the self, are focused upon
in this attention to the liminal.

Among the extremes and taboos that the Gothic explores are
religious profanities, demonism, occultism, necromancy, and incest.
This can be interpreted as a dark side of Enlightenment free-
thinking or the persistence of an increasingly excluded occultist tradition in western culture, one which paradoxically insisted on an
acknowledgment of the continuing existence of magic, religious, and
demonic forces within a more and more secular society.[5] Much of
the apparent supernaturalism in the Gothic is ultimately explained
away, as in the "explained supernaturalism" of Radcliffe's romances,
but on the other hand, much is not. Here science plays a paradoxical role, explaining the previously inexplicable, but also pointing to
new and sometimes sinister capacities bordering on the miraculous.
The mad scientist and the ill-advised experiment play major roles
in Gothic fictions. Science might be seen as pushing rationalism
toward its limits, but in the Gothic it was often shown to include
connections to occultist pre-scientific doctrines, as in Mary Shelley's
account of the university education of her Dr. Frankenstein. In this
and other respects the Gothic merges with supernaturalism and the
fantastic, drawing on folktales and histories of the grotesque monstrosity supposed to result from any meddling with Nature. Cogent
distinctions have been made between the supernatural or mar-
velous, the fantastic, and the uncanny,[6] all of which appear in Gothic
texts but change over time, so that by the later nineteenth century
the uncanny is seen as increasingly dominant when the Gothic
probes deeper into psychological areas, as in Henry James's cele-
brated ghost story, *The Turn of the Screw* (1898).

Gothic interest in extreme states and actions can also be seen to
correlate with widespread social anxieties and fears. Significant
among these are fears having to do with the suppressions of past

traumas and guilt, anxieties concerning class and gender, fear of revolution, worries about the developing powers of science; an increasing suspicion that empire and colonial experience might bring home an unwanted legacy (a suspicion related to xenophobia but also involving a fear of colonial otherness and practices such as Voodoo); post-Darwinian suggestions of possible regression or atavism; and displaced versions of the dread occasioned by syphilis, or much later, by AIDS.

Among the most striking features of the Gothic genre is the style of its architectural settings. In early Gothic these were often medievalist, involving ancient stone buildings with elaborate, "Gothic" arches, buttresses, passageways, and crypts. This was to become the *mise en scene* of Gothicism, replete with trappings of hidden doorways and secret chambers, incomprehensible labyrinths, speaking portraits, and trapdoors. In some respects this was an aspect of the new pleasure in lost "pastness" that intrigued Romantics, an aesthetic appreciation of a previously scorned inheritance. An element no doubt was also distaste for the changes brought by increasing commerce and industrialism that inspired nostalgia for the supposedly simpler and more pleasing structures of the past. But it was also an expression of fear of those structures and the oppressive society they suggested, as the drawings of Piranesi so powerfully indicate. Endless prisons filled with balconies and buttresses that confuse perspective loom over primitive instruments of torture in these studies. Piranesi also serves well to illustrate the *atmosphere* of the Gothic, a chiaroscuro of shadows and indeterminate illumination inducing a sense of futility, despair, and the loss of hope among brutal realities of cruel and conscienceless power. The impression is awful, but also sublime.

Landscapes in the Gothic similarly dwelt on the exposed, inhuman and pitiless nature of mountains, crags, and wastelands. In time these tropes of atmosphere, architecture, and landscape became as much metaphorical as actual, so that a simple house, a room or cellar, could become a Gothic setting, and the mere use of darkness or barrenness could call up the Gothic mood. We could dismiss these trappings as trivial stage machinery, as many critics have in preferring the deeper psychological implications of Gothic novels and stories, or we might, with recent critic Eve Kosofsky Sedgwick, refocus attention on the nature of Gothic *surfaces*, to see what can be read from them.[7] But from an early stage such features can be read as a kind of proto-expressionism, articulating in settings the emotional states within the narrative, as we see in the writing of Edgar Allan Poe.

Ann Radcliffe stressed the importance of *terror* as opposed to *horror*, a distinction that is often blurred in other Gothic works such as M. G. Lewis's *The Monk*, but which nevertheless does offer some useful ways to talk about the emotional affect that is privileged here. In Gothic the terror of what might happen, or might be happening, is largely foregrounded over the visceral horror of the event. But both are frequently present at once in an interplay not unlike the interplay between reason and emotion, unreason and passion. These states are both opposed and related to one another, often in the mind of a protagonist who hovers indecisively between them; and in parallel, in the narrative itself which veers from rational explanation to emotion and intuition. The terror may be unreasonable, but, as we shall see, for example, in Melville's "Benito Cereno" (1856), the more terrible explanation is often the truth, and the horror cannot be averted.

Behind the states of fear and horror, and driving through the tissue of reasonable and rational explanations, loom the outlines of real horrors. In early Gothic this was sometimes the reality of the oppression of women, or children, in a patriarchy that denied them rights. In American Gothic, while this remained a major theme, the trauma and guilt of race and slavery, or fear of what was then called miscegenation, also emerges, along with the settlers' terror of the Indians and the wilderness, and later perhaps some suppressed recognition of Native American genocide. One of the great strengths of the Gothic is its ability to articulate the voice of the "other" within its fancy-dress disguise of stylized contestations. A woman murdered and walled-up in a cellar, her body discovered through the howling of a buried cat, might be read as a voicing of silenced domestic atrocity, and also as connected obliquely with slavery motifs, whether or not that was in fact Poe's explicit "intention" in his story "The Black Cat."[8] In the British novels of the early Gothic the feudal antagonists arguably embody in some respects an emergent middle class anxiety about the previously dominant and still powerful aristocracy, while the religious tyrants of monastery, convent, and inquisition suggest a Protestant distrust and fear of Catholicism. Scenes of disruption, mob action, and even possibly such creatures as Frankenstein's creation may be representative of a fear of the burgeoning working class and a risk of class revolution. While this also holds true to an extent in American Gothic, it is possible to trace certain other social, political, and class fears, such as the fear and distaste generated against specific immigrant groups: the Irish in the mid-nineteenth century, southern and eastern Europeans and Asians later in the century, or against homosexuality in the twentieth century. As David Punter puts it in *The Literature of Terror*, "the middle class displaces the violence of present social structures, conjures them up again as past, and promptly falls under their spell." But the relationship of Gothic to cultural and historical realities is like that of dream, clearly somehow "about" certain fantasies and anxieties, less than coherent in its expression of them.

Notes

1. Leslie Fiedler, for example, in *Love and Death in the American Novel* (1960) says that American literature was from the first "a gothic fiction, non-realistic and negative, sadist and melodramatic." (New York: Delta, 1966) p. 29.

2. When it began in 1817 it was called the *Edinburgh Monthly Magazine*, later *Blackwood's*.

3. Maurice Lévy, "Gothic and the Critical Idiom," in *Gothick: Origins and Innovations*, Allan Lloyd-Smith and Victor Sage, eds. (Amsterdam: Editions Rodopi, 1994) pp. 4, 8.

4. Hector St. John de Crèvecoeur, *Letters From an American Farmer*, 1782.

5. On the occultist tradition, see John Senior, *The Way Down and Out: Occultism in Symbolist Literature* (Ithaca, NY: Cornell University Press, 1959).

6. See Tzvetan Todorov, *The Fantastic* (Ithaca, NY: Cornell University Press, 1975).

7. Eve Kosofsky Sedgwick, *The Persistence of Gothic Conventions* (New York: Methuen, 1986).

8. See Leslie Ginsberg, "Slavery and the Gothic Horror of Poe's 'The Black Cat,'" in *American Gothic: New Interventions in a National Narrative*, Robert Martin and Eric Savoy, eds. (Iowa City: University of Iowa Press, 1998).

Chapter Two

Timeline

(American works are asterisked. Not all of these texts are "Gothic" in full, but they contain Gothic elements.)

1662	*Michael Wigglesworth, "The Day of Doom" sermon
1692–1693	**Salem Witchcraft trials**
1693	*Cotton Mather *The Wonders of the Invisible World* (account of supposed Salem witchcraft written at the request of the judges)
1741	*Jonathan Edwards, "Sinners in the Hands of an Angry God" sermon
1745	Edward Young, "Night Thoughts"
1746	Dom Augustine Calmet, Treatise on Vampires and Revenants: The Phantom World
1748	Samuel Richardson, *Clarissa*
1750	Thomas Gray, "Elegy in a Country Churchyard" (poetry)
1756	Edmund Burke, *A Philosophical Enquiry into the Origin of our Ideas of the Sublime and Beautiful*
1760	James Macpherson, *Ossian* (poetry, passed off as ancient)
1762	Richard Hurd, *Letters on Chivalry and Romance*
1764	Horace Walpole, *The Castle of Otranto;* reissued 1765
1765	Thomas Percy, *Reliques* (collection of ballads)
1768	Horace Walpole, *The Mysterious Mother*

1772	Jacques Cazotte, *The Devil in Love*
1775	**The American War of Independence**
1777	Clara Reeve, *The Old English Baron*
1781	Friedrich Schiller, *Die Rauber* (*The Robbers*) staged in Germany
1782	*Hector St. John de Crèvecouer, *Letters From an American Farmer*
1783	**The American War of Independence ends;** Sophia Lee, *The Recess*
1786	William Beckford, *Vatheck*
1789	**The French Revolution;** Anne Radcliffe, *The Castles of Athlin and Dunbayne* (published anonymously); Friedrich Schiller, *Der Geisterseher* (*The Ghostseer, or, The Apparitionist*)
1790	Anne Radcliffe, *The Romance of the Forest*, and *A Sicilian Romance*; Edmund Burke, *Reflections on the Revolution in France*
1792	Mary Wollstonecraft (mother of the author of *Frankenstein*, Mary Shelley), *A Vindication of the Rights of Women*
1793	Charlotte Smith, *The Old Manor House*
1794	Anne Radcliffe, *The Mysteries of Udolpho;* William Godwin (father of Mary Shelley), *Things as They Are; or, The Adventures of Caleb Williams;* Carl Friedrich Kahlert, *The Necromancer* (English trans.); Regina Maria Roche, *The Children of the Abbey*
1795	Cajetan Tschink, *The Victim of Magical Delusion*
1796	Matthew Gregory Lewis, *The Monk;* American publication of Friedrich Schiller, *Der Geisterseher* (*The Ghostseer*); Anne Radcliffe, *The Castles of Athlin and Dunblane;* Regina Maria Roche, *The Children of the Abbey;* Eliza Parsons, *The Mysterious Warning;* William Godwin, *Political Justice*
1797	Anne Radcliffe, *The Italian*, in both English and American editions; American edition of Clara Reeve,

	The Old English Baron (1778); Karl Grosse, *Horrid Mysteries*
1798	*Charles Brockden Brown, *Wieland; or, The Transformation*; Regina Maria Roche, *The Children of the Abbey* (American edition); Francis Lathom, *The Midnight Bell*; Regina Maria Roche, *Clermont*; Wordsworth and Coleridge, *Lyrical Ballads* (poetry); *Charles Brockden Brown, *Alcuin; or, The Rights of Women*; Matthew Lewis, *The Castle Spectre*
1799	*Charles Brockden Brown, *Edgar Huntley* and *Ormond; or, The Secret Witness*; and *Arthur Mervyn* (1799–1800); William Godwin, *St Leon: A Tale of the Sixteenth Century*; *Philip Freneau, "The House of Night" (poem)
1803	Jane Austen writes *Northanger Abbey* (published 1818)
1805	Charlotte Dacre, *Zofloya, or, The Moor*
1807	**Slave trade banned in British Empire;** Charles Robert Maturin, *Fatal Revenge; or, The Family of Montiori*
1810	Percy Shelley, *Zastrozzi*
1811	*Isaac Mitchell, *The Asylum; or, Alonzo and Melissa; An American Tale, Founded on Fact*
1815	**Slave trade banned in French possessions;** E. T. A. Hoffman's "The Sandman" (in Germany)
1816	Sophia Lee, *The Recess*; E. T. A. Hoffman, *The Devil's Elixirs*, "The Sandman"
1817	Lord Byron, Mary and Percy Shelley, and John Polidori amuse themselves in writing ghost stories near Geneva; *Frankenstein* and Polidori's *The Vampyre* result; Walter Scott, *The Antiquary*; William Godwin, *Mandeville*; Byron, *Manfred* (dramatic poem)
1818	Mary Shelley, *Frankenstein*; Thomas Love Peacock, *Nightmare Abbey*; Jane Austen, *Northanger Abbey*; *Washington Irving, "Rip Van Winkle"

1819	Percy Shelley, *The Cenci* (poetry); John Polidori, *The Vampyre* (published under Byron's name); Walter Scott, *The Bride of Lammermoor*
1820	Charles Robert Maturin, *Melmoth the Wanderer*; J. R. Planché, *The Vampyre, A Romantic Melodrama in Two Acts*
1821	*James Fenimore Cooper, *The Spy*; *Richard Henry Dana, Sr., "Paul Felton"
1822	*Washington Irving, *The Sketch Book of Geoffrey Crayon, Gent.* and *Bracebridge Hall*; *Washington Allston, *Monaldi* (not published until1841); *John Neal, *Logan* (involves mysterious voices, cf. *Wieland*)
1823	*James K. Paulding, *Koningsmarke* (includes a black slave, thought to be a witch)
1824	*Washington Irving, *Tales of A Traveller*, includes "The Adventure of the German Student;" James Hogg, *The Confessions of a Justified Sinner*
1826	*James Fenimore Cooper, *The Last of the Mohicans*
1827	*Hamel the Obeah Man* (Jamaica, anon); *James Fenimore Cooper, *The Prairie*
1828	*John Neal, *Rachel Dyer* (Salem witchcraft)
1829	*James Fenimore Cooper, *The Wept of Wish-ton-Wish* (Gothic episode)
1830	*Nathaniel Hawthorne, "The Hollow of the Three Hills;" *James Fenimore Cooper, *The Water-Witch* (optical trickery); Walter Scott, *Letters on Demonology and Witchcraft*
1831	*James K. Paulding, *The Dutchman's Fireside* (contains comic Gothic); *History of Mary Prince* (black autobiography, Barbados); *James Fenimore Cooper, *The Bravo* (historical novel of Venetian intrigues)
1832	*Nathaniel Hawthorne, "My Kinsman Major Molineux;" *James Fenimore Cooper, *The Heidenmauer; or, the Benedictines, A Legend of the Rhine*; *Washington Irving, *The Alhambra*

1833	*William Gilmore Simms, *Martin Faber*; *Edgar Allan Poe, "MS Found in a Bottle"
1835	*Edgar Allan Poe, "Morella"; *Nathaniel Hawthorne, "Young Goodman Brown," and "The Haunted Mind"; Rebecca Reed, *Six Months in a Convent*
1836	*Nathaniel Hawthorne, *Twice Told-Tales*: "The Minister's Black Veil," "The May-Pole of Merry Mount"; Théophile Gautier, *La morte amoreuse* ("The Beautiful Dead," vampire story); *Robert Montgomery Bird, *Sheppard Lee* (reincarnation); *Maria Monk, *Awful Disclosures of . . . the Hotel dieu Nunnery at Montreal*
1837	*Robert Montgomery Bird, *Nick of the Woods*; Dickens, *Oliver Twist*; *Nathaniel Hawthorne, "The Prophetic Pictures"
1838	*Edgar Allen Poe, "How to Write a Blackwood's Article"; *The Narrative of Arthur Gordon Pym of Nantucket*; *Nathaniel Hawthorne, "Howe's Masquerade"
1839	*Edgar Allan Poe, *Tales of the Grotesque and Arabesque* (includes "Ligeia," "Berenice," "William Wilson," "The Fall of the House of Usher," and "The Conversation of Eiros and Charmion")
1840	*Edgar Allan Poe, "The Man of the Crowd"
1841	*Edgar Allan Poe, "A Descent into the Maelstrom," "The Colloquoy of Monos and Una"
1842	*Edgar Allan Poe, "The Pit and the Pendulum," "The Masque of the Red Death"; Eugène Sue, *The Mysteries of Paris*; W. M. Reynolds, *The Mysteries of London* (serialization—continued until 1856); Edward Bulwer-Lytton, *Zanoni*
1843	*Second volume of Edgar Allan Poe, *Tales* ("The Tell-Tale Heart," "The Black Cat"); *Nathaniel Hawthorne, "The Birth-Mark"

1844	*Nathaniel Hawthorne, "Rappaccini's Daughter"; *Edgar Allan Poe, "A Tale of the Ragged Mountains," "Premature Burial"; *George Lippard, *The Quaker City or, the Monks of Monk Hall;* G. W. M. Reynolds, *The Mysteries of London* (1844–1848)
1845	*Edgar Allan Poe, "The Raven," "The Imp of the Perverse," and "The Facts in the Case of M. Valdemar"
1846	*Edgar Allan Poe, "The Cask of Amontillado"; *Nathaniel Hawthorne, *Mosses From an Old Manse*
1847	Emily Brontë, *Wuthering Heights;* Charlotte Brontë, *Jane Eyre;* James Rymer, *Varney the Vampire*
1848	**Year of Revolution in France;** *Edgar Allan Poe, *Eureka* (cosmological philosophical essay)
1849	**Edgar Allan Poe dies in mysterious circumstances in Baltimore;** William Harrison Ainsworth, *The Lancashire Witches*
1850	*Nathaniel Hawthorne, *The Scarlet Letter,* "Ethan Brand"; *Herman Melville, *Moby-Dick*
1851	*Nathaniel Hawthorne, *The House of the Seven Gables;* Sheridan Le Fanu, *Ghost Stories and Tales of Mystery*
1852	*Harriet Beecher Stowe, *Uncle Tom's Cabin* (includes Gothic episodes); *Herman Melville, *Pierre, or The Ambiguities;* *Nathaniel Hawthorne, *The Blithedale Romance* (some Gothic episodes); Charles Dickens, *Bleak House*
1853	Charlotte Brontë, *Villette*
1856	*Herman Melville, *The Piazza Tales,* "Benito Cereno," and "The Bell Tower"
1859	Charles Darwin, *The Origin of the Species;* Edward Bulwer-Lytton, "The Haunters and the Haunted: or The House and the Brain"; George Eliot, "The Lifted Veil"
1860	**American Civil War begins;** *Nathaniel Hawthorne, *The Marble Faun;* Wilkie Collins, *The Woman in White*

1863	**American Emancipation Proclamation**
1864	J. Sheridan Le Fanu, *Uncle Silas*
1865	**End of American Civil War**
1866	*Louisa May Alcott, "Behind a Mask: or, A Woman's Power"
1868	Wilkie Collins, *The Moonstone*
1869	Charles Dickens, *The Mystery of Edwin Drood* (unfinished)
1871	Charles Darwin, *The Descent of Man*
1872	J. Sheridan Le Fanu, *In a Glass Darkly* (includes the famous female vampire story "Carmilla")
1880	*William Dean Howells, *The Undiscovered Country*
1881	*Henry James, *The Portrait of a Lady*
1885	**Legal penalties against homosexuality increased by the Labouchère Amendment in Britain;** H. Rider Haggard, *King Solomon's Mines*
1886	Robert Louis Stevenson, *The Strange Case of Dr. Jekyll and Mr. Hyde*; H. Rider Haggard, *She*
1890	*William Dean Howells, *The Shadow of a Dream*; Arthur Machen, *The Great God Pan*; Vernon Lee, *Hauntings*
1891	Charlotte Perkins Gilman, "The Yellow Wallpaper"; Oscar Wilde, *The Portrait of Dorian Gray*; *Ambrose Bierce, *Tales of Soldiers and Civilians*
1892	*Ambrose Bierce, *In the Midst of Life* (stories)
1893	*Ambrose Bierce, *Can Such Things Be?* (stories)
1894	Arthur Machen, *The Great God Pan* and *The Inmost Light*
1895	*Robert W. Chambers, *The King in Yellow*; *Frank Norris *Vandover and the Brute* (published in 1914); Marie Corelli, *The Sorrows of Satan*; George MacDonald, *Lilith*; Arthur Machen, *The Three Imposters*
1896	*Harold Frederic, *The Damnation of Theron Ware*; H. G. Wells, *The Island of Dr. Moreau*

1897	Bram Stoker, *Dracula*; *Emma Dawson, *The Itinerant House* (stories); Richard Marsh, *The Beetle*
1898	*Henry James, *The Turn of the Screw*
1899	*Frank Norris, *McTeague*; Sigmund Freud, *The Interpretation of Dreams*
1900	*Stephen Crane, *Maggie: A Girl of the Streets* (Gothic episodes)
1901	*Henry James, *The Sacred Fount* (telepathy)
1902	*Henry James, *The Wings of the Dove*; Joseph Conrad, *Heart of Darkness*
1903	*Mary E. Wilkins Freeman, *The Wind in the Rosebush*; Bram Stoker, *The Jewel of Seven Stars*; *William Dean Howells, *Questionable Shapes*
1904	*Henry James, *The Golden Bowl*; M. R. James, *Ghost Stories of an Antiquary*
1907	*William Dean Howells, *Between the Dark and the Daylight* (stories); *Jack London, *The Iron Heel*; Arthur Machen, *The Hill of Dreams*
1908	*Henry James, "The Jolly Corner"; William Hope Hodgson, *The House on the Borderland*
1910	*Edith Wharton, "The Eyes"
1911	Bram Stoker, *The Lair of the White Worm*; *F. Marion Crawford, *Wandering Ghosts*
1914–1918	**First World War**
1914	*Edith Wharton, "The Triumph of Night"; Otto Rank, *The Double* (psychoanalysis)
1915	*Edith Wharton, "Kerfol"
1917	*Henry James, *The Sense of the Past*
1918	**Suffrage for British women**
1919	**Suffrage for American women**; Sigmund Freud, "Das Unheimliche" ("The Uncanny"); *James Branch Cabell, *Jurgen*; Robert Wiene, dir., *The Cabinet of Dr. Caligari*
1920	Sigmund Freud, "Beyond the Pleasure Principle"

1922	F. W. Murneau, dir., *Nosferatu* (German film based on *Dracula*); David Lindsay, *The Haunted Woman*
1925	*Edith Wharton, "Bewitched," and "Miss Mary Pask"
1927	*Howard Phillips Lovecraft, *The Case of Charles Dexter Ward*
1929	George de Lisser, *The White Witch of Rosehall* (West Indian Gothic)
1930	Katherine Ann Porter, "Flowering Judas"
1931	*William Faulkner, *Sanctuary*; *Edith Wharton, "Pomegranate Seed"; Todd Browning, dir., *Dracula* (with Bella Lugosi, Universal); James Whale, dir., *Frankenstein* (with Boris Karloff, Paramount)
1932	*William Faulkner, *Light in August*; Karl Freund, dir., *The Mummy* (with Boris Karloff, Universal); Victor Halperin, dir., *White Zombie* (United Artists); Reuben Mamoulian, dir., *Dr. Jekyll and Mr. Hyde*; Carl Dreyer, dir., *Vampyr*
1933	*Nathaniel West, *Miss Lonelyhearts*
1934	*Isak Dineson (Karen Blixen), *Seven Gothic Tales*
1935	James Whale, dir., *Bride of Frankenstein* (Universal)
1936	*William Faulkner, *Absalom! Absalom!*; *Djuna Barnes, *Nightwood*
1937	*Edith Wharton, *Ghosts*: "All Souls"
1938	Daphne Du Maurier, *Rebecca*
1939–1945	**Second World War**
1939	*Nathaniel West, *The Day of the Locust*; Robert Siodmak, dir.,*The Spiral Staircase* (RKO); Mervyn Peake, *Titus Groan*
1940	Alfred Hitchcock, dir., *Rebecca*; *Richard Wright, *Native Son* (Gothic episodes)
1941	August Derleth, *Someone in the Dark*
1942	*Eudora Welty, *The Robber Bridegroom*; Jacques Tourneur, dir., *Cat People* (RKO)
1943	Jacques Tourneur, dir., *I Walked With a Zombie* (RKO)

1944	Lewis Allen, dir., *The Uninvited*
1945	*H. P. Lovecraft and August Derleth, *The Lurker at the Threshold*
1948	*Truman Capote, *Other Voices, Other Rooms*
1949	*John Hawkes, *The Cannibal*; *Paul Bowles, *The Sheltering Sky*
1950	Billy Wilder, dir., *Sunset Boulevard* (Paramount); Mervyn Peake, *Gormenghast*
1951	*John Hawkes, *The Beetle Leg*; *William Styron, *Lie Down in Darkness*
1952	*Flannery O'Connor, *Wise Blood*
1954	Isaac Dinesen, *Seven Gothic Tales*
1956	Don Siegel, dir., *Invasion of the Body Snatchers*
1957	*Flannery O'Connor, *The Artificial Nigger*; Terence Fisher, dir., *The Curse of Frankenstein* (first Gothic film from Hammer Studios)
1958	*Vladimir Nabokov, *Lolita*
1959	*Shirley Jackson, *The Haunting of Hill House* (became 1963 film, *The Haunting*); *Tennessee Williams, *Sweet Bird of Youth*; *William Burroughs, *The Naked Lunch*; *James Purdy, *Malcolm*; Robert Bloch, *Psycho*
1960	*John Hawkes, *The Lime Twig*; *Flannery O'Connor, *The Violent Bear It Away*; *The House of Usher* begins Roger Corman's Edgar Allan Poe film series; Wolf Rilla, dir., *Village of the Damned* (MGM); Michael Powell, dir., *Peeping Tom*; Alfred Hitchcock, dir., *Psycho*
1961	*The Innocents* (Jack Clayton's film adaptation of *The Turn of the Screw*); *Joseph Heller, *Catch-22*
1962	Ray Bradbury, *Something Wicked This Way Comes*
1963	*The Haunting* (Robert Wise's film of *The Haunting of Hill House*); *Thomas Pynchon, *V*; *Sylvia Plath, *The Bell Jar*; *John Rechy, *City of Night*

1964	*Hubert Selby, *Last Exit to Brooklyn;* *John Hawkes, *Second Skin*
1965	*Flannery O'Connor, *Everything That Rises Must Converge* (stories); *Norman Mailer, *An American Dream;* *Jerzy Kosinski, *The Painted Bird;* Roman Polanski, dir., *Repulsion*
1966	Jean Rhys, *Wide Sargasso Sea* (reprise of *Jane Eyre,* telling the story of Bertha, Rochester's Jamaican wife); *Thomas Pynchon, *The Crying of Lot 49;* *Kurt Vonnegut, *Mother Night;* *Truman Capote, *In Cold Blood*
1967	*William Styron, *The Confessions of Nat Turner;* *Susan Sontag, *Death Kit*
1968	Roman Polanski, dir., *Rosemary's Baby;* *Joyce Carol Oates, *Expensive People;* George A. Romero, dir., *Night of the Living Dead*
1969	*Kurt Vonnegut, *Slaughterhouse-Five*
1970	J. G. Ballard, *The Atrocity Exhibition*
1971	*William Peter Blatty, *The Exorcist;* *John Hawkes, *The Blood Oranges*
1972	Angela Carter, *The Infernal Desire Machines of Dr. Hoffman;* *Margaret Atwood, *Surfacing*
1973	**US forces leave Vietnam;** William Friedkin, dir., *The Exorcist;* *Thomas Pynchon, *Gravity's Rainbow*
1974	*Richard Brautigan, *The Hawkline Monster: A Gothic Western;* *Stephen King, *Carrie;* *John Hawkes, *Death, Sleep and the Traveller*
1975	*Stephen King, *Salem's Lot*
1976	*Anne Rice, *Interview With The Vampire;* Brian de Palma, dir., *Carrie;* *John Hawkes, *Travesty*
1977	*Stephen King, *The Shining;* *David Seltzer, *The Omen*
1978	John Carpenter, dir., *Halloween*

1979	Angela Carter, *The Bloody Chamber* (stories); Stanley Kubrick, dir., *The Shining*; Ridley Scott, dir., *Alien*; Warner Herzog, dir., *Nosferatu*
1980	*John Hawkes, *The Passion Artist*; *Suzy McKee Charnas, *The Vampire Tapestry*
1981	*Thomas Harris, *Red Dragon*; *William Burroughs, *Cities of the Red Night*
1982	*Joyce Carol Oates, *The Bloodsmoor Romance*; *Stephen King, *Danse Macabre*; Ridley Scott, dir., *Blade Runner*; Steven Spielberg, dir., *Poltergeist*; *William Burroughs, *Cities of the Red Night*
1983	Susan Hill, *The Woman in Black*; *Stephen King, *Pet Semetary*
1984	*William Gibson, *Neuromancer*; *John Updike, *The Witches of Eastwick*; Iain Banks, *The Wasp Factory*; Jody Scott, *I, Vampire*; Wes Craven, dir., *A Nightmare on Elm Street*; S. P. Somtow, *Vampire Junction*
1985	*William Gaddis, *Carpenter's Gothic*; *Gloria Naylor, *Linden Hills* (Afro-American Gothic); *Margaret Atwood, *The Handmaid's Tale*; *Anne Rice, *The Vampire Lestat*
1986	David Lynch, dir., *Blue Velvet*; *Robert Coover, *Gerald's Party*; *Paul Auster, *The New York Trilogy*; John Banville, *Mefisto*
1987	*Toni Morrison, *Beloved*; *Paul Auster, *In the Country of Last Things*; Alan Parker, dir., *Angel Heart*; Joel Schumaker, dir., *The Lost Boys*; Kathryn Bigelow, dir., *Near Dark*
1988	*Stephen King, *The Tommy-Knockers*; *Poppy Z. Brite, *Lost Souls*; Clive Barker, *The Books of Blood*; David Cronenberg, dir., *Dead Ringers*; Patrick McGrath, *Blood and Water, and Other Tales*
1989	*Thomas Harris, *The Silence of the Lambs*; *Dennis Cooper, *Closer*; John Banville, *The Book of Evidence*

1990	*Stephen King, *Four Past Midnight; Twin Peaks* (David Lynch TV series); *Thomas Pynchon, *Vineland;* Tim Burton, dir., *Edward Scissorhands*
1991	*Bret Easton Ellis, *American Psycho;* Patrick McGrath, *Spider;* *Dennis Cooper, *Frisk;* Jonathan Demme, dir., *The Silence of the Lambs*
1992	Mayra Montero, *The Red of His Shadow* (Haitian Gothic); Francis Ford Coppola, dir., *Bram Stoker's Dracula;* *Poppy Z. Brite, *Lost Souls*
1993	*Pat Califa, "The Vampire;" *The X-Files* (TV series begins); Iain Banks, *The Crow Road* and *Complicity*
1994	*Joyce Carol Oates, *The Haunted: Tales of the Grotesque;* *Poppy Z. Brite, *Swamp Foetus* and *Love in Vein;* Kenneth Branagh, dir., *Mary Shelley's Frankenstein*
1995	*Joyce Carol Oates, *Zombie;* David Fincher, dir., *Se7en*
1996	*Mayra Montero, *In the Palm of Darkness;* Stephen Ferris, dir., *Mary Reilly* (version of *Jekyll and Hyde* based on Valerie Martin's 1991 novel)
1997	Iain Banks, *A Song of Stone*
1998	John Carpenter, dir., *Vampires*
1999	*Thomas Harris, *Hannibal*
2000	*Peter Straub, *Magic Terror: Seven Tales*
2001	*The Others* (film influenced by *Turn of the Screw*)
2002	Will Self, *Dorian: An Imitation*

Chapter Three

How to Read American Gothic

This chapter provides an introduction to some of the underlying themes in American Gothic and offers an overview of the more important writers in this genre, some of whom will be studied in detail in Chapters Four and Five.

Widely reviled as infantile, depraved, and potentially corrupting, American Gothic appealed to the popular audience in a rapidly growing readership, itself a consequence of private circulating libraries, the development of cheap printing methods, and an explosive growth in magazine production and consumption at the beginning of the nineteenth century.[1] The stark and sensational events and descriptions appealed to a relatively unsophisticated new audience, while amusing many of the better educated both as a leisure diversion and as a field in which previously unexamined aspects of society might be explored. In opening such subjects to literature the role of the newspapers was important: accounts of crime or other aberrant doings in the popular press, along with a concern with the behavior of the people, the dominant political force in the new American democracy, increased general interest in what had been dismissed as below polite consideration. Political anxieties about the spread of radical ideas and the predicted instability of the new republican and democratic experiment also underlie this early American Gothic, while later, a growing popular interest in psychology and deviance became a further element to intrigue a wide readership.

Certain aspects of the American experience may be understood as inherently Gothic: religious intensities, frontier immensities, isolation, and violence; above all, perhaps, the shadows cast by slavery and racial attitudes. Romanticism, in aesthetics and to an extent also in philosophy, increasingly replaced the Scottish "Common Sense" philosophy that shaped American thought up to about 1830; this new philosophy tended to privilege the Gothic mode in its concentration on subjectivity, the inner life and the imagination, and the aesthetics of the Sublime. The psychoanalytical potential of Gothic in providing a metaphorical representation of trauma and anxiety in its readership will be explored in Chapters Five and Six, along with the ways in which American Gothic might be seen to offer a "voice" for the culturally silenced, and the repressed events of American history. These are complex and fascinating aspects of the reading experience offered by this strikingly persistent form of fiction. In *Love and Death in the American Novel*, Leslie Fiedler claims that American fiction has been "bewilderingly and embarrassingly, a gothic fiction, non-realistic and negative, sadist and melodramatic—a literature of darkness and the grotesque in a land of light and affirmation."[2] The claim may seem extravagant, but it is borne out when even an arch-realist like Henry James turns out to be, one might say, a closet Gothicist, and not only in his ghost stories, just as William Faulkner's "Yoknapatawpha County" contains a haunting southern Gothic, in past and present.

To be useful in describing American writing the term Gothic has to be interpreted quite broadly, not least because of some significant differences in topographical and cultural conditions. Even at the time of the Gothic's first popularity the American writers who engaged with the form, such as Charles Brockden Brown or Edgar Allan Poe, developed a version that shows differences from the English or European tradition. James Fenimore Cooper complained in 1828 that there were no suitable materials for a writer to be found in the new country, "no annals for the historian . . . no obscure fictions for the writer of romance." That sense of difficulty in finding imaginative sustenance was echoed by Nathaniel Hawthorne, who acknowledged in 1859 the "broad and simple daylight" and "common-place prosperity" of his country, so different from the shadow and mystery and sense of gloomy wrong that the ruins of Italy suggested. Without a feudal past, or those relics so important to the English or European Gothicist, castles and monasteries and legends, the American landscape seemed inherently resistant to Gothic stories and settings. But Brown and Poe had already forged an American Gothic—or rather Gothics since their directions were quite different—that shows how the culturally specific anxieties and tensions of the new country could determine alternative settings and plots to renew the genre. To see this we should consider what it was about castles and wild scenery, feudal aristocracies and monastic oppressions that had made them so potent for their contemporary audience.

One reason for the original invention and popularity of the Gothic mode was a near revolution in aesthetics and in philosophy, of which the figureheads were Edmund Burke and Immanuel Kant. Burke's *Philosophical Inquiry into the Origin of our Ideas of the Sublime and Beautiful* (1756) helped to redirect attention to the aesthetic power of the "Sublime," showing how even the emotion of fear might be pleasurable in the right context. What had been seen previously as barbaric, monstrous, or terrifying could alternatively be experienced as sublimely affecting through its production of powerful emotional reactions in the observer. Mountains, precipices, violent seas, or even descriptions of pain might, it followed, be preferred to tranquil and ordered landscapes; Gothic churches or medieval castles to Palladian classically proportioned architecture. The eighteenth century cultivated an appreciation of sentiment[3] which in the Romantic movement was to become a fascination with passions. Meditations on mortality as in Thomas Gray's "Elegy in a Country Churchyard" (1750) or Edward Young's "Night Thoughts" (1745) could lead on to an interest in morbid states, or violent, tragic death. Gardens were now laid out to imitate nature rather than more formally ordered, and mock ruins were built in convenient spots to suggest the pleasures and pathos of antiquity. Tours began to visit wild and untamed scenery: the Lake District, Scotland and Switzerland, even Derbyshire, all found new appreciation. Kant's philosophical ideas, although no doubt too complex for most readers of Gothic romances, were popularized as a revolution in thought, with a stress on subjective and intuitive sources of knowledge (a distortion of Kant's argument that understanding must depend on a prior ability to apprehend time, for example, or space). Intuition, popularized in this way, suggested that inward contemplation could result in deeper knowledge than rationality; the "Higher Reason" might be more profound than mere calculation:

ideas that energized Romantic aesthetics and invited attention to inspiration within the self, best realized at night and in solitude, as in the "Hymns of Night" by Novalis. Much of the early Gothic was concerned with the aesthetics of wildness and sublimity, and the difficulties of correct subjective knowledge; both elements well suited to American circumstances, with the wilderness (or later urban labyrinths) replacing the unknowable and menacing castle or monastery, and new perplexities about knowledge derived from unreliable senses or mental derangement substituted for the unfathomable motives of European villains.

Because the first substantial American efforts coincided with the great period of British and European Gothicism, American fiction began in a Gothic mode. The examples of the British novelist William Godwin and of German romances like Ludwig Tieck's *The Victim of Magical Delusion* (1795) or Friedrich von Schiller's *The Ghost-Seer* (1795) played an important part in inspiring Charles Brockden Brown's early novels, and the Germans similarly provided material for Washington Irving's Gothic satires. A little later Edgar Allan Poe worked in the vein of the sensationalist *Blackwood's Edinburgh Magazine*, producing tales that did not unfortunately achieve the commercial popularity he expected, largely because the literary marketplace had already moved on by the 1830s and 1840s. Nathaniel Hawthorne fully realized the possibilities of resonance between the Gothic tradition and the American past, and Herman Melville used Gothic to articulate his darkly coded understanding of what lay beneath the new nation's optimistic surfaces.

That darker note concerned in part the legacy of slavery and racial discrimination, which was to inform many subsequent fictions of southern Gothic and is still a principal energizer of the genre, as in Toni Morrison's *Beloved* (1987). Another theme may be identified in the psychological possibilities of Gothicism, again a major element in Brown's novels, developed through Poe and Hawthorne's tales and powerfully at work in Henry James's ghost stories and even his major fictions. The advantage—perhaps even inevitability —of the Gothic form in articulating the concerns of the unvoiced "other" has meant that the position of the female in a predominantly masculinist culture provided another important strand in American Gothicism, instanced best by Charlotte Perkins Gilman's story "The

Yellow Wallpaper." Recently, while the southern Gothic tradition has modulated from Faulkner, Truman Capote, and Flannery O'Connor into an exploration of the history of the racially "othered," there can also be identified a strain of urban Gothicism, in the work of James Purdy, John Hawkes, John Rechy, or Brett Easton Ellis, and what might be called techno-Gothic, as in Thomas Pynchon's *V* (1963), *Gravity's Rainbow* (1973), and *The Crying of Lot 49* (1966); or cyber-Gothic, as in William Gibson's novels and stories. To summarize, then, although American Gothicists participated in a wider literary tradition, the circumstances of their own history and the stresses of their particular cultural and political institutions meant that a series of significant inflections determined a Gothicism that differs considerably from British or European versions.

Philip Freneau (1752–1832) struck the American Gothic note early in his graveyard-poem "The House of Night" (1799):

> Let others draw from smiling skies their theme,
> And tell of climes that boast unfading light,
> I draw a darker scene, replete with gloom,
> *I sing the horrors of the House of Night.*

He went on to give a lurid picture of the death of Death, with coal-black chariot and "Spectres attending, in black weeds array'd." But it was Charles Brockden Brown (1771–1810) who most thoroughly founded the Gothic tradition in American fiction with his novels *Wieland, Ormond, Edgar Huntly*, and *Arthur Mervyn*, written between 1798 and 1800. Brown's novels exploited Ann Radcliffe's vein of "explained supernaturalism," using ventriloquism, somnambulism, or charnel-house scenes of plague to create their Gothic effects. William Godwin was another and more important mentor, for Brown's work, like his, is based on rationalist precepts and is now increasingly seen to contain political implications.

Wieland (1798) begins with the baffling death of Wieland senior, a religious fanatic mysteriously consumed by a fireball in his garden-house temple of worship. His children Clara and Theodore —unwisely—convert the temple into a summer house and live on the estate in tranquillity until some uncanny voices trigger Theodore Wieland's own lurking religious mania. Clara relates the terrible story of the discovery of the mangled remains of Wieland's wife and children, and comes to realize that Theodore, in obedience to his voices, intends to kill her too. Responsibility for the whole disaster is eventually traced to Carwin, a ventriloquist who had used his strange gift to divert attention from his minor misdemeanors. Even Clara's blaming of Carwin is delusional, however, for the story has shown that the roots of irrationality lie deeper than mere surface causes (and indeed may involve Wieland's incestuous feelings toward his sister). Such self-reflexive subtleties are characteristic in Brown's novels.

In *Edgar Huntly* (1799) the narrator attempts to help a disturbed somnambulist, Clithero, but similarly falls victim to sleepwalking and mental disturbance, hiding papers from himself, and wandering in the wilderness of Norwalk. In one episode Huntly falls into a cave. He loses consciousness but wakes to find himself threatened by silent Indians. Huntly kills one with a hatchet, shoots three more, and bayonets a fifth—an act he describes as "cruel lenity." He has himself become savage, out of the necessity of his own psychic constitution, because his parents were butchered by Indians in a quintessentially American primal scene. This adaptation of Gothic conventions to the American landscape is not simply a literary convenience; it is also a significant pointer to the racial antagonism, guilt, and displacement that has driven much subsequent Gothic writing. In *Arthur Mervyn* (1799), Brown invented the American urban Gothic, in which the civilized city of Philadelphia is transformed through plague into an unknowable labyrinth of horrors, and in *Ormond* (1799), another urban Gothic work, he imagined an adherent of a notorious European secret society, the "Illuminati," coming into the American environment. These books refer obliquely, often through interpolated tales of minor characters, to European political instability and particularly to fears aroused by the terror of the French Revolution, especially perhaps as this had been represented by Edmund Burke in his *Reflections on the Revolution in France* (1790).

Some of Edgar Allan Poe's work seems to follow in the patterns set by Brown: the indeterminate urban situations, the nightmare intensities, and above all, the confusions of consciousness as the protagonist's madness destabilizes narrative and setting. Like Brown, fundamentally a rationalist who generally stops short of supernaturalism, Poe as a later writer was, however, also much influenced by Romanticism, and particularly by German Romantic irony.[4] This is demonstrated in his interest in extremes of consciousness, in episodes of near-death states or dreamlike intensities, and his underlying macabre humor that delights in the reversal of expectations. Before Poe, the American artist Washington Allston had shown how Gothicists might theorize the darker side of the Romantic ideal in his lectures and his novella Monaldi (written in 1822). An American painter, and a friend of the English Romantic Coleridge, Allston argued in his "Lectures on Art" that the beautiful and the sublime have their dark analogue descending to the ugly and then rising again to complete the circle. " . . . [I]n this dark segment," he claimed, "will be found the startling union of deepening discords— still deepening as it rises from the Ugly to the Loathsome, the Horrible, the Frightful, the Appalling."[5] Poe's interest in precisely those qualities as the route to deeper illumination is what raised his work above Blackwood's Magazine sensationalism and made him subsequently a favorite of the French Symbolists. Another influence on Poe was one of the most prolific American writers of the early period, John Neal (1793–1876), who wrote several Gothic novels between 1820 and 1840 including Logan (1822), about hereditary family madness in the wilderness, and Rachel Dyer (1828) on the Salem witchcraft episode of 1692, which also later informed Nathaniel Hawthorne's "Alice Doane's Appeal." Other early Gothicists included James Kirke Paulding (1778–1860), who collaborated with Washington Irving on the magazine Salmagundi (1807–1808), and William Gilmore Simms (1806–1870), whose Martin Faber (1833) drew on both Godwin and Brown. Even James Fenimore Cooper incorporated Gothic elements into his novels, especially in The Spy (1821), a story of the underside of the American Revolution, and his tale of Venetian intrigue, The Bravo (1831). Robert Montgomery Bird (1806–1854) echoed the Indian-hating theme of Brown's Edgar Huntly in his novel Nick of the Woods (1837), the extraordinary tale of a schizophrenic peaceful-Quaker/ Indian-killer, Nathan Slaughter, who engraves crosses on the bodies of his victims, exemplifying the potential Gothicism of racism and the dark American forests. Later, in a sensationalist and hugely popular novel, The Quaker City or, The Monks of Monk Hall (1844),

George Lippard developed more possibilities of urban Gothic, describing a fantastic secret underside of Quaker Philadelphia. Lippard's mixture of sensuality and radical social thought owed much to "Monk" Lewis, and to Charles Brockden Brown, to whom in fact he dedicated the book.

But beyond all these is the figure of Edgar Allan Poe, who developed a new incisiveness in Gothic writing through his conception of "unity of effect," a concern for the reading experience that left a deep impress both on American and European Gothic developments; and through his invention of the macabre detective story, which inaugurated another lasting genre. Poe's Gothic tales, such as "Ligeia" or "The Fall of the House of Usher," combined unspeakable frisson with a tantalizing psychological complexity that continues to unfold in response to new critical discourses, whether of Jacques Lacan, Jacques Derrida, Barbara Johnson, or other poststructuralists.[6] Conventionally divided into the tales of "imagination" and those of "ratiocination," in practice his stories of both types are examples of different strains within the Gothic, the drive toward mystery and the fantastic, and the corresponding drive toward explanation. The mystery stories invite and challenge interpretation, while the detective stories, such as "The Murders in the Rue Morgue," also incorporate elements of fantastic excess. A persistent mocking humor is to be found in these as well as his more overtly comic tales, reminiscent of the work of Washington Irving (1783–1859), if more savage and without Irving's more comfortable end-of-story recuperations. One of Irving's stories, in fact, "The Adventure of the German Student" (1824), is almost exactly in the vein that Poe made his own, with its sinister celebration of what Poe called the most poetical of topics, the death of a beautiful woman, and its explanatory invocation of madness. Poe *internalized* the Gothic nightmare, claiming in his Preface to *Tales of the Grotesque and Arabesque* (1839), "my terror is not of Germany, but of the soul,"[7] thus opening the way for the psychological ghost story; he also *domesticated* it in such tales as "The Black Cat," a "mere series of household events" which concludes with the loathed animal discovered feeding off the head of a walled-up corpse—the narrator's murdered wife. Poe's work still shows the effects of late eighteenth-century rationalism in its American form, which was heavily influenced by the Scottish Common Sense philosophers: the drive toward explanation and understanding of Gothic events through mental disorder, and the sense of stopping short of supernaturalism; but at the same time, he was clearly also a product of the Romantic movement, in that his tales show the compelling effects of disorder in the imaginative creation of his protagonists' worlds, without a fussy recourse to normalizing narrative frameworks.

Nathaniel Hawthorne (1806–1864) similarly internalized and domesticated the Gothic to explore its insights into the psychology of everyday life, and its applicability to history. In Hawthorne's hands the Gothic is *performed*: it is not allowed to direct the form of the narrative but is instead manipulated and distorted for purposes that include a recognition of its origins in destabilized personal and political situations. His tales are full of magic or fetish objects: speaking portraits, fatal shawls, broken fountains, ghostly prophecies, artificial flowers, and cryptic veils; but these are characteristically unpacked to show their range of historical and personal meanings. The scarlet letter itself in his novel *The Scarlet Letter* (1850)—introduced by a standard Gothic scenario, the discovery of a strange old manuscript—is an example of a totemic magic object which fascinates not so much for its strange powers as for the rich variety of meanings it is shown to contain. Similarly the deadly shawl of "Lady Eleanore's Mantle" exudes a literal pestilence, but it is at the same time an emblem of the pestilential effects of class in aristocratic isolation, and of the arrogance of beauty. Hawthorne uses mirrors, magical portraits, and the effects of uncertain light to produce a mood of Gothic strangeness, rather than to develop fully Gothic narratives. In *The Scarlet Letter*, the relationship between Dimmesdale and Chillingworth echoes Poe's "Willam Wilson" and Simms's *Martin Faber*, with, behind them, Maturin's *Melmoth*. But Hawthorne's version of the demonic double is focused on the psychic cost of the Faustian bargain and its reciprocal endorsement by the victim. We find familiar Gothic figures in the magnetic and saturnine Hollingsworth of *The Blithedale Romance* (1852), the sinister monk or model and family secrets of *The Marble Faun* (1860), the ancestral curse of the Pyncheons in *The House of the Seven Gables*, or the witchcraft of "Young Goodman Brown."[8] In each instance, however, the Gothic elements are enlisted in the service of a heightened normality, using extreme cases—of the Faustian pact, the mad scientist, preternatural knowledge—to illuminate the influence of the past in the present, or the damage caused by ambition, hypocrisy, and the denial of personal truths.

These were the elements that caused Herman Melville (1819–1891) to recognize a hell-fired darkness in Hawthorne's writing, an identification that had perhaps as much to do with Melville's own concerns as those of his fellow writer. The sense of evil that Hawthorne had found buried in the Puritan experience, and the "heart" that was its product, was generalized in Melville's Conradian vision of a world so profoundly diabolised by the distortions of slavery and aggressive capitalism as to seem evil at its very centre. The beneficent nature hymned by Emerson and Thoreau concealed a violent rapacity that *Moby-Dick* (1851) detailed, as much in man as in the sharks, or the malevolent uncanny whale itself. In his compelling novella "Benito Cereno," Melville prefigured Conrad's *Heart of Darkness* in exploring the deformations due to racism, and his urban-Gothic sentimental thriller *Pierre* (1852) investigated a tangle of incest and inherited deception that overwhelmed his narrative skills in a manner reminiscent of Hawthorne's last unfinished novels "The Dolliver Romance," "The Ancestral Footstep," or "Dr. Grimshawe's Secret." What most closely links the three great American Gothicists of this period—Poe, Hawthorne, and Melville—is their exploration of "negative Romanticism," the blackness of vision when Romantic inspiration succumbs to an equally overwhelming but far bleaker subjectivity.

The shadows of patriarchy, slavery, and racism, as of Puritan extremes of the imagination and the political horror of a failed utopianism, fall across these works of American Gothic and direct its shape toward a concern with social and political issues as well as toward an agonized introspection concerning the evil that lies within the self. Because Gothic is of its nature extravagant and concerned with the dark side of society, and because it is in some ways freed by its status as absurd fantasy, this form is perhaps more able than realism to incorporate unresolved contractions within the culture, or to express as in dream logic the hidden desires and fears that more considered and "reasonable" perspectives would shrug off or repress. But it must be remembered in reading this material that it is, first and foremost, *fiction*, and not disguised political and social polemic. Writers of Gothic aim to entertain—themselves and their audience—rather than covertly instruct. The shadows that we see: of class anxieties, racial conflicts and genocidal guilts, domestic oppressions, the persistence of the past in the present; these are not the reasons for the writing, they are "what happens" in the process of the writing, the more or less conscious conditions of its being, and sometimes even, perhaps, the effect of the unconsciousness of the writer. There is then, a risk of over-coherent interpretation, as though the Gothic writer set out to express a specific concern and then thoughtfully chose the Gothic form to present it best. But Henry James, to give just one telling example, wrote the *Turn of the Screw* as a magazine commission for a Christmas ghost story. So to conclude this chapter on how to read American Gothic—and how to read this book—we need to remember that the Gothic is fantasy and amusement, games and fancy dress, entertainment that engages with its readers on many different levels from trauma to laughter. In analyzing it we find that it stands for many things, but first and always it is *for itself.*

Notes

1. Donald A. Ringe, *American Gothic* (Lexington: University Press of Kentucky, 1982) pp. 14–16.

2. Leslie Fiedler, *Love and Death in the American Novel*, 1960 (New York: Delta, 1966) p. 29.

3. See, for example, Laurence Sterne, *A Sentimental Journey* (1768).

4. As has been shown by G. R. Thompson in *Poe's Fiction: Romantic Irony in the Gothic Tales* (Madison: University of Wisconsin Press, 1973), and in Thompson's Introduction to *Romantic Gothic Tales, 1790–1840* (New York: Harper and Row, 1979) pp. 13–38.

5. Washington Allston, *Lectures on Art, and Monaldi*, R. H. Dana, ed., 1850 (Gainsville, FL: Scholars Facsimiles and Reprints, 1967).

6. Lacan's essay and Barbara Johnson's response can be found in Rupert Con Davis and Ronald Schleifer, eds., *Contemporary Literary Criticism* (New York and London: Longman, 1989).

7. See also Ian Walker, "The 'Legitimate Sources' of Terror in 'The Fall of the House of Usher,'" *Modern Language Review*, 61 (October 1966) pp. 585–592.

8. See Chapter Six for more detailed readings.

Chapter Four

Key Texts

The craze for Gothic fiction begun by Walpole and developed by Matthew Gregory Lewis, William Godwin, and Ann Radcliffe, along with the German writers Friedrich von Schiller and Ludwig Tieck, found an enthusiastic readership in North America, despite—or perhaps partly because of—regular denunciation from the pulpit. The rationalist perspective of the dominant American culture, deriving from John Locke and the Scottish Common Sense philosophers Lord Kames and Hugh Blair, and subsequently Thomas Reid and Dugald Stewart, thought tales of spectres and superstition an affront to reason and decency, which no doubt compounded their attraction for the young writers who were struggling to invent an American literature comparable to that of Europe. Charles Brockden Brown, Edgar Allan Poe, Nathaniel Hawthorne, and Herman Melville, the great originators of American fiction, were much influenced by the Gothic fashion, Washington Irving satirized it, and James Fenimore Cooper exploited it in his novels *The Spy*, *The Last of the Mohicans*, and *The Prairie*.

Four indigenous features were decisive in producing a powerful and long-lasting American variant of the Gothic: the frontier, the Puritan legacy, race, and political utopianism.

In the early years of the colonies and the young United States, the settlers were acutely conscious that they lived on the verge of a vast wilderness, a land of threat as much as material promise, where many lived in isolation or in small settlements with the memories and sometimes justified fears of Indian warfare. The legends of seventeenth-century witchcraft in Salem provided for Hawthorne and John Neal some of those "annals for the historian" that Cooper required. The Puritan consciousness itself, although waning in this period, had established a profoundly "Gothic" imagination of good and evil, and the perilous human experience. Two famous texts in particular, Michael Wigglesworth's "Day of Doom" and Jonathan Edward's "Sinners in the Hands of an Angry God" illustrate this inheritance:

> All filthy facts, and secret acts,
> however closely done,
> And long concealed, are there revealed
> before the mid-day sun.
> Deeds of the night shunning the light,
> which darkest corners sought,
> To fearfull blame, and endless shame,
> are there most justly brought.
> —*The Day of Doom* (1662)

> That world of misery, that lake of burning brimstone is extended abroad under you. There is the dreadful pit of the glowing flames of the wrath of God; there is hell's wide gaping mouth open; and you have nothing to stand upon, nor anything to take hold of; there is nothing between you and hell but the air; it is only the power and mere pleasure of God that holds you up.
> —*Sinners in the Hands of an Angry God* (1741)

If the tendency of these Puritan exhortations was largely to develop a sense of guilt and dread, they also fostered a tendency to think of sin and virtue in terms of black and white, the kingdom of light and also the kingdom of darkness. But the actual conjunction of black and white in American society through its unprecedented dependence on slavery, like the conflict between settlers and Native Americans, gave another twist to the development of American Gothic. The power of blackness, to borrow the title of Harry Levin's critique of the contrasts within American Romances, was also, as Toni Morrison has recently argued in *Playing in the Dark*,[1] a power of definition of the "other," the resident non-American whose abjection supported the self-definition of the dominant whites.

Again, as Jean Baudrillard has remarked, America is "a utopia which has behaved from the beginning as though it were already achieved."[2] The utopian visions of freedom and prosperity that brought the early settlers to North America gained new vigor from Enlightenment arguments about the possibility of an ideal society, and were enshrined in the founding constitutional principles of the United States. But along with utopian inspiration came more pessimistic insights into the dangers of trusting society to the undisciplined rule of the majority, fear of faction in democratic government, the rule of the mob, and the danger of a collapse of the whole grand experiment. In the early years of the nineteenth century, as the franchise widened, such anxieties provided a political undertone in fiction as in the rest of public life.

These factors directed the American imagination toward Manichean formulations of good and evil, and as Richard Chase says focused it on alienation and disorder; or, in Leslie Fiedler's words, as we have seen, led American fiction to become "bewilderingly and embarrassingly, a gothic fiction, non-realistic and negative, sadist and melodramatic—a literature of darkness and the grotesque in a land of light and affirmation."[3] At the peak of Gothic's popularity in America, when the last decade of the eighteenth century saw a flood of imported English and German works circulating in the booksellers' catalogues, Charles Brockden Brown's novels demonstrate how his Philadelphian's empiricist and Enlightenment temper picked up on the technique of "explained supernaturalism" that had characterized Ann Radcliffe's work, and also dominated the many imported German romances—Schiller's *The Ghost-Seer* (1789), Kahlert's *The Necromancer* (1794), or Tschink's *The Victim of Magical Delusion* (1795), wherein seemingly supernatural events are explained to be the products of mental delusion. Most notably, the curious voices heard by Theodore Wieland in Brockden Brown's novel *Wieland* (1798), which inspire him to murder his family, originate in the ventriloquism practiced by the interloper Carwin for his own shabby purposes. But whereas in the European novels these misapprehensions are largely gratuitous (mistaking the nocturnal activities of bands of robbers for supernatural interventions, for example), Brown enlarges their scope of implication to significant psychological and political conclusions.

The Wieland family has had a curious history: arriving in America to be a missionary to the Indians, the elder Wieland fails in his project, but becomes a successful entrepreneur (and slave owner) while retaining his intense religious belief. On his estate beside the Schuykill River, he builds himself a small temple where one evening he is consumed by mysterious fire, leaving as he dies an enigmatic account that leaves open the possibility of some supernatural element in his death. His orphaned children, Clara and Theodore Wieland, establish for themselves what is effectively a private utopia, turning the temple into a summer house where they hold free-thinking discussions and readings of poetry and classical literature with their friends, Henri Pleyel and his sister Catherine— who becomes Wieland's wife and mother of his children. A striking example of the extreme isolation of their little community is Clara's note that six years of uninterrupted happiness had passed since her brother's marriage, during which the sounds of war in the distance served only "to enhance our enjoyment by affording objects of comparison. The Indians were repulsed on the one side, and Canada was conquered on the other. Revolutions and battles, however calamitous to those who occupied the scene, contributed in some sort to our happiness, by agitating our minds with curiosity, and furnishing causes of patriotic exultation."[4] Into this Arcadia comes Carwin, a mysterious wandering figure originally from Ireland, whom we later discover to have been brought up in an Illuminati-like secret society with rationalist but subversive aims. Carwin's almost magical power of ventriloquy, which he uses for such purposes as the seduction of Clara's maid, sets off Wieland's latent religious monomania: he murders his wife and children, thinking it the will of God, who then demands of him also the sacrifice of his beloved sister Clara. But realizing his error at last, Wieland kills himself instead of Clara, who then narrates the story in letters to her friends.

The Wielands' utopia has implicit parallels with the newly constituted United States: it is rationalist, based on enlightenment principles, and significantly lacks reference to any external authority. The children have been "saved from the corruption and tyranny of colleges and boarding schools" and left to their own guidance for religious education. The dreadful collapse of this happy and independent society could suggest a pessimism about the future of self-government, as Jane Tomkins points out: "Brown's picture of the disintegration of the Wielands' miniature society is a more or less direct reflection of Federalist scepticism about the efficacy of religion and education in preparing citizens to govern themselves" and so, "the novel's plot offers a direct refutation of the Republican faith in men's capacity to govern themselves without the supports and constraints of an established social order."[5] This would perhaps explain Brown's curious action: upon finishing the book, he sent a copy directly to Thomas Jefferson, then vice president of the new United States. Of course there might be other, and less noble, reasons for an unknown author to draw his work to the attention of America's leading intellectual, but the thrust of Brown's implicit critique of naive utopianism seems clear enough.

Besides these possible political implications, *Wieland* also offers a devastating attack on the then-popular psychology of Sensations. His fellow Philadelphian, the famous Dr. Benjamin Rush, was one of the leading theorists of Sensationist psychology, which explained the mind as simply a product of responses to sensation. But what happens, asks Brown's story, if the sensations themselves are untrustworthy or are misinterpreted according to some inner imperative? Theodore Wieland is the most extreme example, but his sister Clara, and even their rationalist friend Pleyel also fall victim to this. Pleyel refuses to believe Clara's protestations of sexual innocence, insisting instead upon the evidence of his own senses, which are in fact misled by Carwin. Brown rehearses this dilemma in many of his subsequent novels, eventually coming to the conclusion that the inner direction provided by faith provides the only reliable answer.

There is also a psycho-sexual undertow in the novel, to do with why Wieland's mania takes the particular form that it does, and why Clara herself has a prophetic dream in the summer house that her beloved brother is a danger to her: "I remembered the gulf to which my brother's invitation had conducted me; I remembered that, when on the brink of danger, the author of my peril was depicted by my fears in his form. Thus realized were the creatures of prophetic sleep, and of wakeful terror" (28, 29). At the time when the terrible events begin, Clara is expecting Pleyel's proposal of marriage. That her sexuality is awakening, too, is evident from the strange fixation that she develops on first encountering the ugly but magnetic Carwin: sketching his face, and spending the whole of a stormy day contemplating this portrait. Wieland's brutal destruction

of his wife and children, and his projected murder of Clara, suggest
clearly enough a pattern of repressed incestuous desire, emerging
explosively at the point when Clara moves toward independence
and sexual initiation. It is in awaiting Clara's return home that
Wieland's mania actually begins, and in her house that he hears the
voice requiring him to sacrifice his wife as a proof of his faith.

Such political, philosophical, and psychological implications
seem to justify Brown's claim that in *Wieland*:

> The incidents related are extraordinary and rare. Some of
> them perhaps, approach as nearly to the nature of miracles
> as can be done by that which is not truly miraculous. . . .
> Some readers may think the conduct of the younger
> Wieland impossible. In support of this possibility the
> Writer must appeal to Physicians and to men conversant
> with the latent springs and occasional perversions of the
> human mind (3).

Francis Carwin, the self-serving utopian schemer Brown posited as
a threat to the stability of the Wielands, has his own life story
appended to the novel as *Memoirs of Carwin, The Biloquist*. This
curious account does little to throw light on the troubling aspects
of *Wieland*, but illustrates Brown's fascination with deluded ratio-
nalists who subordinate means to ends, and sacrifice principles in
order to achieve results. He developed this interest further in his
novel *Ormond* (1799), in which the virtuous Constantia Dudley
falls prey to the ingenious manipulations of a member of a secret
society, trained like Carwin in remarkable skills, and similarly
employing them for his own devious purposes. Much influenced by
the Gothic rationalism of William Godwin, Brown offers an all-
knowing, all-seeing, Schedoni-ish villain who becomes obsessed
with taking Constantia's virginity. Like Clara Wieland and other
Gothic heroines, Constantia Dudley is a paragon of female virtue,
with a feminist independence and self-reliance which only lead her
into situations of terror and danger, and which inflame the patriarchal male. A proponent of women's rights himself (and writer on
the topic in *Alcuin; or, The Rights of Women*, 1798), Brown here
develops a theme that is largely implicit in the sporadic efforts at

independence by heroines of the English Gothic novel into an explicit interrogation of sexual politics.

The landscape of the Gothic in America initially emulated English and European models, and where European castles and monasteries were not transported to the new world, it borrowed from English graveyard poetry to invoke scenes of melancholy shadow. But Brown was also learning to use a specifically American landscape for chiaroscuro effects, first in the shadowy intricacies of the Wieland estate at night, and later in the wilderness of Norwalk, where Edgar Huntly is driven by his obsessions. *Edgar Huntly* (1799)[6] develops through landscape the psychological Gothicism begun in *Wieland*, and which was subsequently to characterize the majority of American Gothic fictions from Poe to James.

Huntly, disturbed by the unexplained murder of his close friend Waldegrave, feels guilt that he is to benefit from this tragedy, and is further disturbed by having mislaid some embarrassing letters that he had been asked by his friend to destroy, but which we discover he has in fact hidden while sleepwalking, like the later hero of Wilkie Collins's *The Moonstone* (1868). His unresolved concerns draw him back to the scene of the murder, a large elm tree where he discovers a mysterious figure digging in the earth. This encounter, and his effort to discover this stranger's secret, begins Huntly's series of circuitous wanderings in the intricate wilderness maze of Norwalk, pursuing Clithero Edny who turns out to be, in many respects, Huntly's double, not least in that they both sleepwalk. Norwalk is rough and inaccessible country, where the unconscious aspects of Huntly's obsessive pursuit seem to be embodied in the scenery:

> It was a maze, oblique, circuitous, upward and downward, in a degree which could only take place in a region so remarkably irregular in surface, so abounding with hillocks and steeps, and pits and brooks as *Solebury*. It seemed to be the whole end of his labours to bewilder or fatigue his pursuer, to pierce into the deepest thickets, to plunge into the darkest cavities, to ascend the most difficult heights, and approach the slippery and tremulous verge of the dizziest precipice (23).

Labyrinths are a significant Gothic trope, as Fred Botting notes in *Gothic*, in terms that would apply well to *Edgar Huntly*: "The city, a gloomy forest or dark labyrinth itself, became a site of nocturnal corruption and violence, a locus of real horror; the family became a place rendered threatening and uncanny by the haunting return of past transgressions and attendant guilt on an everyday world shrouded in strangeness."[7]

On one of his somnambulatory nights Huntly goes to his bed as usual but awakens in pain and darkness, to find that he has fallen into a pit within a cavern. He experiences feelings of terror and fear of being buried alive which Brown, good Gothicist that he is, draws out over several pages. At the center of Huntly's circular wanderings in the figurative and physical wilderness maze is this cavern, and in it he discovers and kills a panther, which sustains him until he has the strength to find his way out. But a second cave, near at hand, contains another avatar of the wilderness, a group of sleeping Indians. His own parents and sibling had been killed by marauding Indians, which makes Huntly more of an Indian-hater than a benevolent Rousseau-like admirer of the noble savage; and his antipathy is encouraged by discovering the plight of their captive, a young girl. Huntly kills the guard with a hatchet, rescues the girl, and subsequently dispatches three of the Indians with a musket found in their possession (but recognized as his very own, stolen from his uncle's house). He kills the final Indian adversary with the bayonet attached to his gun: "I left the savage where he lay, but made prize of his tomhawk. . . . Prompted by some freak of fancy, I stuck his musquet in the ground, and left it standing upright in the middle of the road" (203). Huntly's flamboyant "freak of fancy" helps to establish the centrality of this seemingly unrelated episode: at the heart of the American Gothic wilderness is the savage Indian, and the overdetermined compulsion of the settler to kill and to signal his triumph over the barbaric in a supposed distinction from the primitive, which unmistakably includes a doubling of his own nature with the savage.

The theme of race which subtly pervades the American Gothic is thus introduced at the heart of Brown's narrative. It reemerges in such books as William Montgomery Bird's *Nick of the Woods* (1837), in which a demented Indian-killer leaves a bloody cross drawn on the breasts of his victims. The Indians believe him to be an evil spirit, called the Jibbenainosay, but he is in fact an outwardly pacifist Quaker, aptly named Nathan Slaughter, who has been driven insane by the treacherous murder and scalping of his wife and children by the Shawnee chief Wenonga.

In an astute comment on *Edgar Huntly*, Leslie Fiedler remarks that the change of myth from European prototypes, such as the ruined castle to the forest and cave, involves a profound change of meaning:

> In the American gothic, that is to say, the heathen, unredeemed wilderness and not the monuments of a dying class, nature and not society becomes the symbol of evil. Similarly not the aristocrat but the Indian . . . the savage colored man is postulated as the embodiment of villainy. [The American Gothic becomes] a Calvinist exposé of natural human corruption rather than an enlightened attack on a debased ruling class or entrenched superstition. The European gothic identified blackness with the super-ego and was therefore revolutionary in its implications; the American gothic (at least as far as it followed the example of Brown) identified evil with the id and was therefore conservative at its deepest level of implication. . . .[8]

In his urban Gothic landscapes, which is to say in the novels *Arthur Mervyn* and *Ormond* to which I shall return, we do find Brown following the European model. But another observation is also in order here: the American Gothic identified blackness not simply with evil but with *racial* "blackness."

Oddly perhaps, the *Gothic* possibilities of conflict with the Native Americans were not greatly drawn on by other writers, even by the master of Indian conflict plots, James Fenimore Cooper, whose Gothic motifs, while appearing in *The Last of the Mohicans* (1826), are found more largely in quasi-European fictions such as *The Bravo* (1831), set the Venice at the time of the Doges, or in the twilight landscape of *The Spy* (1821), his novel about a double agent during the Revolutionary War. But Cooper, like Brown, did appreciate some of the Gothic possibilities of the American wilderness, as a scene of quasi-judicial execution in *The Prairie* demonstrates.

Ishmael Bush hangs his brother-in-law, Abiram White, for the murder of his son, by leaving him noosed on a narrow ledge to fall. Bush listens from a distance in the night, hearing unearthly shrieks from the wind, and finally one last cry in which there can be no delusion and "to which the imagination could lend no horror." This is what we might call a Gothic realism, using the resources of the wilderness and the primitive emotions of the rough settlers for its effect.

Cooper's worrying at the margins of civilization and savagery announced a new thematic that was to develop ultimately into the Western genre, on one hand, and into Southern Gothic on the other. Edgar Allan Poe, an early exponent of the latter, shows in his strange novel *Arthur Gordon Pym* (1837) how the shadow of white racism may fall even within a comic narrative. *Pym*'s preposterous plot involves stowaways, mutinies, shipwrecks, cannibalism, a Flying Dutchman ghost ship, and travel to the ends of the world. It is Gothic in its evocation of claustrophobic terror, when Pym is hiding in the dark hull of a ship, but also and much more powerfully in its descriptions of the fearsome natives of Tsalal who cannot abide the color white, have black teeth, and live among rocks which resemble corded bales of cotton, except that they too are black. The hoax plot concludes with Pym sailing toward a giant milky-white figure, which as one of Henry James's characters remembers, was indeed "a thing to show, by the way, what imagination Americans *could* have."[9]

Poe, a southerner from Richmond, shows a racism subtly etched throughout, like the natural hieroglyphics of his peculiar invented land in *Pym*, and it emerges on occasion with demonic energy. In his story "Hop Frog," for example, a much abused court jester dwarf has his revenge on a cruel king and his courtiers by encouraging them to dress up as chained gorillas. He then cunningly strings their chain up to a great chandelier, and sets their tarred bodies on fire in a grotesque approximation to southern lynchings.

For the most part, however, Poe turned his back on specifically American settings and invented an indeterminate quasi-European setting for his Gothic tales. His stories of morbid introversion employed such stylized Gothic items as the ancient house of Usher, the incomprehensible architecture of the English boarding school in "William Wilson," or the baronial Gothic tower room of "Ligeia," but these are divorced from any social or historical resonance so that they become more like symbolist motifs; a technique that was in fact later admired by Baudelaire and other French Symbolists. The "spiralling intensification" of his narrative technique, as David Punter well describes it,[10] gave an extra dimension to situations not uncommon in the *Blackwood's Magazine* of the time, and the immediacy and suddenness of his first-person narration developed the sensationalism of European Gothic (or of Brown) into a sharper focus. Scenes of exquisite terror, as in the discovery by the demented narrator of "Berenice" that his nightmare of removing his cousin's teeth while she yet lived must be the truth, or the exposure of the wife's walled-up corpse with the cat feeding on her head in "The Black Cat," push the charnel-house elements of literary Gothic toward a fascination with horror for its own sake that culminates in the horror film (to which Poe's work very directly contributed in the films of, for example, Roger Corman).

Supernaturalism is *suggested* in many of Poe's tales of terror, but it is rarely their essential point, and is frequently explained away by the protagonist's evident insanity. The narrator sees his beloved dead Ligeia reanimated in the body of his abused new wife, Rowena; the corpse of M. Valdemar speaks from his mesmeric trance (only to say, "Let me die," and collapse in a putrifying mess as soon as the spell is removed); the fatal embrace of Usher and his supposedly dead sister engenders a collapse of the whole House of Usher; and the message inadvertently daubed on the sail of the ghost ship in "MS Found in a Bottle" spells out a cryptic mirroring of our quest for meaning and knowledge in the one word, DISCOVERY; but in none of these episodes of failed epistemological utopias do we find anything beyond the horrific *materiality* of death itself. Nor do most attempts to find psychological explanations—as in identifications of Roderick Usher with the super-ego and his sister Madeleine with the id, or Roderick with the mind and Madeleine with the body—seem wholly convincing. Poe may be explicable himself in terms of Freudian assumptions of unresolved Oedipality, as Marie Bonaparte has argued at length, but his fiction does not entirely resolve itself into such a coherent pattern. Poe's great contribution to psychological acuity lies more in his identification of a human spirit of *perversity*, detailed in the "The Imp of the Perverse" but also to be seen in "Usher," "The Black Cat," and "The Tell-Tale Heart."

This anti-Utopian thematic of "perversity" had been explored in a preliminary way by Brown, when Arthur Mervyn's self-deluding projects of benevolence result in quite opposite consequences to those he intended (although perhaps they *are* related to his unexamined drives). In *Edgar Huntly* too, the narrator's good intentions backfire in ways that suggest his own inner conflicts. Most memorably he informs the maniac Clithero that the woman he believed he had killed is still alive and living near New York. At the good news Clithero immediately sets off again to kill her, this mother figure whose supposed death has caused his mania of grief. The "primal scene" behind this novel is convoluted: Clithero inadvertently killed Mrs. Lorimer's adored but vicious brother in a fight, and so, afraid that the discovery of this will cause her to die of a broken heart, he decided it would be kindest to murder her, too, before she learns of it. Clithero decribes how he prepared to strike at the sleeping woman with a dagger, only to have his hand held back by Mrs. Lorimer herself: the figure in the bed was her daughter, his own betrothed. Mrs. Lorimer collapsed, seemingly killed by this shock, and so Clithero fled to his exile in Norwalk.

Perversity also shadows Carwin's actions in *Wieland*, and Ormond's rationally benevolent plans are perversely distorted by his powerful personal desires. But Poe takes a further step, making the perverse desire to vex the self into the central motivation of his characters, and removing the previous eighteenth-century clutter of rationalist reflection and commentary so that the self-damaging impulse stands out in sharp relief and beyond explanation. The first line of his tale, "The Man of the Crowd," includes the quotation "es lässt sich nicht lesen"—"it does not permit itself to be read"—which is precisely the case with his own Gothic sensationalism: there is a dark impulse beyond understanding which wreaks havoc, operating in complete contradiction to the normative assumption of the early United States polity that individuals will always seek to act in their own best interests (and therefore might be trusted with democratic self-government and capitalist freedom of enterprise).

"The Man of the Crowd," set in London but obviously relevant to the new American scene, offers a study of one such aberrant individual, pursued by a fascinated (and it seems equally perverse) narrator. First noticed in the early evening, this curious figure roams the city streets among crowds of returning workers, then heads for the busy nightspots, always seeking to be one of the throng. In the small hours he is to be seen desperately seeking company among the few remaining night wanderers, and is visibly relieved by the return of the urban mob in the morning. The narrator finds in his mind a confused sense aroused by the figure: ideas of "vast mental power, of caution, of penuriousness, of avarice, of coolness, of malice, of blood-thirstiness, of triumph, of merriment, of excessive terror, of intense —of extreme—despair."[11] All the qualities of the urban throng are here in contradictory conjunction, suggestive of the promiscuous dangers of democracy. This story, a foretaste of urban Gothic, does not have a plot and is without any significant action. The only clue to the man's behavior is his clothing: through a rent in his ragged dress the narrator glimpses a dagger, but also a diamond and richer linen beneath the outer rags. This man, the narrator insists, is "the type and the genius of deep crime." It is as though Poe senses the possibilities of urban Gothic, as it was later developed for example in Stevenson's *Dr. Jekyll and Mr. Hyde*, but does not yet see how to explore it further.

The urban landscape could serve as a modern version of the incomprehensible castle or monastery of early Gothic, but to do so required a considerable thematic inflection that several early American writers struggled to discover. Brown had similarly attempted to read the significance of the urban space in *Arthur Mervyn*, where the Yellow Fever plague turns Philadelphia into a Night Town, and in *Ormond* again we see a charnel vision due to the outbreak of the fever. But George Lippard, in his best-selling novel *The Quaker City, or, The Monks of Monk Hall* (1844) invented an alternative Philadelphia, comprised of rakes, rogues, and cripples, all involved with a Gothic whorehouse; the secret life supposedly behind the virtuous city's facade. Lippard's pornographic take on the Gothic, reminiscent of Lewis's *The Monk*, combined salacious scenes with social protest against corruption and libertinism, a popular recipe also not unlike the work of Eugene Sue, and later the English writer George Reynolds. The melodramatic possibilities of city life as discovered by Sue and Balzac, with the secret interconnections of high and low society, and the suddenness of transition in a crowded, promiscuous metropolis (well described in Peter Brooks' study, *The Melodramatic Imagination*[12]), was to prove immensely popular, although here it was perhaps more to do with *The Quaker City's* steamy voyeurism than its pretensions to reform. In *Beneath the American Renaissance*, David S. Reynolds details the American development of this kind of writing, showing that the more famous names of the American canon used such motifs quite as often as Lippard, John Neal, or George Thompson, albeit in a manner designed to appease their respectable audience.[13] Among them was Herman Melville, who turned to the urban shocker in a bid for popularity after the failure of *Moby-Dick's* reception. In *Pierre* (1852), Melville deployed a *menage à trois* with incestuous elements in a setting of urban degradation: his aristocratic young writer hero, on discovering that his adored father had sired an illegitimate daughter, Isabel, feels that he must restore the family honor by marrying her, because he cannot dishonor his father's name by admitting her as his sister, while yet maintaining the rights of his existing fiancée, Lucy. This predictably results in a life of poverty and shame, followed by a dramatic death scene, though it did not, unfortunately for Melville, result in the large sales his lurid plot anticipated.

The urban landscapes of the Gothic, however, are just one aspect of the complex adaptations made by American writers. Poe's stylized use of Gothic motifs points toward the intense and economical invocations of Gothic elements in the work of Melville, Nathaniel Hawthorne, and later Ambrose Bierce and Henry James. But unlike these later writers' work, much of Poe's Gothic has a burlesque element.

By the early nineteenth century, the highest point of the Gothic vogue had passed and it frequently became the target for satires and parodies, notably in Jane Austen's *Northanger Abbey* of 1818, and Thomas Love Peacock's *Nightmare Abbey* of the same year. Some of Poe's tales are overtly comic, such as "The Psyche Zenobia, or, How to Write a *Blackwood* Article," in which a narrator details her sensations as her head is slowly cut off by the hand of a giant clock and falls to the ground. But others, including his most famous stories, "The Black Cat," "Ligeia," "The Tell-Tale Heart," and "The Fall of the House of Usher," are played straight-faced in a way that G. R. Thompson has identified as the humor of German Romantic irony. Before Poe, Washington Irving had exploited the comic possibilities of the Gothic tall tale in such stories as "The Adventure of the German Student," "The Spectre Bridegroom," or "Dolph Heyliger." In "The German Student" (1824), a dreamy young student in Paris at the time of the Terror in the French Revolution swears himself forever to a beautiful stranger, but she is found dead on his bed the next morning. When the investigating police remove her black diamond-clasped neckband, her head falls onto the floor. A policeman is asked if he knows the woman. "Do I?" he exclaims, ". . . she was guillotined yesterday!" Then Irving's narrator attests to the undoubted truth of his story: "I had it from the best authority. The student told it me himself. I saw him in a madhouse in Paris." Other writers, such as William Gilmore Simms, and later John Pendleton Kennedy and William Cullen Bryant, also employed a light touch with Gothic elements in their fictions. So as Poe knew, American readers were familiar with Gothic pastiche, and it is only surprising that so little of the close critical attention Poe's work has received has acknowledged the comic element in his preposterous stories.

Trying to write in a sunnier—or at least a less gloomy—tone than he took in *The Scarlet Letter*, Nathaniel Hawthorne attempted comic Gothic in his novel *The House of the Seven Gables* (1851). This concerns a house in Salem whose occupants have regularly been the victims of "Maule's Curse." Maule owned the land that Colonel Pyncheon wanted as the site of his home, and when falsely convicted of witchcraft and destined to be hanged, Maule had cursed Pyncheon, saying (in the words of one of the 1692 Salem witch trial's real victims): "God will give him blood to drink." Colonel Pyncheon duly died choking on his own blood, and thereafter his descendants regularly succumbed to the family curse; which provides Hawthorne the material for a contemporary satire on the evil-doing and hypocrisy of respectable villains like the later Judge Pyncheon, whose character he likens to a magnificent palace with a corpse rotting beneath. The House of the Seven Gables, erected on a shameful rotting corpse, is a version of the Gothic haunted castle, brought up to date and now containing a cent shop selling miscellaneous items. But Hawthorne's serious involvement with his theme of rapacious misappropriation and the evils of inherited wealth overwhelms his comedy to produce a disturbingly sinister effect. It is likely that his own sense of having suffered from the political chicanery of a man very like Pyncheon, one Charles Upham who helped oust Hawthorne from his customs post by false accusations, sharpened the malice of his pen. In the novel's most memorable scene, the author taunts Judge Pyncheon after he has died from the traditional family stroke, in thirteen pages of invective:

> What! Thou art not stirred by this last appeal? No; not a jot! And there we see a fly—one of your common houseflies, such as are always buzzing on the window-pane—which has smelt out Governor Pyncheon, and alights now on his forehead, now on his chin, and now, Heaven help us, is creeping over the bridge of his nose, towards the would-be chief-magistrate's wide-open eyes! Canst thou not brush the fly away? Art thou too sluggish? Thou man, that hadst so many busy projects, yesterday! Art thou too weak, that wast so powerful? Not brush away a fly! Nay, then, we give thee up!

Hawthorne's necrophobic taunting here resembles one of Emily Dickinson's most horrifying poems:

> I heard a Fly buzz—when I died—
> The Stillness in the Room
> Was like the Stillness in the Air—
> Between the Heaves of Storm
>
> The Eyes around—had wrung them dry—
> And Breaths were gathering firm
> For that last onset—when the King
> Be witnessed—in the Room—
>
> I willed my Keepsakes—Signed away
> What portion of me be
> Assignable—And then it was
> There interposed a Fly—
>
> With Blue—uncertain stumbling Buzz—
> Between the light—and me—
> And then the Windows failed—and then
> I could not see to see—

Since the fly is the traditional symbol of Beelzebub, what might seem at first an innocent example of domestic pathos is an introduction to appalling horror: the inward light of the Christian resurrection has been blocked by the buzzing of the fly, the King of Hell, and since this communication is from one already dead, the implication seems to be that all hope of salvation has been denied.

Dickinson's poem, like Hawthorne's description of the necrophilic fly exploring the face of the dead Judge, exemplifies how American writers increasingly came to strike the Gothic note in macabre *detailing* rather than by invoking the genre *in toto*. This is also how the Gothic element occurs in Hawthorne's *The Scarlet Letter* (1850), itself an instance of the particular legacy of Puritan intensity noted earlier. The Salem witchcraft era became for several writers a repository of that gloomy and mysterious past that otherwise seemed unfruitfully absent to the American imagination. John Neal in *Rachel Dyer* (1828) had adopted the 1692 Salem trials as the basis for a popular novel, as did several other authors. In *The Scarlet Letter*, however, Hawthorne uses the Salem episode not directly, but rather as a darkening and enriching context for his story of seduction, betrayal, and shame. The governor's mansion, for example, is decorated with cabalistic inscriptions, Mistress Hibbins is supposed to be a witch, the forest is an unknowable darkness like a castle, the scarlet letter appears in the sky and is inscripted on the guilty minister's chest, Hester's husband Chillingworth is a shamanistic demon figure whose pursuit of Dimmesdale is relentless—in fact Dimmesdale has in this story something of the role of the persecuted female in traditional Gothic, tyrannized into self-mutilation and ultimately death by his adversary. But Hawthorne's Gothic here is preeminently *psychological*, building on Poe's internalizing, and anticipating Henry James's use of the Gothic in his ghost stories; the horror is now within the self. The dark intensity of Puritan imagination, bordering on mania, is also seen in Hawthorne's "Young Goodman Brown" and "The Minister's Black Veil" as well as "Ethan Brand." In each of these tales the protagonist is afflicted by a religious depravity that grotesquely distorts the mindscape.

In his 1850 review of Hawthorne's *Mosses From an Old Manse*, Melville said that he admired the "great power of blackness" in him, derived "from that Calvinistic sense of Innate Depravity and Original Sin, from whose visitations, in some shape or other, no deeply thinking mind is always and wholly free." This did indeed continue to preoccupy Hawthorne, whether in the lighter Gothic fantasies of "Rappacinni's Daughter," the grotesquerie of "The May-Pole of Merrymount" and "My Cousin Major Moulineux," or the Roman art world of *The Marble Faun*.

The most overtly Gothic of Hawthorne's novels, *The Marble Faun* (1860) envisages the European past as a chronicle of horrors, and Rome itself as a labyrinth of crime and intrigue, built insecurely over a sea of blood, and riddled with the Catacombs where some of the most significant events take place. The almost impenetrable plot unites a vision of prelapsarian innocence to the Gothic horror of a sinister monk-like artists' model, who pursues Miriam and is murdered by her lover Donatello at her silent instigation. Miriam is herself obscurely a version of Beatrice Cenci, the girl whose portrait by Guido Reni was much admired in the mid-nineteenth century for its ambiguous linkage of innocent beauty with the double guilt of incest and murder, making her "double-hooded," as Melville memorably expressed the source of the picture's strange fascination, "by the black crape of the two most horrible crimes . . . possible to civilized humanity—incest and parricide."[14]

The unspeakableness of this quintessential Gothic emblem was Hawthorne's undoing; this novel falters under the weight of its Gothic mystifications just as his last Gothic works somehow could not quite discover their own plots. It is perhaps not coincidental that Melville also related his dark heroine Isabel in *Pierre* (1852) to Beatrice Cenci, and that novel too foundered in what the narrator terms her "ever creeping and condensing haze of ambiguities." As the Gothic moved into the realm of psychological terror it encountered the risk that its authors could be overwhelmed by the very themes that compelled them toward it.

Melville's powerful story "Benito Cereno" (1856) brings together the psychological Gothic just mentioned with the racial and political aspects introduced earlier.[15] The Spanish slave ship, the *San Dominick*, encountered at a remote uninhabited island off Chile by a Northern American captain, Amasa Delano, has dark secrets. It appears to him first in the morning mists as resembling a monastery perched on the Pyrenees, inhabited by cowled monks, and subsequently as like some crumbling, deserted chateau, with formal gardens of trailing seaweed and wormy balustrades that threaten to drop the unwary Delano into the depths. The story itself is formally Gothic in its features of indeterminacy, the epistemological quest for the truth, and the constant windings, false clues, and reversals that incapacitate the reader as much as the innocent sea captain in his Isabella or Emily role. There are incessant references to enchantment, the hull is hearse-like, with a wen on its side, the negroes are sphinx-like, the sailors enigmatic, and the ship's bell has a graveyard toll. The hypochondriacal, Usher-like Benito Cereno himself is read by Delano as a Schedoni villain, set on tricking his way into control of the American's ship; his slave Babo is merely seen as a model of the humble docility of the black servant. But Delano has read it all wrong: as the ship's name might have told him, it suggests the ship is *without master,* or rather, as the oval sternpiece implies in showing two *masked* figures, one of whom is holding his adversary down with his foot on the other's neck, the roles are reversed and Babo is the master both of Cereno and the ship. In all, the situation suggests the master is slave to the servant, and inferentially, to hold slaves is in fact to be held by them, in that state of anxiety of insurrection that allows only at most an ever-challenged, hysterical authority. More subtly, by returning in tableau form to this oval sternpiece motif at the denouement, when *Delano* himself sets his foot on the neck of the finally unmasked Babo, Melville's story implies a hypocritical collusion of the North with the Peculiar Institution of the South at the time of impending pre-Civil War tension. Delano and Cereno are thus doubles of a sort, as their names imply.

That racism is the energy that drives this compelling story to a pitch of terror is apparent in what might be called its "surplus" features. The negroes are represented in a Manichean reversal of extremes: from being perceived as wholly subservient, docile, and with engaging animal innocence ("there's mere naked nature for you" Delano comments fondly on watching the females nurse their children, just as he haplessly discourses on the pleasing faithfulness and dexterity seen in Babo's deft shaving of his master with a cutthroat razor); from this illustration of naive stereotypes of the black slave, the text then swerves to an opposite extreme: the slaves have not only engaged in a rebellion which Melville's mostly Northern readers might find legitimate; they have done so with an excess rapacity and cruelty that goes beyond even what can be spoken. Perhaps cannibalism is implied in the clean-picked bones of the ship's concealed skeleton figure-head; perhaps something even worse. At all events, Melville brings us to a sense of what he called, in *Billy-Budd* (1891), "natural depravity," a "depravity according to nature" as he enigmatically construes it, beyond what is explicable. His ending of the story, with Babo's head impaled on a pole, but still looking toward the monastery where Benito will shortly die of his exposure to evil, possibly inspired Conrad's conclusion in *Heart of Darkness*. Delano asks Cereno why he is not able to recover from his experience:

> "But the past is passed; why moralize upon it. See, yon bright sun has forgotten it all, and the blue sea, and the blue sky; these have turned over new leaves."
>
> "Because they have no memory," he dejectedly replied; "because they are not human."
>
> "You are saved: what has cast such a shadow upon you?"
>
> "The negro" (90).

Harriet Beecher Stowe, while maintaining a simpler perspective regarding the horrors of slavery, also found the Gothic useful in pressing home her abolitionist argument in *Uncle Tom's Cabin* (1852).[16] It might be remarked, however, that the surprise in this hugely influential novel is not so much that she has occasional recourse to the Gothic as that it is not wholly a Gothic work. When Eliza flees the vicious slave traders with her child, slipping out of the tavern where they have come to recapture her in the evening, and fleeing across moving blocks of ice on the frozen river, we have a perfect Gothic tableau. But the author resists this in presenting the episode without the expected Gothic accoutrements of anxiety, suspense, and delay. The reason seems to be the centrality of Christian faith in Stowe's world view: Eliza will be secure because God is with her in the escape. Similarly Tom's horrific suffering and death at the Legree plantation is removed from Gothic terror by his noble simplicity of faith, shared by the text itself. Nor does even the death of the angelic child Eva allow any opening to the Gothic, for death even more than life is seen as an access to the triumphal realm of Jesus. But in one episode Stowe does give the Gothic full sway. Cassy and her fellow slave Emmeline, both sexual victims of Simon Legree, arrange their escape by exploiting the supernaturalism of Legree and his henchmen and hiding in the supposedly haunted attic until the search is called off. Cassy appears to Legree in the night, perhaps in his dream:

> But finally, there came over his sleep a shadow, a horror, an apprehension of something dreadful hanging over him. It was his mother's shroud, he thought; but Cassy had it, holding it up and showing it to him. He heard a confused noise of screams and groanings; and, with it all he knew he was asleep, and he struggled to wake himself. He was half awake. He was sure something was coming into his room. He knew the door was opening, but he could not stir hand or foot. At last he turned, with a start; the door was open, and he saw a hand putting out his light (366).

A ghostly figure in white whispers to him "Come! come! come!" as he lies sweating with terror, then the thing is gone and he finds the door securely locked. This episode is clearly a grace-note in Cassy's escape plan, but the effects of his discovery of a lock of little Eva's hair provide an even more fully Gothic scene. Legree has destroyed his mother's keepsake curl because the memory of her reminds him of his own evil; yet when he comes across the fetish object that memorializes Eva he reads the curl as the return of his mother's hair: "the long shining curl of fair hair, —hair which, like a living thing, twined itself around Legree's fingers" (—like the charnel worms, comments Susan Wolstenholme in *Gothic (Re)Visions*, that wrapped themselves around the fingers of the fallen nun Agnes in *The Monk*, in the dungeons under the [suggestively named] "St. Clare" convent). The fetishized and "petrifying" hair, like that of the Medusa in Freud's analysis,[17] represents femininity as terrifying, a reading which "provides a figurative account of how fear of the maternal becomes transmuted to hatred, not only of femininity but also of racial darkness (because within the novel this fear of the maternal is cast as explanatory myth of Legree's debased character. Evidently Legree displaces this hatred/fear of the feminine onto the slaves)."[18]

To find the fear of the feminine at the root of the most Gothic episode of *Uncle Tom's Cabin* will hardly surprise readers of the American Gothic, at least from Poe onwards. "Ligeia," "Usher," "Berenice," "Morella," even "The Murders in the Rue Morgue," where sadistic violence is practiced on the mother and daughter victims (by an Ourang-Outan, of course, which removes any human male complicity in the violation) are all exemplary of Poe's "rational" decision that the death of a beautiful woman must be the literary theme most productive of beauty. Irving's "German Student" Gothic comedy of decapitation, as well as the now largely forgotten early American Gothic stories, Richard Henry Dana, Sr.'s "Paul Felton" (1821) and Washington Allston's *Monaldi* (1822), tales of husbands who are driven magically to murder their beloved wives; Hawthorne's nervous admiration of powerful women and sadistic elaboration of their demise (in, for example, the death and subsequent accidental mutilation of Zenobia's body in *The Blithedale Romance* [1851]); Melville's sense of the threat posed by Isabel in *Pierre*; James's registration of the damage caused by the innocent governess in *The Turn of the Screw* and the not-so-innocent Kate Croy in *The Wings of the Dove:* all these register an acute anxiety about the role of the feminine in nineteenth-century culture, and suggest how a deep gender-anxiety fed into the production of the Gothic. The political agitation for women's rights may well be linked subterraneously to ascriptions of uncanny power to the female, although that connection is rarely made overtly (with the possible exception of James's novel *The Bostonians*, 1886).

But the perception of women's imperilled situation also created a further reach of Gothic, one written by women and conveying a sense of their own fears and oppression. Charlotte Perkins Gilman's "The Yellow Wallpaper" (1892) is a powerful expression of the Gothicism inherent in the experience of patriarchal society. Her heroine, condemned to a therapeutic regime that amounts to imprisonment by her husband and his apparently kindly sister, identifies with the figure of a creeping old woman that she perceives behind the wallpaper pattern of the room where she is confined. By the end of the story she has effectively herself become the spectral woman: "I've got out at last. . . . And I've pulled off most of the paper, so you can't put me back!"[19] Other writers of ghost stories, including Emma

Dawson, Mary Wilkins Freeman, and Edith Wharton, similarly used Gothic treatments to express female experience.

Ambrose Bierce (1842–1914?), who at the end of his life mysteriously disappeared on a trip to Mexico, never displayed much Romantic sensibility but showed instead the profound cynicism often associated with the loss of illusion that many felt in post-Civil War America. He mastered a particularly virulent form of satire, and produced a number of Gothic tales collected in *In the Midst of Life* (1892) and *Can Such Things Be?* (1893), which combine the macabre with astute psychology. His protégé, Emma Dawson, wrote ghost stories with an intermixture of sexuality, sadism, and the uncanny, collected in *The Itinerant House* (1897), which takes its title from a story about a haunted house in San Francisco; one that crops up in various locations as it is physically transplanted according to the Californian practice. Mary E. Wilkins Freeman developed a similar body of work in the stories collected in *The Wind in the Rosebush* (1903), of which "Louella Miller" might be the strongest example. Louella is an ideal Victorian wife: charming, helpless, a little prone to hysteria—the killer of six, for everyone who comes near her dies.

W. D. Howells (1837–1920) is best known as a realist writer and urbane editor, the "Dean of American letters," as he was sometimes called. But Howells too was fascinated by the nightside and wrote several powerful ventures into the Gothic/Uncanny including the stories in *Between the Dark and the Daylight* (1907) and *The Shadow of a Dream* (1890). Robert W. Chamber's extraordinary fantasy of 1895, *The King in Yellow*, invokes Ambrose Bierce's imaginary places, Carcosa and Hali (from "An Inhabitant of Carcosa") and describes a degenerate play, itself also titled "The King in Yellow," which is supposedly so devastating in its beauty and its depravity that even reading it opens the door to corruption and death. The next year, 1896, saw Harold Frederic's story of a priest's temptation and fall, *The Damnation of Theron Ware*, which plays off a Hawthornesque subjective engagement against the formal techniques of realism to produce a disturbingly skewed narrative of the priest Theron Ware's seduction and downfall.

Henry James (1843–1916), who is similarly regarded as a largely realist writer, infused his work with Gothicism, from his early stories written in imitation of Hawthorne through the last intricate novels of despair and redemption. But James's Gothic—although not altogether without its ghosts, as in *The Portrait of a Lady* (1881)—is more internalized, a Gothicism running riot in metaphor and mood rather than made explicit in narrative. In *The Portrait of a Lady* (1881), for example, Isabel Archer is immured, not so much in a stone prison but through her husband's "fine" but appalling mind (he has in effect "collected" her along with her money), of which she takes the measure like some Radcliffean innocent discovering the dimensions of her dungeon.

> Then the shadows began to gather; it was as if Osmond deliberately, almost malignantly, had put the lights out one by one. The dusk at first was vague and thin, and she could still see her way in it. But it steadily increased, and if here and there it had occasionally lifted, there were certain corners of her life that were impenetrably black. These shadows were not an emanation from her own mind. . . . They were a part of her husband's very presence.[20]

In *The Wings of the Dove* (1902), a strong sense of evil is generated through the machinations of Kate Croy against the heiress Milly Theale, culminating in a Gothicized episode in a wintry storm-lashed Venice, and in *The Golden Bowl* (1904) the images of entrapment and stalking produce a sense of uncanny horror even in conventional domestic scenes: a bridge game, a stroll in the gardens. Gender roles may be reversed, for the villain is female as often as not, and the innocent victim male, but the full machinery of Gothic horror is unleashed within the metaphorical structures of the texts. Two of James's most powerful stories, "The Turn of the Screw" (1898) and "The Jolly Corner" (1908), demonstrate the horror of overwhelming delusion, as the Governess in the first attempts to comprehend what she sees as demonic possession in her small charges, and Spencer Brydon in "The Jolly Corner" tries to confront the spectre of his *alter ego*, but instead finds himself overcome by its horrifying presence. Although sometimes regarded as divorced from the concerns of everyday life, James's work derives its force from an apprehension of the underlying structures in his society—in these tales, for example, the unspoken secret of child abuse, or the pernicious effects of *rentier* capitalism—and his ability to interrelate such personal and social pressures gives his work a terrifying undertone. Edith Wharton shared his interest in Gothic ghost stories, which in her hands also often explored the unspoken territory of sexual oppression; the best are collected in *Ghosts* (1937).

In a totally different vein, more related to the phantasmagoric Scientism of Arthur Machen, Algenon Blackwood, or Bram Stoker's *The Great White Worm*, H. P. Lovecraft invented a New England science-fiction bestiary conjured up in baroque prose, and filled with incantatory notions of strange and terrible books, or awful knowledge shared only by the few. His obscene "Old Ones" fantasies entwined racial stereotyping with naturalist psychology and senti-mental archaic mysticism in the horrors of "Cthulthu."

William Faulkner (1897–1962) wrote some tales that clearly belong in the Gothic tradition, like "A Rose For Emily," although most of his work, like James's, would seem not to invite such inter-pretation. If, however, the Gothic is best described as a fiction con-cerned with the horrifying impress of past (but also sometimes present) institutions and events, Faulkner's version of southern his-tory must be seen as a profoundly Gothic vision, not simply in its echoes of the form, as at the end of *Absalom! Absalom!* (1936), when the mansion cracks apart like Poe's House of Usher, but in its deeper logic, imbued as it is with entrapment and despair, flight and pursuit, the inescapability of the past in the present, or the extreme pressures of racial hostilities and a lost southern mythos. *Sanctuary* (1931) is an example of more contemporary Gothicism, while *Light in August* (1932) invites comparison with William Godwin's *Caleb Willams*. Faulkner's world of Yoknapatawpha County is a Scott-like effort of intense re-imagination, combining the extravagance of Jacobean tragedy with an intense naturalistic violence. The line goes back, of course, through the Gothic passages of Stowe's *Uncle Tom's Cabin* to the race-generated Gothicism of Bird's Indian-hater, and the early fictional encounter with Indians in Brown's *Edgar Huntly*. Faulkner's distinction, however, is to show how nothing less than the Gothic mode is fully able to express the reality of the South. Since his writing a whole genre of southern Gothic has been iden-tified, in the work of Truman Capote, Carson McCullers, and Flannery O'Connor. Recently Toni Morrison has developed a new kind of southern Gothicism, from the non-white perspective, to express the atrocity of black experience in the South in *Beloved* (1987), in which the nightmare past is reexperienced through a "spiteful" haunted house and the revenant of a murdered child. Another recent version of Southern Gothic has been Anne Rice's *Interview with a Vampire* series, which draws upon the languid, decadent traditions of American plantation life to refresh an arguably tired genre.

To many American writers the Gothic has come to seem the most appropriate mode for dealing with contemporary experience; its distant but all-controlling institutions, its mechanisms of alienation and destruction, and its continuing atrocities. Frequently the Gothic appears as simply one of a range of resources, like the Gothic-comedy toward the end of Vladimir Nabokov's *Lolita* (1955), or the night scenes in John Hawkes' *The Lime Twig* (1960), or Joseph Heller's *Catch-22* (1961). Equally it may operate at a subordinate level throughout novels that are not predominantly Gothic. Thomas Pynchon developed a form of techno-Gothic influenced by science fiction in *V* (1963) and *Gravity's Rainbow* (1973), and his *The Crying of Lot 49* (1966) is a controlled exercise in Gothic hysteria. Much of William Burroughs' work could be described as Gothic phantasmagoria, as could a host of other novels, like Stephen Schneck's *The Night Clerk*, or such recent thrillers as Thomas Harris's *Red Dragon, Hannibal,* and *The Silence of the Lambs.* William Gaddis offers an homage to the genre in *Carpenter's Gothic*, as does Richard Brautigan in *The Hawkline Monster: A Gothic Western.* Joyce Carol Oates has a number of distinguished Gothic novels, such as *The Bloodsmoor Romance*, and Susan Sontag's *Death Kit* similarly belongs to the genre. The most striking recent departure is perhaps William Gibson's cyber-Gothic in the *Neuromancer* series of books, where the process of *internalizing* that has characterized development of the Gothic mode for two centuries opens out again, now into a *shared* inner landscape created by the integration of mind and computer; a new fantastic realm operating again according to the original Gothic principles. Gibson's is a fantastic reality, as much so as Maturin's, Beckford's, or Hogg's, but it is driven by a disturbing new integration, no longer neurosis or religious hysteria but instead a terrifying *interspace* where the imaginary and the real change places.

Notes

1. Harry Levin, *The Power of Blackness* (New York: Vintage, 1958); Toni Morrison, *Playing in the Dark: Whiteness and the Literary Imagination* (Cambridge, MA: Harvard University Press, 1992).

2. Jean Baudrillard, *America* (London and New York: Verso, 1986) p. 28.

3. Leslie Fiedler, *Love and Death in the American Novel*, 1960 (New York: Delta, 1966) p. 29.

4. Charles Brockden Brown, *Wieland, or, The Transformation*, 1798 (New York: Harcourt Brace and World, facsimilie of 1926 ed.) pp. 28, 29. This provides an interesting comparison with Washington Irving's comic Gothic fable "Rip Van Winkle," in which the Revolutionary War is forgotten.

5. Jane Tomkins, *Sensational Designs: The Cultural Work of American Fiction 1790–1860* (New York: Oxford University Press, 1985) pp. 48, 49.

6. Charles Brockden Brown, *Edgar Huntly; or, Memoirs of a Sleepwalker*, 1799 (Kent, OH: Kent State University Press, Bicentennial Edition, 1984).

7. Fred Botting, *Gothic* (London and New York: Routledge, 1996) pp. 7, 11.

8. Leslie Fiedler, *Love and Death in the American Novel*, 1960 (New York: Delta, 1966) pp. 160, 161.

9. Henry James, *The Golden Bowl*, 1904 (Harmondsworth, England: Penguin Books, 1985) p. 42.

10. David Punter, *The Literature of Terror* (London: Longman, 1980) p. 203.

11. *Selected Writings of Edgar Allan Poe*, Edward H. Davidson, ed. (Boston: Houghton Mifflin, 1956) p. 135.

12. Peter Brooks, *The Melodramatic Imagination: Balzac, James, Melodrama and the Mode of Excess* (New York: Columbia University Press, 1985).

13. David S. Reynolds, *Beneath the American Renaissance: The Subversive Imagination in the Age of Emerson and Whitman* (Cambridge, MA: Harvard University Press, 1989) pp. 169–211.

14. Herman Melville, *Pierre; or, The Ambiguities*, 1852 (New York: New American Library, 1964) p. 393. See also Chapter Five.

15. Herman Melville, *Selected Tales and Poems* (New York: Holt, Rinehart and Winston, 1950).

16. Harriet Beecher Stowe, *Uncle Tom's Cabin*, 1852 (New York: Norton, 1994).

17. Regarding Freud on the Medusa's head, see Allan Lloyd-Smith, *Uncanny American Fiction*, pp. 161–162.

18. Susan Wolstenhome, *Gothic (Re)Visions: Writing Women as Readers* (New York: State University of New York Press, 1993) pp. 88, 90.

19. See Chapters Five and Six for more discussion of this story.

20. Henry James, *The Portrait of A Lady*, 1881 (New York: New American Library, 1963) p. 392.

Chapter Five

Major Themes in American Gothic

Gothic Heritage: Rationalism and Perversity

Ormond (1799), one of Charles Brockden Brown's most potent novels concerning the hopes and fears of the early Republic, shows how European influences in American Gothic writing were not simply instrumental in matters of style or imitated plot, but carried material of genuine anxiety: in this case, the fear of European rationalism and radicalism, and the absence of a sustaining American polity capable of defending the individual against such terrors. The question was all the more urgent for Brown because the French Revolution was so recent and so compelling in its possibilities and its failures, and because Brown himself shared in many respects the rational and secular perspectives of the new age. Most of his novels explored the benefits and the limits of Godwinian rationalism, considering such issues as the rights of man—and as significantly—of women; the obligations of benevolence and the perils of ill-informed good intentions; the limits of knowledge derived from the senses and experience; and also the propensity later theorized by Poe toward perverseness in acting against the self's own best interests. Although most of Brown's protagonists mean well, they are consistently deceived—by others, by their own senses and their own hidden drives, but most of all by their own innate perversity. As Arthur Mervyn expresses it, "The constitution of my mind is doubtless singular and perverse; yet that opinion, perhaps, is the fruit of my ignorance. It may be by no means uncommon for men to fashion their conclusions in opposition to evidence and *probability*, and so as to feed their malice and subvert their happiness."[1] Another bewildered hero, Henry Colden, asks what causes his "incurable folly? —this rooted incapacity of acting as every motive, generous and selfish, combine to recommend? Constitution; habit; insanity; the dominion of some evil spirit, who insinuates his baneful power between the *will* and the *act*," is his conclusion.[2]

Ormond himself—the villain, not the hero of his novel—brings to America enormous talents and a complete lack of morality. His ability to spy on others is almost preternatural, his commitment to himself absolute, and his rationalism devastating. For him "considerations of justice and pity were made, by a fatal perverseness of reasoning, champions and bulwarks of [his] most atrocious mistakes."[3] He sets his formidable abilities to work on the seduction of Constantia Dudley, another rational being, who proves eventually to be his match, killing him with a penknife in a lonely house in Brown's melodramatic Gothic climax. The seduction plot is less significant than Brown's demonstrations of a Philadelphia threatened by chaos from the Yellow Fever plague; the helpless sufferings of the worthy Dudleys (Constantia and her father, reduced to penury), and the all powerful machinations of European immorality represented in Ormond. Constantia defeats him because her own rationalism stops short at the preservation of her virtue, against what Ormond in his obsessive rationalism ridicules as "this injury without a name or substance."[4]

The character of Ormond explores some of the possible consequences of William Godwin's rationalism, to which Brown himself largely subscribed. Brown claims, for example, that man is no more than a cog in the social system, "He was part of a machine, and as such had not power to withhold his agency," just as Godwin, in his *Thoughts on Man*, had argued that "man is a machine, that he is governed by external impulses, and is to be regarded as the medium only through the intervention of which previously existing causes are enabled to produce certain effects."[5] Rationalism is undermined from several directions. It tends to remove all values from moral and social systems, leading to catastrophes on the political level (such as the French Revolution), and on the personal level (such as the threat to Constantia's virtue). It is damaged by an irreducible perversity in the self, such that good intentions prove suspect, and people do *not* will what would be best for them; and it is often seen by

Brown as being in the service of irrational drives, such as Ormond's lust. It is, besides, fatally weakened by failures in perception: Constantia thinks, for example, that Ormond is a paragon of honesty like herself, saying bemusedly "All you know, all you wish, and all you purpose, are known to others as soon as yourself" (VI 248). This is far from truth, it is simply due to Ormond's pretence of transparency. In fact, in Berlin he had fallen in with "schemers and reasoners who aimed at the new-modeling of the world, and the subversion of all that has hitherto been conceived elementary and fundamental in the constitution of man and of government." He concealed where the seat of this new empire should be "—whether on the shore of an *austral* continent, or in the heart of desert America—."[6]

Brown seems to see a fatal weakness in the American emphasis on rational progressivism and the optimistic throwing off of the past. Reason and benevolence were consistently assaulted in his novels, by amoral free thinkers with a European background like Ormond or Carwin in *Wieland* (who is also associated with a radical European secret society), and from within by the fault lines of naiveté and madness, as we see in Clara and Theodore Wieland, Constantia, Arthur Mervyn, and Edgar Huntley. Horror lurks below utopian surfaces: in cities plagued by fever and social breakdown; in the wilderness with its natural labyrinths, darkness, and legacies of native Indian hostilities; and ultimately, within the self.

Reason in the Age of Reason provided no bulwark for Brown against horror—in fact, as in France, it might lead to it—and he turned to writing sentimental novels in which the conundrum could be resolved by faith and propriety, before ceasing to write novels altogether, becoming a magazine editor instead. But for Edgar Allan Poe the interplay between reason and horror released the energies of his most powerful work, and led him toward the creation of the detective genre.

"The Murders in the Rue Morgue," a founding story of detection, pits Poe's detective August Dupin's "ratiocinative" calm against the hysteria of a depraved action, in which a mother and her daughter have been violently murdered, and the daughter's body thrust up a chimney in a locked room. Dupin solves the case precisely because, in a sense, it is unsolvable, *not* amenable to reason. He deduces that such unreasonable action cannot be human, and triumphantly convicts an escaped great ape of the crime (on not altogether convincing evidence[7]). The crisis or breakdown of reason gave Poe his great theme: a crisis overcome in the detective stories, but overpowering the minds of his other deranged narrators. For Poe, reason seems a masquerade, adopted only when convenient—as in his celebratory analysis of his own poem "The Raven" in "The Philosophy of Composition"—but more often undermined by the material realm (we might call it, after Lacan, the "real") that refuses submission to its rule. Those violated bodies, that chimney and locked space, cannot be fully subdued even by Dupin's majestic thought processes, and arguably least of all by a shifting of responsibility to what is outside of human agency.

Poe's culture was dominated by reason, in the form of the "Common Sense" school of philosophy—even more popular in America than in Scotland where it originated—which insisted on a simple material world, fully understood by the senses and the judgment, and based securely on experience (along with a supposedly innate moral sense).[8] This philosophy provided a refutation of Berkeley's subjectivity and Hume's skepticism but in Poe's time was becoming increasingly outmaneuvered by variants of transcendental "Reason" derived ultimately from Kant. The realization that the "Common Sense" model of experience based on reflection on the evidence of the senses could not account for even the most basic experience of time or space, which must instead depend upon innate qualities of the mind, allowed popularizers of the New Philosophy to claim the existence of Higher Reason, accessible by intuition and introspection. Poe's fiction plays around this theme, showing how his narrators attempt to contain their irrational experiences, drives, and desires within the rational framework. "True!—nervous—very, very dreadfully nervous I had been and am; but why *will* you say that I am mad?," the narrator of "The Tell-Tale Heart" begins, before explaining his reason for murder: "Object there was none. Passion there was none. I loved the old man. He had never wronged me. . . . I think it was his eye! Yes, it was this!"[9] He rants on: ". . . this is the point. You fancy me mad. Madmen know nothing. But you should have seen *me*. You should have seen how wisely I proceeded—with what caution, with what foresight—with what dissimulation I went to work!" (195). These merely *calculating* attributes of mind, as Dupin observes in "The Purloined Letter," are limited; the Minister D—is not only a mathematician but also a poet, and therefore he, like the equally intuitive Dupin, rises above them.

That the murderer's fixation in "The Tell-Tale Heart" should be with the physical eye itself, however, reminds that Poe's approaches to the Higher Reason and eternal truths were mostly limited to his poetry: his *prose* continually confronts the immediate, viscerally abject, material real of the body; or the corpse. Death is perpetually confronted in Poe's fiction, but the doorway to the eternal opens only to the horror of this intransigent "real." In "The Facts in the Case of M. Valdemar," for example, the subject is put into a mesmeric trance before death. He dies, but remains in a suspended animation and still retains the power of speech. A letter Poe wrote in July 1844 suggested that he might himself believe in a mesmeric ability to see beyond the grave: "At death, the worm is the butterfly, still material, but of a matter unrecognized by our organs—recognized occasionally perhaps, by the sleep-walker directly—without organs—through the mesmeric medium. Thus a sleep-walker may see ghosts."[10] In Poe's story, however, when Valdemar speaks, it is only to groan "I am dead" and "Let me die!" The ending of the story has Valdemar's body collapse into a putrefying liquid on the bed, stressing the corporeality of the body and its abjection; we are given no "beyond." Less purulently, another of Poe's narrators reads a word that has appeared on a sail he idly dabbed with tar when it was folded on the deck of a ghost ship. Unfurled it allows him a communication from the further realm. Like a sardonic mirror of his aspiration, however, it reads only DISCOVERY. Lady Madeleine Usher returns from the grave to fall upon her brother and drag him with her into death; Ligiea reanimates the body of the replacement wife Rowena—but the story ends there, she offers no message except horror; supposedly dead Berenice shrieks in his dream as her sleep-walking cousin Egaeus pulls the teeth that obsess him from her catatonic body; and so on. Endlessly "modern" or even "postmodern," Poe in these ways points the way toward *abjection* in horror, which will be discussed later in more detail.

Puritanism

It may seem surprising to link the seemingly godless Poe to the after-shocks of Puritanism, but that may be a significant aspect of his evo-cations of horror and terror. The horrific immediacy of his fallen worlds offers a hellish vision of the depraved and demonic human will;[11] his poetry addresses an angelic realm but those in the unre-deemed world below register it only as a charnel-house filled with tormented minds and bodies. The highly calibrated introspection of his narrators, watching their minds slip away or realizing the extent of their sins and corruption; the fear of Catholicism in "The Pit and the Pendulum," or the exploration of southern European revenge culture in "The Cask of Amontillado," all suggest that Poe might be seen as possessing a Puritan imagination, but largely without com-pensatory notions of grace. Melville wrote of Hawthorne's "Calvinistic sense of Innate Depravity and Original Sin, from whose visitations, in some shape or other, no deeply thinking mind is always and wholly free."[12] Equally, we might say, from which no deeply thinking *American* mind of the period could be free. Poe, then, might be seen as a man of his time in another sense than that noted by Edward Davidson, when he says that "[Poe] brought to lit-erature and to critical theory a mind which was, *in part*, out of the eighteenth century and thus hardly romantic at all—a mind which believed in the values of clarity, precision, and reason of the pre-ceding century which had reached from Pope to Dr. Johnson" (ital-ics added).[13] Another *part* was surely that great imaginative input for the American, the perspectives and images from hell-fired Puritanism. Poe's tales of tormented sinners propose a kind of dark necessity, for which their explanations provide only rationalized jus-tifications. The predestinarianism underlying Calvinism represents man as helplessly working out a fate he can only pretend to choose, which in Poe's hands prefigures an absurdist, existentialist mod-ernism, as in the explanation that it is simply the old man's eye that provides the motive for murder in "The Tell-Tale Heart"; but equally, as in "Ligeia," it can suggest a dark, puritanical view of earthly follies: ". . . the play is the tragedy, 'Man,'/ And its hero the Conqueror Worm."[14] It might be argued, in fact, that even Poe's apparent early identification of the unconscious is a product of this

Calvinist sense of how destiny spins against intention and rationality, producing a sense of an inexorable drive toward something that might not be consciously wished for—ultimately, of course, death.

The Gothic Object, "The Thing"

Nathaniel Hawthorne felt the heat of Puritanism more directly and consciously as, while not himself Puritan or even particularly religious,[15] he was a descendant of the Judge Hathorne who played a key role in the Salem witchcraft trials in 1692, like the infamous supernaturalist Cotton Mather; a lineage Hawthorne ruefully acknowledges in the "Custom House" sketch that introduces *The Scarlet Letter*. "I, the present writer, as their representative, hereby take shame upon myself for their sakes, and pray that any curse incurred by them—as I have heard, and as the dreary and unprosperous condition of the race, for many a long year back, would argue to exist— may be now and henceforth removed."[16] In "The Custom House" Hawthorne describes finding the ancient scarlet letter "A" bound up with an old manuscript (itself another Gothic trope) that tells its story. As he holds the Letter it seems to burn: "I felt a sensation not altogether physical, yet almost so, as of burning heat; and as if the letter were not of red cloth but red-hot iron" (25). Hawthorne's ironic tone here is of a piece with his treatment of the Gothic more generally: the nightmares of the Puritan imagination are reencountered in a minor key, now as much in the mind as in the fictional reality. The spectral fire of the scarlet letter, which as like a "red-hot iron" of the mind burns into Hester's consciousness, occurs also in "Young Goodman Brown," when the haunted woods during the Black Mass seem "all on fire, blazing high into the night" but the fire, like the "liquid flame"—or water reddened by the fire, or blood?—in the occult font, disappears when Brown manages to resist the hallucinatory evil ceremony and, the "hanging twig, that had been all on fire, besprinkled his cheek with the coldest dew."[17] Once burned by the spectral fire Goodman Brown becomes "a stern, a sad, a darkly meditative, a distrustful, if not a desperate man" after "the night of that fearful dream" (123, 124). Instead of the literal, visceral, horrors of Poe's tales, Hawthorne explores the Puritan imagination as it warps its inheritors, men like Brown, or the Reverend Hooper of "The

Minister's Black Veil," who takes to his death the secret of why he wears the awful veil that terrifies his congregation.

Hooper's veil is given no explanation, or rather, as is characteristic of Hawthorne it is "over-determined"; we are offered *too many* explanations. The villagers are left to speculate on why Hooper should always wear his black veil, and they assume that it represents a penance for some secret sin. Hawthorne has taken a familiar Gothic device, the mysterious veil, and centered it as the obsessive focus of the text: it might represent penitence, a consciousness of personal wrongdoing, or it could be a figure for the sins of everyone. But as an object it develops its own power, even over Hooper himself. The dread of the village children causes him to feel that "a preternatural horror was interwoven with the threads of the black crepe" (153), and his own antipathy to the veil is so great that he never passes before a mirror or drinks at a still fountain in case he should see himself. Even his intended wife Elizabeth is unable to see through the veil, and although wondering if it indicates some mental disease: "in an instant, as it were, a new feeling took the place of sorrow; her eyes were fixed insensibly on the black veil, when, like a sudden twilight in the air, its terrors fell around her" (152). This figure of an enigmatic "something else," replete with meanings but not decipherable, can be said to haunt American Gothic writing. The scarlet letter is one example, Melville's unreadable white whale Moby-Dick is another. In Melville's "Bartleby the Scrivener," his melancholic copyist endlessly replies to every effort to make him participate in the work and life around him "I would prefer not to"; his enigmatic response is neither a something nor a nothing. To this we might add the teeth of Poe's "Berenice," his black bird of night in "The Raven," the sail writing in "MS Found in a Bottle," the hieroglyphics in *Arthur Gordon Pym*; or, in poetry, Emily Dickinson's "There's a certain slant of light":

> When it comes; the landscape listens—
> shadows hold their breath—
> When it goes, 'tis like the distance
> On the look of Death—
> (Poem 320)[18]

Other examples include Hawthorne's "Lady Eleanore's Mantle," or the girl, the flowers and the fountain in "Rappaccini's Daughter." A much later manifestation might be the golden bowl itself in Henry James's novel *The Golden Bowl* (1904). Such "fetish objects" may be interpreted in several ways. For literary criticism they provide examples of symbolism: coalescences of possible meanings within a text, often repeated to produce a particular aesthetic shaping and organization. In philosophical terms it is possible to read the mute but transcendent object as related—if mostly negatively—to the American Transcendentalists' assumption of a benign and readable Nature, a Nature that speaks a truer language than the corrupted versions we use and prompts Emerson's ambition to "fasten words again to visible things."[19] There is the suggestion of an occultist tradition in which certain objects may have unnatural powers; or alternatively there is a foretaste of a phenomenological encounter with the otherness of things in the world (things-in-themselves) and the oppression these may occasion in human attempts to disguise them with meaning. Psychologically such fixations would have been read by contemporaries as examples of obsessions, fixed ideas, monomanias; psychoanalytically by a later audience as displacements of responses to trauma and frustrated desire and, in Lacanian terms, the Real as opposed to the real, the recognition that the world is not comprehensible within the Symbolic realm of acculturated structures of thought.

Such enigmas of the American Gothic can be shown to have recuperable social and historical meanings, the problem—and the game—however, is that they exceed all these. In the case of "The Minister's Black Veil," for example, it is quite evident that one of the meanings ascribed to the veil has profound resonance with the Calvinist view that the world is already and always "fallen"; all are sinners and most are doomed. "Young Goodman Brown" also finds this in the woods, when he finds that the demonic participants in the Black Mass are all those people he had most respected, and even his beloved young wife Faith is among the congregation. Hooper's wearing of the black veil suggests that this is how a true Puritan must see the world (and he does become a most effective clergyman through inspiring a sense of dread, despite his kindness). Equally the veil allows Hawthorne to explore the idea that nobody can really be known, even to those closest to him, like Elizabeth, Hooper's lover. And it allows for some rather pat moralizing for a reader who does not delve too deeply: Hooper is wrong to see the world only in this way; surely he should balance the shadow with the light? Similarly shouldn't Giovanni in "Rappacinni's Daughter" realize that the physical poisonousness of his adored Beatrice and her fatal flowers only shroud her deeper spiritual truth and beauty; or Young Goodman Brown simply accept his neighbors' failings and his own instead of leading a dark and disappointed life after his dream of the forest? In the same way, Poe's bereaved lover in "The Raven" is clearly anticipating and exploiting the inevitable answer of the bird: "Nevermore." And isn't Egaeus's fixation with his cousin Berenice's teeth to be understood as a fetishism related to the fantasy of the "vagina dentata"? If this were "explained Gothic" like Ann Radcliffe's, the mysterious portrait or whatever other magical object would have such a natural "realistic" explanation: Hooper's black veil would be stripped away in the revelation of his reasons for wearing it—a sin, a crime, a failure, a promise. But in this enigmatic American version the Gothic object is allowed its own life, remaining stubbornly resistant to interpretation, however persuasive. Like the scarlet letter its meanings twist and turn as events and attitudes organize themselves around it, so that what might have been a minor element, a Gothic grace-note or piece of mysterious scenery, colonizes other realms of meaning—or, indeed, non-meaning, refusal to mean. That refusal to mean might itself be seen historically, of course: in a culture so obstinately insistent on the everyday, the optimistic, the progressive and the common-sensical, the "naysaying" (as Melville called it) of the artist required a stubborn refusal to allow meaning to be suborned by conventional understanding, an insistence upon a flickering negation of whatever cultural nets that could be brought to capture it. This is, in part, what makes American writing of the nineteenth century so modern: it anticipates the existential and the absurd in a Kafkaesque resistance to the too easily understood. And this is also what makes it uncanny.

The Uncanny in American Gothic

Freud's account of the uncanny in his profoundly influential essay "Das Unheimliche" (1919) identified some of its features as a strangeness within the familiar, "everything that ought to have remained . . . secret and hidden but has come to light";[20] repetition, coincidence, animism, and other archaic beliefs; an inability to imagine one's own death leading to fear of the "double"; and the fear of castration, which he identified with the fear of losing one's eyes. Many of these features recur in the American Gothic. The German word for the uncanny, *das Unheimliche*, carries the meaning of the unhomely: it can be understood as equivalent to the "domestic terror" which so aptly describes much of the work of American Gothicists. The house, not the castle, becomes the site of trauma; its terror deriving from the familiar inmates instead of some external threat, and its terror therefore what Poe called a terror of the soul, and not of Germany.

Poe's story "The Black Cat" announces itself as "a simple tale of domestic events" and indeed remains such, however macabre those events turn out to be. The previously animal-loving narrator turns against his affectionate cat, Pluto, putting out one of the creature's eyes with a penknife in a fit of "gin-nurtured" fiendish malevolence of the sort his patient wife has had to endure. The spirit of PER-VERSENESS (capitalized in Poe's text), this "unfathomable longing of the soul to *vex itself*" (201), urges him on until he hangs the animal from a tree in his garden. After a fire consumes his house that night, one wall only remains, and on it is impressed in *bas relief* a gigantic cat, with a rope about its neck. In his "half-sentiment that seemed, but was not remorse," the haunted narrator adopts another black cat, closely resembling the first, except for a patch of white fur on its breast. Only after it follows him home does he realize, next morning, that like Pluto "it had also been deprived of one of its eyes." He again comes to loathe this second cat for its affectionate closeness. The white patch of fur then takes on by degrees "a rigorous distinctness of outline," the image of "a hideous—of a ghastly thing—of the GALLOWS!" (203, 204). As this cat almost trips him on his cellar stairs, he swings at it with an axe which, when his wife restrains him, he buries instead in *her* brain. To conceal her body, the narrator walls it up in the cellar, and significantly enjoys his first tranquil night's sleep since the introduction of the cat. But perversely tapping on the wall of the cellar in the presence of suspicious police officers he provokes from the hidden recess a hideous scream, "utterly anomalous and inhuman—a howl!—a wailing shriek, half of horror and half of triumph, such as might have arisen only out of hell, conjointly from the throats of the damned in their agony and of the demons that exult in their damnation" (207). The wall is soon pulled down and there follows a moment of voyeuristic horror:

> The corpse, already greatly decayed and clotted with gore, stood erect before the spectators. Upon its head, with red extended mouth and solitary eye of fire, sat the hideous beast whose craft had seduced me into murder, and whose informing voice had consigned me to the hangman (208).

This tale is a variant of the sensational fiction popular in the 1830s and 1840s, to be found in *Blackwood's Edinburgh Magazine*, or the work of American novelists such as John Neal, George Thompson, or George Lippard. David Reynolds has shown in his study of such literature that Poe's versions are, in fact, generally more restrained and more tightly focused than the enthusiastic but often incoherent accounts of violence and sexual depravity that found a mass market in his America.[21] The story ostensibly has a temperance motif, but as with much of this literature of "dark reform" the improving sentiment acts rather as a cover for the performance than its true *raison d'être*. It has also been seen as a story containing racial and anti-slavery motifs: the use of the pet black animal as comparable to a sentimentalizing of the slave; an echo of lynching in its fate.[22] But more than this it seems an exercise in the *uncanny* as Freud was later to theorize it in his essay. In fact, the story displays almost a roll call of the features that Freud brings into focus in "Das Unheimliche": to repeat some of them; a strangeness within the familiar, the emergence of what "ought to have remained secret and hidden"; repetition, coincidence, animism, and archaic beliefs; the inability to imagine one's own death leading to fear of the "double"; and also the fear of castration, associated for Freud with the fear of losing one's eyes. Whether in fact the story is experienced as uncanny may depend on the reading experience—the uncanny in literature is, above all, a reading effect[23]—but it certainly fulfills Freud's description of the factors involved in producing that effect, and particularly the most important element: the strange within the familiar, what is hidden and should not but nevertheless does come to light. The discovery of the walled-up corpse provides an exact figuration of this process (just as the cat seems to represent the castration fear, animism and other archaic beliefs, and the representation of one's own death; imagined as the self alive in the tomb). But *what*, exactly, is hidden and comes to be revealed may be another matter. As we have seen, the cat's blackness may suggest a racial inflection, its lynching a southern trauma. More openly, the cat seems to represent the wife, onto whom the blow is so easily deflected. The narrator feels no remorse, nor does he express surprise at his action, instead he remarks nonchalantly: "She fell dead upon the spot, without a groan. This hideous murder accomplished, I set myself forthwith, and with entire deliberation, to the task of concealing the body" (205). Attentive readers will have noticed that his wife, who was superstitious, had "made frequent allusion to the ancient popular notion, which regarded all black cats as witches in disguise. Not that she was ever serious upon this point. . . ." (200). Not, in any event, as serious as the narrator proves to be. The cat is an avatar of the witch; the wife is killed instead of the cat. Misogyny, then, is part of that strangeness within the familiar: the *woman* is walled up, only to break out and return. The howling of the immured cat, likened to the howling of the damned and their tormenters, suggests as clearly as does the doubled *William Wilson* that Poe is finding external correlatives for internal divisions of the mind. And perhaps more horror is lurking behind the wall of what ought to be hidden but comes to light: what sustained the cat with its "red extended mouth" during those four days in the tomb?

Another aspect of the uncanny is suggested in this story, this "most wild, yet homely narrative" (199), through the narrator's asides on perverseness. He consistently finds himself acting against his expectations; finding, for example a dislike for the new animal that is "just the reverse of what I had anticipated" (203). Where he should find the most familiar, he finds the strange, and formulates his view of the spirit of PERVERSENESS to account for it:

> Of this spirit philosophy takes no account. Yet I am not more sure that my soul lives, than I am that perverseness is one of the primitive impulses of the human heart—one of the indivisible primary faculties, or sentiments, which give

direction to the character of Man. Who has not, a hundred times, found himself committing a vile or a silly action, for no other reason than because he knows he should *not*? Have we not a perpetual inclination, in the teeth of our best judgment, to violate that which is *Law*, merely because we understand it to be such? This spirit of perverseness, I say, came to my final overthrow. It was this unfathomable longing of the soul *to vex itself*—to offer violence to its own nature—to do wrong for the wrong's sake only—that urged me to continue and finally to consummate the injury I had afflicted upon the unoffending brute. One morning, in cool blood, I slipped a noose about its neck and hung it to the limb of a tree; —hung it with the tears streaming from my eyes, and with the bitterest remorse at my heart; —hung it *because* I knew that it had loved me, and *because* I felt it had given me no reason of offence; —hung it *because* I knew that in so doing I was committing a sin—a deadly sin that would so jeopardize my immortal soul as to place it—if such a thing were possible—even beyond the reach of the infinite mercy of the Most Merciful and Most Terrible God (202).

The aspiration of the Gothic villain is here reduced to bathos as he imagines his immortal soul to be beyond the reach of the (sardonically noted) infinite mercy (and terrible power) of his God for a mere act of cruelty to an animal.[24] But the further reach of this extends to the issue of the uncanny, the alienating experience of unconscious compulsion, and the feeling of being in the control of something other than the familiar self; a doubling within. His explication of perverseness of course extends to the indifferently accepted murder of his wife, and although it is explained in the language of Phrenology and the Will, familiar jargon of the then current psychology, it serves to open up a fissure in the usual assumptions of agency, just as it does in "The Tell-Tale Heart" or "The Imp of the Perverse," or Arthur Gordon Pym's swooning fall from a cliff, to be caught in the arms of the dusky Dirk Peters.

Another direction is pointed by this tale, the uncanny death and return of the woman, such as we see in "Ligeia," "Morella," and Irving's "German Student," and more will be said of the concept of abjectification of the woman in a later section.

Frontier Gothic, Gothic Nature

In his Preface to *Edgar Huntley* (1799), Charles Brockden Brown wrote disparagingly of the means adopted by earlier authors for engaging the reader's sympathy and passions: "Puerile superstition and exploded manners; Gothic castles and chimeras, are the materials usually employed for this end." In his view, "the incidents of Indian hostility, and the perils of the western wilderness, are far more suitable; and, for a native of America to overlook these, would admit of no apology" (3). The incidents of Indian hostility do play a significant role in his novel, and the perils of the wilderness— although not one that many would now see as western—provides a labyrinthine setting that replaces the European windings of convent or castle corridors and dungeons. His Norwalk wilderness is remarkably barren and indeterminate, a place that comes to seem a wilderness of the bewildered mind as much as nature when Huntley sleepwalks his way into its confusions. This is not the picturesque landscape of Ann Radcliffe's European Gothic, but a more abstractly sinister place where the dungeon becomes a cave and its prisoner has no memory of how he came to be there: "Methought I was the victim of some tyrant who had thrust me into a dungeon of his fortress, and left me no power to determine whether he intended I should perish with famine, or linger out a long life in hopeless imprisonment" (161, 162). The tropes of the Gothic seem almost reassuring in comparison with the not-knowing emptiness the American confronts here. Similarly, the threat of a living death is entertained up in a Poe-esque manner: "I had fallen into seeming death and my friends had confined me to a tomb, from which a resurrection was impossible. That in such a case, my limbs would have been confined to a coffin, and my coffin to a grave, and that I should instantly have been suffocated, did not occur to destroy my supposition" (162). The Gothic chimeras are conjured up and exploited even as they are rejected, pointing the way toward the subsequent path of American Gothic, in which the feudal armory of European progenitors is reinterpreted as largely indicative of inward states of mind, and abstracted into metaphor.

In Melville's *Moby-Dick* the frontier Gothic persists within an ostensibly naturalistic whaling tale.[25] The Pequod, for example, is presented as "a ship of the old school," long seasoned and weather stained, her old hull's complexion darkened, her venerable bows looking bearded, and her ancient decks "worn and wrinkled, like the pilgrim-worshipped flagstone in Canterbury Cathedral where Beckett bled" (105). But more than this:

> She was apparelled like any barbaric Ethiopian emperor, his neck heavy with pendants of polished ivory. She was a thing of trophies. A cannibal of a craft, tricking herself forth in the chased bones of her enemies. All round, her unpanelled, open bulwarks were garnished like one continuous jaw, with the long sharp teeth of the sperm whale, inserted there for pins. . . . She sported a tiller; and that tiller was in one mass, curiously carved from the long narrow jaw of her hereditary foe (106).

This ship is cannibal, almost alive, barbaric in its trophy wearing, destined to hunt its "hereditary" enemy, the sperm whale (or more particularly, Moby-Dick). Cannibalism was one of Melville's important themes, providing the plot for his early success *Typee* (1846) and making a disturbing undertone in "Benito Cereno." It was also, as H. L. Malchow points out in his "Gothic Images of Race in Nineteenth Century England," a significant element within Gothic more generally, informing what we might call Colonial or Empire Gothic, and, of course, implicit in stories of vampirism. The Pequod (named after an "extinct" Indian tribe) has a further demonic aspect too, as appears in the chapter called "The Try-Works," when the whale blubber is rendered down over a great hearth:

> As they narrated to each other their unholy adventures, their tales of terror told in words of mirth; as their uncivilized laughter forked upwards out of them, like the flames from the furnace; as to and fro, in their front, the harpooners wildly gesticulated with their huge pronged forks and dippers; as the wind howled on, and the sea leaped, and the ship groaned and dived, and yet steadfastly shot her red hell further and further into the blackness of the sea and the night, and scornfully champed the white bone in her mouth, and viciously spat round her on all sides; then the rushing Pequod, freighted with savages and laden with fire,

and burning a corpse, and plunging into that blackness of darkness, seemed the material counterpart of her monomaniac commander's soul (540).

Ahab himself seems a frantically exacerbated version of the Gothic villain, magnetically imposing his will on the crew as he pursues his own demented purposes. He is possessed by hatred and the desire for revenge on the whale that took his leg and his manhood, literally possessed in the demonic sense such that he becomes not a man but a thing—"the tormented spirit that glared out of bodily eyes, when what seemed Ahab rushed from his room, was but for the time a vacated thing, a formless, somnambulistic being, a ray of living light, to be sure, but without an object to color, and therefore a blankness in itself" (272)—in other words, and picking up the theme of savagery that threads through the book, a zombie. That theme of savagery can be understood as colonial Gothic, legends of supernatural otherness in exotic places and non-white peoples. Melville domesticates this theme to an extent in the amiable and admirable Queequeg, whose body is tattooed over with mysterious hieroglyphics and whose similarly decorated coffin that he prepares when ill (before deciding, and managing, not to die after all) is the salvation of Ishmael in the end. But the other representatives of this colonial Gothic theme remain terrifyingly other, especially Fedallah, one of "the mysterious shadows I had seen creeping on board the Pequod during the dim Nantucket dawn" who is connected to the "enigmatical hintings of the unaccountable Elijah" (294): "such a creature as civilized, domestic people in the temperate zone only see in their dreams, and that but dimly; but the like of whom now and then glide among the unchanging Asiatic communities" (308), a phantom from the dawn of time made real. Fedallah reinforces the supernaturalism that lingers in the very rigging of the Pequod and its mad quest. Ahab has an immutable appointment with the whale and fate, to which he journeys as on iron rails (as he had previously to the prophesied loss of his leg, according to the enigmatic Elijah as the voyage begins); a fate that undermines whatever rational skepticism Ishmael can bring to bear on matters.

The pact in which Ahab makes the crew swear to follow his purpose is a piece of stage-managed necromancy. But there is a "hollow laugh" from the hold, "presaging vibrations" from the winds in the rigging, a "hollow flap of the sails against the mast," which Ahab ignores (222). He hands around a baptismal drink "hot as Satan's hoof": "It spiralizes in ye; forks out at the serpent-snapping eye" (223). Ahab touches the axis of their crossed harpoons, and then,

> . . . while so doing, suddenly and nervously twitched them; meanwhile, glancing intently from Starbuck to Stubb; from Stubb to Flask. It seemed as though, by some nameless, interior volition, he would fain have shocked them into the same fiery emotion accumulated within the Leyden jar of his own magnetic life. . . . "In vain!" cried Ahab; "but maybe, 'tis well. For did ye three but once take the full-forced shock, then mine own electric thing, that had per-chance expired from out me. Perchance, too, it would have dropped ye dead" (224).

He follows this with ceremonial draughts from the harpoon sock-ets, as they all swear death to the Whale: "Commend the murder-ous chalices! Bestow them, ye who are now made parties to this indissoluble league" (225). At this Starbuck turns pale and shivers.

Melville's use here of the pseudo-scientific language of mes-merism, or "animal magnetism," is in the tradition of mid-century American Gothic, allowing a plausible naturalistic reading while taking advantage of the mysterious realms being uncovered by con-temporary science, much as Poe used the vague scienticism of con-temporary psychology, or the stranger ideas of "metempsychosis" and "natural sentience" in his stories. The natural and the supernat-ural are allowed complementary existence through metaphor, allowing the fantastic to emerge within a framing attitude of scien-tific disbelief. So it is when Ahab adapts technological metaphor as he reflects that "my one cogged circle fits all their various wheels, and they revolve" (226), or addresses the gods: "Swerve me? Ye can-not swerve me, else ye swerve yourselves! . . . The path to my fixed purpose is laid with iron rails, whereon my soul is grooved to run. . . . Naught's an obstacle, naught's an angle to the iron way!" (227) On one hand this inexorable rushing on like the new railway has a political dimension, as an allusion to America's supposed manifest destiny.[26] But on the other hand it equally proposes a supernatural fatalism in Ahab's prophesied destiny, his quest and inevitable rendezvous with the whale.

But Melville's most startling contribution to nineteenth-century frontier Gothic comes in Ishmael's extended meditation on the whiteness of the whale. In this chapter Ishmael attempts to understand his "nameless horror" concerning Moby-Dick: "It was the whiteness of the whale that above all things appalled me" (252, 253). He begins with the more usual positive qualities of whiteness (including, however, the element of racism involved in its supposedly "giving the white man ideal mastership over every dusky tribe" to which Queequeg's nobility has already offered a rebuttal), before noting that "there yet lurks an elusive something in the innermost idea of this hue, which strikes more of panic to the soul than that redness which affrights in blood" (255). The abhorrent mildness of white creatures in nature, the polar bear, the "smooth, flaky whiteness" that makes the white shark or the albatross such "transcendent horrors" (255); these and the famous white steed of the prairies in Indian folklore give whiteness a peculiar significance, borne out in the idea of the strangely hideous albino, suggesting the "supernaturalism of this hue" (258). The "White Hoods of Ghent," masked in "the snowy symbol of their faction" (and disturbingly anticipating American Ku Klux Klan robes), or the White Friars (Carmelites), like the whiteness of ghosts, the pallor of the dead, also "evoke such an eyeless statue in the soul" (259). But the most devastating part of Ishmael's argument lies in its extension to the whole of the "natural" world: "Though in many of its aspects the visible world seems formed in love, the invisible spheres were formed in fright" (263).

> Is it that by its indefiniteness it shadows forth the heartless voids and immensities of the universe, and thus stabs us from behind with the thought of annihilation, when beholding the white depths of the milky way? Or is it, that as in essence whiteness is not so much a color as the visible absence of color, and at the same time the concrete of all colors; is it for these reasons that there is such a dumb blankness, full of meaning, in a wide landscape of snows— a colorless, all-color of atheism from which we shrink? And when we consider that other theory of the natural philosophers, that all other earthly hues—every stately or lovely

emblazoning—the sweet tinges of sunset skies and woods; yea and the gilded velvets of butterflies, and the butterfly cheeks of young girls; all these are but subtile deceits, not actually inherent in substances, but only laid on from without; so that all deified nature absolutely paints like the harlot, whose allurements cover nothing but the charnel-house within; and when we proceed further, and consider that the mystical cosmetic which produces every one of her hues, the great principle of light, for ever remains white or colorless in itself, and, if operating without medium upon matter, would touch all objects, even tulips and roses, with its own blank tinge—pondering all this, the palsied universe lies before us a leper (264).

The science here—that color depends upon the refraction of light caused by the wavelength of the surface on which it falls, and also its illusory effect upon the mind of the observer—allows Melville to explore a universe of palsied horror and meaninglessness, over which a mere surface of color and warmth is projected. It is a horror beyond the horror of conventional Gothic, but with something in common with the fallen world of Puritan exegesis, though without the consolation of even a fearsome God behind it. There is perhaps an echo of Poe's great white figure at the end of *Arthur Gordon Pym* (1838): " . . . there arose in our pathway a shrouded human figure, very far larger in its proportions than any dweller among men. And the hue of the skin of the figure was of the perfect whiteness of the snow."[27] And there may also be some relation to Poe's imaginary island of Tsalal, whose black inhabitants are terrified by the color white.[28] But Melville's evocation of terror in whiteness goes far beyond Poe's, and has greater implications.

Surprisingly, Ishmael's disturbing reflections actually mirror Ralph Waldo Emerson's view that Nature itself is a great—although in his view tranquil and benevolent—*apparition*. Melville's hugely influential contemporary, the intellectual leader of the mid-century American transcendentalist movement, Emerson thought that the world of tangible things should be seen as an illusion, a projection through consciousness of the universal over-soul, creating a world that is consistent only because God—Emerson derived his pantheist spirit of the universe as much from Eastern philosophy and

Berkeleyan Idealism as from his Puritan religious inheritance—
"never jests with us."[29] His confidence in the benevolence of a
sustaining world spirit led him to some assertions that Melville annotated in his own copy of Emerson as signals of fatuous complacency,
but which seem to have inspired both an educational unfolding in
Ishmael and a negative refiguring in Ahab. Emerson's view in
"Nature" (1836) was that the world should be seen as "phenomenal,"
rather than material. Idealism "beholds the whole circle of persons
and things, of actions and events, of country and religion, not as
painfully accumulated, atom after atom, act after act, in an aged
creeping Past, but as one vast picture which God paints upon the
instant eternity for the contemplation of the soul" (48). But in his
later and more disenchanted essay, "Experience" (1844), Emerson
came closer to a Melvillean sense of that phenomenal world: "All
things swim and glitter. Our life is not so much threatened as our
perception. Ghostlike we glide through nature, and should not know
our place again" (255). When Ishmael reports on the dangers of a
masthead reverie he seems to have the earlier Emerson in mind:

> . . . [so] lulled into such an opium-like listlessness of
> vacant, unconscious reverie is this absent-minded youth by
> the blending cadences of waves with thoughts, that at last
> he loses his identity; takes the mystic ocean at his feet for
> the visible image of that deep, blue, bottomless soul, per-
> vading mankind and nature; and every strange, half-seen,
> gliding beautiful thing that eludes him; every dimly-
> discovered uprising fin of some undiscernible form, seems
> to him the embodiment of those elusive thoughts that only
> people the soul by continually flitting through it. In this
> enchanted mood, thy spirit ebbs away to whence it came;
> becomes diffused through space and time; like Cranmer's
> sprinkled Pantheistic ashes, forming at last a part of every
> shore the whole world over (214).

Given that Thomas Cranmer was burned as a heretic in 1556, the
subdued reference is by no means innocent, and it is swiftly followed by terror: "But while this sleep, this dream is on ye, move your
hand or foot an inch; slip your hold at all; and your identity comes
back in horror. Over Descartian vortices you hover. And perhaps at
mid-day, in the fairest weather, with one half-throttled shriek you

drop through that transparent air into the summer sea, no more to rise for ever. Heed it well, ye Pantheists" (215).

Ishmael's rebuttal of the Ideal philosophy and optimistic Pantheism might be the common sense response to transcendentalism, which Emerson admitted in "Nature" was easily burlesqued (42). Sometimes Emerson offered a comfortable confidence in the beneficent "Supreme Being" that acts through ourselves, that "does not build up nature around us, but puts it forth through us, as the life of the tree puts forth new branches and leaves through the pores of the old. As a plant upon the earth, so a man rests upon the bosom of God; he is nourished by unfailing fountains, and draws at his need inexhaustible powers" (50).[30] Melville's quarrel with these views was most profoundly figured in Ahab, who subscribes to transcendentalist doctrines in a much more disturbing way than the masthead dreamer. Like Emerson, Ahab affirms that nature is only a veil of illusion, but behind that veil he sees malevolence: "Hark ye yet again,—the little lower level. All visible objects, man, are but as pasteboard masks. But in each event—in the living act, the undoubted deed—there some unknown but still reasoning thing puts forth the mouldings of its features from behind the unreasoning mask. If man will strike, strike through the mask! How can the prisoner reach outside except by thrusting through the wall?" (220). This is the distinctive theme and deepest insight of American Gothic, the sense that there is something *behind*, which may not be, as in European Gothic, the Past, but some perpetual and present Otherness, hidden within, behind, somehow below the apparently benign "natural" surface.

In his book *Frontier Gothic* David Mogen writes that the "American myth of metamorphosis is inextricably linked with Gothic emotions: terror and horror, feelings of helpless victimization by forces from without that may after all be projected from within, a dread of annihilation more overwhelming than that induced by any merely physical threat."[31] D. H. Lawrence saw the American culture as haunted,[32] (an insight that Leslie Fiedler later developed in *The Return of the Vanishing American*[33]), haunted, as Mogen puts it, "by the ghosts of subdued Indian cultures, ghosts which either induce madness or enter into our awareness in ways we cannot comprehend" (22). That would be one source of the terror evoked by the American experience, along with "the desolation wrought by progress, the psychological deprivation of alienation, and the threatening but revolutionary possibilities that appear when civilized conventions are left behind" (23). In that American sense, Melville's horror comes along in the ship, certainly, with Ahab or Fedallah; but it is also *already out there* in the South Seas, in the hideous ferocity of the cannibal sharks, the fangs beneath the beautiful surface of the sea, "treacherously hidden beneath the loveliest tints of azure" (*Moby-Dick* 364), behind the overwhelming whiteness of the whale.

In Melville's novella "Benito Cereno" the horror straggles into port in a crippled slave ship, dismasted by severe weather and turned inside out by a secret insurrection. The Yankee skipper Amasa Delano, who encounters the ship, owes his survival ironically enough to his Emersonian optimism and consequent obtuseness: if he ever suspected the truth of the *San Dominick* he would be murdered at once. Yet again the horror from "out there" proves to be also a horror from within: since slavery is so American, the Spanish slave ship can be viewed from Melville's perspective as at root a product of the American system, and the story inferentially as a comment on that system. At the end of his documentary addendum, Melville says: "If the Deposition have served as the key to fit into the lock of the complications which precede it, then, as a vault whose door has been flung back, the San Dominick's hull lies open today."[34] *If*, indeed. The Deposition only adds to the enigma of the story, offering a not quite exact fit with the narrative. Mystery remains, a precipitate from the clash of interpretations when like a Gothic portrait the ship's sternpiece, showing "a dark satyr in a mask, holding his foot on the prostrate neck of a writing figure, likewise masked" (6) comes to life in the scene in which the American is finally attacked. Delano's "left hand, on one side, again clutched the half-reclined Don Benito, heedless that he was in a speechless faint, while his right foot, on the other side, ground the prostrate negro" (67, 68). In this movement from impenetrable emblem to epiphanic action, the meanings of the story are condensed. We are shown the involvement of the apparently innocent Northern states of America in the institution of slavery, while at the same time we are presented with a dazzling cascade of inversions inherent in the Hegelian question of who really is master, the master who lives in fear of insurrection, or the slave who fully understands freedom through its very absence? Melville does not stop there, however, as his ending opens another vista, anticipating Joseph Conrad's *Heart of Darkness*:[35] "You are saved," says Delano to Benito Cereno, "What has cast such a shadow upon you?"/ "The negro" (90).

"The negro" here contains more than a simple horror at the treachery of Babo, the leader of the slave insurrection whose rebellion would seem justified by the cruelties of slavery. Babo and his companions have indulged in what to a reader of the day would certainly seem an excess of violence, and even diabolical evil. The shrouded figurehead of the ship is unveiled to be a human skeleton; mutely offering "chalky comment on the words chalked below, *Follow your leader*" (69). These bones (of Don Alexandro, the owner) were prepared in a particular way, the terrified Cereno mysteriously states, that "the negroes afterwards told the deponent, but which he, as long as reason is left him, can never divulge" (85). Eric Sundquist has shown how the excesses of this insurrection may reflect American fears roused by the Haitian rebellion of the 1790s, a persistent source of nightmare for American Southerners in the early nineteenth century.[36] The implication of cannibalism is a familiar Gothic and racist trope of the period, as H. L. Malchow illustrates in his chapter on this widely held assumption about South Sea islanders and others in *Gothic Images of Race*.[37] But as I have suggested in Chapter Three, Melville's text goes beyond this in its supernatural inferences, as is seen most powerfully in the unexpected use of active verbs in this, the final paragraph:

Some months after, dragged to the gibbet at the tail of a mule, the black *met* his voiceless end. The body was burned to ashes, but for many days, the head, that hive of subtlety, fixed on a pole in the Plaza, *met*, unabashed, the gaze of the whites; and across the Plaza *looked* towards St Bartholomew's church, in whose vaults *slept* then, as now, the recovered bones of Aranda: and across the Rimac bridge *looked* towards the monastery, on Mount Agonia without; where, three months after being dismissed by the court, Benito Cereno, borne on the bier, did, indeed, *follow* his leader (91, italics added).

These active verbs mock Christian assurances of resurrection; there is an afterlife, they imply, but a demonic one. Aranda's bones are "recovered," but not saved in the redemptive sense. Instead Babo's head broods on over the scene, gazing toward his victims. Here Melville's Gothic transcends race as it contemplates what he elsewhere calls "natural depravity," a depravity that is considerably beyond any Calvinistic sense of man's fallenness, and sees rather an evil or depravity, "according to nature." That other sort of depravity, displayed by Claggart in *Billy Budd* —"to cross from a normal nature to him one must cross 'the deadly space between'"—is beyond explanation, "not engendered by vicious training or corrupting books or licentious living, but born with him" and suggestive of the Holy Writ's "mysteries of iniquity" (320–323), a devilishness within or beyond nature like the devilishness suggested by the whiteness of the whale.

That demonic element in nature is sensed in many other American Gothic texts. In one of the first, Brown's short story "Somnambulism: A Fragment,"[38] it is suggested through the maniac Handyside's mocking cries in the night-time forests—if indeed they are Handyside's; in Bierce's "The Death of Halpin Frayser," it is there in the woods as mocking laughter, as it is in Hawthorne's "Young Goodman Brown." If there *is* something "out there," it seems to be evil.

In Ambrose Bierce's ghost story, "The Death of Halpin Frayser," the protagonist dreams of walking along a dusty road, and turning into "a road less travelled," in the ruts of which is a crimson liquid that he takes to be blood. With the liquid and a twig he writes feverishly in his red-leather pocket book, while he hears a strange low and wild peal of laughter growing nearer.

> [Frayser] had but one thought: to complete his written appeal to the benign powers who, traversing the haunted wood, might some time rescue him if he should be denied the blessing of annihilation. He wrote with terrible rapidity, the twig in his fingers rilling blood without renewal; but in the middle of a sentence his hands denied their service to his will, his arms fell to his sides, the book to the earth; and powerless to move or cry out, he found himself staring into the sharply drawn face and blank, dead eyes of his own

> mother, standing white and silent in the garments of the
> grave![39]

This extraordinary apparition seems to cause his death: at all events
he *is* later found dead, evidently strangled, and his body in a rigid
attitude of "desperate but ineffectual resistance—to what?" (25).
What is more, he is found dead on the grave of one Catherine Larue,
who is, it turns out—although unknown to him, having taken
another name through her remarriage—his mother.

As is customary in Bierce's supernatural fictions, the reader is
lured toward a realistic explanation: the investigating detectives on
the track of the madman called Larue, assume that this man, the
mother's second husband, having killed her in his mania, now
haunts her grave and kills Frayser in his turn. But, as is also customary in Bierce's writing, the possible realistic explanation is only the
top layer of a series of deeper insights and ironic alternatives below
the surface.

One of these layers ironically addresses the question of the fictionality of the fiction: the writing that Halpin Frayser dreams he is
so anxious to finish with his twig dipped in blood (or wrote earlier
in his book using red ink?) turns out to be a poem in the manner of
his ancestor Myron Bayne, a once famous "Colonial bard"—not
unlike Philip Frenau it would seem since the poem resembles his
American landscape in "The House of Night"—although Frayser,
while poetic in inclination, had never actually been a poet. The
abruptly broken-off manuscript foretells the enchanted wood in
which he meets his death, in which

> Conspiring spirits whispered in the gloom,
> Halfheard, the stilly secrets of the tomb.
> With blood the trees were all adrip; the leaves
> Shone in the witch light with a ruddy bloom.

Bierce's interest in the uncanniness of writing itself is reinforced by
his characteristic production of narrative uncertainties, as sections
on Frayser's subjective experience alternate with a retrospective history of his life and the experiences of the two detectives who find
his body.

Within the retrospective section Bierce investigates the unusually close relationship between Halpin and his delightful mother, based in part upon a shared secret admiration for Myron Bayne's poetry, a thing not to be admitted in their practical Southern family:

> Their common guilt in respect of that was an added tie between them. If in Halpin's youth his mother had 'spoiled' him he had assuredly done his part toward being spoiled. As he grew to such manhood as is attainable by a Southerner who does not care which way elections go, the attachment between him and his beautiful mother—whom from early childhood he had called Katy—became yearly stronger and more tender. In these two romantic natures was manifest in a signal way that neglected phenomenon, the dominance of the sexual element in all the relations of life, strengthening, softening, and beautifying even those of consanguity. The two were nearly inseparable, and by strangers observing their manners were not infrequently mistaken for lovers (15).

Bierce's dry humor as he describes this semi-incestuous relationship is unmistakable. Halpin's decision to visit California—where he will be "Shanghied" and lose all contact with his family for many years—is of course opposed by his loving mother, who in a dream sees Myron Bayne pointing to Halpin's portrait, now painted with a face cloth "such as we put on the dead." "And I saw below the edge of the cloth the marks of hands on your throat—forgive me, but we have not been used to keep such things from each other. Perhaps you have another interpretation. Perhaps it does not mean that you will go to California. Or maybe you will take me with you?" (16). Halpin's immediate reaction is that the dream "foreshadowed a more simple and immediate, if less tragic, disaster than a visit to the Pacific coast. It was Halpin Frayser's impression that he was to be garroted on his native heath" (16). Given the ultimate outcome, for "heath" the reader might well be expected to read "hearth" and thus find the threat nearer to home, especially when Mrs. Frayser complains of her "stiff" fingers and suggests the medicinal springs in California might be of assistance. While she remains charming as ever, "Katy" Frayser's subtly implied threat, so immediately noted by her adoring son, suggests another side to this loving mother, fulfilled in her later monstrous aspect:

> The apparition confronting the dreamer in the wood—the thing so like, yet so unlike, his mother—was horrible! It stirred no love nor longing in his heart; it came unattended with pleasant memories of a golden past—inspired no sentiment of any kind; all the finer emotions were swallowed up in fear. He tried to turn and run from before it, but his legs were as lead; he was unable to lift his feet from the ground. His arms hung helpless at his sides; of his eyes only he retained control, and these he did not dare remove from the lustreless orbs of the apparition, which he knew was not a soul without a body, but that most dreadful of all existences infesting that haunted wood—a body without a soul! In its blank stare was neither love, nor pity, nor intelligence —nothing to which to address an appeal for mercy. . . .
>
> For a time, which seemed so long that the world grew grey with age and sin, and the haunted forest, having fulfilled its purpose in this monstrous culmination of its terrors, vanished out of his consciousness with all its sights and sounds, the apparition stood within a pace, regarding him with the mindless malevolence of a wild brute; then thrust its hands forward and sprang upon him with appalling ferocity! . . .
>
> Borne backward to the earth, he saw above him the dead and drawn face within a hand's-breadth of his own, and then all was black. . . . and Halpin Frayser dreamed that he was dead (18, 19).

The thing behind nature, the thing behind even the veil of a mother's love (that exemplification of nature's benignity) is a terror without any apparent reason, a zombie with "the mindless malevolence of a wild brute."

Such demonic hollowness behind nature is there again in Bierce's enigmatic tale, "An Inhabitant of Carcosa." In this sketch, a wanderer finds himself on a bleak and desolate plain, among strangely shaped rocks that "seemed to have an understanding with one another and to exchange looks of uncomfortable significance" (241). A canopy of low leaden clouds hangs over the landscape like a visible curse. There are no birds, beasts, or insects, although a lynx trots past. The oddly shaped stones seem to be of an ancient graveyard. Then at a distance a man appears, "half naked, half clad in skins" carrying in one hand a bow and arrow, in the other a blazing torch with a trail of black smoke. It is neither night nor day, or somehow, it is both: "I saw even the stars in the absence of daylight" (245). At last the traveller recognizes his own grave, with its ancient date of death "and then I knew that these were the ruins of the ancient and famous city of Carcosa" (246). We too know where we are: this is the country of the negative Sublime, the occulted landscape of despair of Poe's Ushers and "Ulalume," Brown's Norwalk, Richard Henry Dana, Sr.'s blasted heath of "Paul Fenton," Hawthorne's forest of "Young Goodman Brown," Melville's treacherous ocean in *Moby-Dick* or at the beginning of "Benito Cereno." We find in the end that this particular landscape is supposedly not American, for the account is "imparted to the medium Bayrolles by the spirit Hoseib Alar Robardin." But such places, like Poe's pseudo-European settings, go beyond geography just as they go beyond the pathetic fallacy; they are more than representations of subjectivity and aspire to an active malevolence of their own. The land itself is evil, like the setting of Frayser's dream. The affectless or threatening landscape suggests a dead Mother Nature's implacable gaze. It seems reminiscent of the desacralized or even diabolical Nature in Ishmael's "Whiteness" chapter in *Moby-Dick*. It also looks forward to the secularized landscapes of the American Naturalists, Norris, Dreiser, or Crane. But here, in place of the diabolical laughter of Frayser's tale, or the idiot boy and devil's child Abel in "Paul Fenton," or the lunatic Handyside in "Somnambulism," we find a silent savage, whose description surely brings back to mind the Native American. In this respect, at least, D. H. Lawrence's insights into the haunted American land as somehow cursed by the fate of its original inhabitants seems imaginatively borne out in a wide range of writings; the evil of this effective genocide, like the evil of slavery, underlies the American Imaginary. But there is perhaps something more too, a terror of the land itself, its emptiness, its implacability; simply a sense of its vast, lonely, and possibly hostile space that informs the American Gothic and, ultimately, resists any rational explanation. As Robert Frost put it, "We were the land's / Before the land was ours." "The Gothic wilderness," says David Mogen in *Frontier Gothic*, "is a profoundly American symbol of an ambiguous relationship to the land, of an alienation that was first articulated when, in the words of Peter N. Carroll, the Puritans perceived 'beneath the florid plenty of the New World . . . the Devil lurking in the wilderness.'"[40]

The Gothic Inner Life: Domestic Abjection

If the devil lurked in the wilderness for American Gothicists, he might more easily be found nearer to hand—at home, in fact. The suggested echo of "heath/hearth" in "Halpin Frayser" anticipates Freud's unpacking of the uncanny as "das Unheimliche," in which heimliche may mean homely, domestic, thus leading to his recognition of the uncanny as in part at least, the strange within the familiar: "that class of the frightening which leads back to what is known of old and long familiar."[41] In the course of the nineteenth century, American Gothic came closer to home, shedding the exotic locations and extreme caricatures of, say, *The Monk*, *Melmoth the Wanderer*, or later, *Dracula*, in preference for a more domestic unease and a psychological Gothic, with close relation to the uncanny and the ghost story. The tendency was there from the beginning, as we saw in Brown's Wieland family or Poe's tales of domestic nightmare, a product of the inconvenient absence of castles and the heavy footstep of the European past, but also no doubt a legacy of intense Puritan introspection and a relative "thinness" of society and available "usable," past.

A key example of such domestic Gothic is Charlotte Perkins Gilman's story, "The Yellow Wallpaper" (1892), briefly mentioned in Chapter Four. In this tale, a young mother suffering from what now might be seen as post-natal depression, is confined to an upstairs nursery in an old house (described as an "ancestral hall"), rented for the summer by her doctor husband. Her regimen, satirizing that of Dr. S. Weir Mitchell, a famous contemporary consultant who had disastrously treated Gilman,[42] is strict: she is not allowed excitements, even those produced by her favorite activity of writing. The windows of the room are ominously barred, as those of a nursery might be—or the chamber of a confined lunatic—and she is left alone for long periods to contemplate the unpleasant patterns of the yellow wallpaper. This madwoman in the attic, for so she is treated by her husband and his sister, sees the eccentric, writhing pattern in the wallpaper to represent another set of bars, behind which she makes out eventually the figure of "a woman stooping down and creeping about behind that pattern."[43] This figure is echoed in one that she sees outside in the garden below, a stooped little old woman, and both seem to be perhaps versions of herself, in her subjugation and threatened annihilation as a person. There is a track smudged around the walls of the room at the level of a creeping figure; by the end of the story it seems as likely to have been made by the narrator as by some previous occupant of this madwoman's chamber, with its heavy window bars and badly gnawed, nailed-down bedstead. "I can creep smoothly on the floor," she says at the end of the story, "and my shoulder just fits in that long smooch around the wall, so I can not lose my way" (495). The use of a deranged narrator reminds of Poe's tales, but unlike those, the reader of "The Yellow Wallpaper" is invited to see an underlying rationality in her position. She is smothered with kindness, but smothered nevertheless. Her husband John laughs at her fear of the wallpaper, saying that "after the wallpaper was changed it would be the heavy bedstead, and then the barred windows, and then that gate at the top of the stairs, and so on" (488). He infantilizes her, calling her a "blessed little goose" (488). "And dear John gathered me in his arms and just carried me up the stairs and laid me on the bed, and sat and read to me until it tired my head" (491). Ominously the narrator mentions that she has secreted a piece of rope, which produces an even more disturbing possibility at the end of the story, when the narrator has psychically merged with the wallpaper figure but feels she has freed herself: "'I've got out at last,' said I, 'in spite of you and Jane. And I've pulled off most of the paper, so you can't put me back!'" In this ambiguous ending Gilman possibly suggests that the narrator has tried to hang herself:

> I've got a rope up here that even Jennie did not find. If that woman does get out, and tries to get away, I can tie her!

But I forgot I couldn't reach far without anything to stand on! The bed will *not* move. I tried to lift or push it till I was lame, and then I got so angry I bit a little piece off at one corner—but it hurt my teeth.

Then I peeled off all the paper I could reach standing on the floor. It sticks horribly. And the pattern just enjoys it. All those strangled heads and bulbous eyes and waddling fungus growths just shriek with derision!

I am getting angry enough to do something desperate. To jump out of the window would be admirable exercise, but the bars are too strong even to try. Besides I wouldn't do it of course! I know well enough that a step like that is improper and might be misconstrued.

I don't like to look out of the window even—there are so many of those creeping women, and they creep so fast.

I wonder if they all came out of that wallpaper as I did? But I am securely fastened now by my well-hidden rope— you don't get *me* out in the road there (495).

If she is "securely fastened" by the rope, is there hinted another meaning to her "creeping" at the climax of the story? John enters the room and faints "right across my path, so that I had to creep over him!" (496). Perhaps creeping here might suggest hanging?

In *The Madwoman in the Attic,* Sandra Gilbert and Susan Gubar bravely read this ending as some sort of triumph: "John's unmasculine swoon of surprise is the least of the triumphs Gilman imagines for her madwoman. More significant are the madwoman's own imaginings and creations, mirages of health and freedom with which her author endows her like a fairy godmother showering gold on a sleeping heroine. The woman from behind the wallpaper creeps away, for instance, creeps far and fast on the long road, in broad daylight. 'I have watched her sometimes away off in the open country,' says the narrator, 'creeping as fast as a cloud shadow in a high wind.'"[44] But that bold reading attempts to turn a horrific defeat into a triumph, as if we were to conclude that Poe's narrators in "The Black Cat," "The Tell-Tale Heart," or "The Imp of the Perverse" pay a worthwhile price in losing their minds.

A more persuasive interpretation of implicit subversion of the patriarchy in "The Yellow Wallpaper" might be one that acknowledges that the narrator gains insight only at the risk of her sanity, and possibly her life, and considers the story in terms of what Julia Kristeva calls "abjection." In *The Powers of Horror* (1982), Kristeva says:

> The abject has only one quality of the object—that of being opposed to *I*. If the object, however, through its opposition, settles me within the fragile texture of a desire for meaning, which, as a matter of fact, makes me ceaselessly and infinitely homologous to it, what is *abject*, on the contrary, the jettisoned object, is radically excluded and draws me towards the place where meaning collapses. . . . And yet, from its place of banishment, the abject does not cease challenging its master. Without a sign (for him), it beseeches a discharge, a convulsion, a crying out. . . . A massive and sudden emergence of uncanniness, which, familiar as it might have been in an opaque and forgotten life, now harries me as radically separate, loathsome. Not me, not that. But not nothing either. . . . A weight of meaninglessness, about which there is nothing insignificant, and which crushes me.[45]

At its simplest this might concern the loathing of an item of food, a piece of filth, waste, or dung. A wound, a defilement, or the corpse is an ultimate example; not as signifying death but as "the most sickening of wastes"—the corpse is "a border that has encroached upon everything." "It is thus not lack of cleanliness or health that causes abjection, but what disturbs identity, order, system" (2–4). Kristeva moves from this phenomenology of horror to finding an echo of "jouissance" in the abject: "jouissance alone causes the abject to exist as such . . . one joys in it. . . . Violently and painfully." She sees its victims as fascinated, even submissive and willing (9). That suggests another possible version of the "triumph" felt by Gilman's narrator.

The nastiness of the yellow wallpaper is contained partly in its repellent pattern, but also in its color and smell. The pattern is vile, with a "strange provoking formless sort of figure, that seems to skulk about behind that silly and conspicuous front design" (489), not arranged in any kind of repetition or symmetry; in which "the bloated curves and flourishes—a kind of debased Romanesque with *delirium tremens*—go waddling up and down in isolated columns of fatuity . . . great slanting waves of optic horror; like a lot of wallowing sea-weeds in full chase" (490). The "outside pattern is a florid arabesque, reminding one of a fungus. If you can imagine a toadstool in joints, an interminable string of toadstools, budding and sprouting in endless convolutions—why, that is something like it" (492). By the end of the narrative its "strangled heads and bulbous eyes and waddling fungus growths just shriek with derision" (495). But in addition, the "color is repellant [sic], almost revolting; a smouldering unclean yellow. . . . It is a dull yet lurid orange in some places, a sickly sulphur tint in others" (487). It is "a sickly, penetrative suggestive yellow. It makes me think of all the yellow things I ever saw —not beautiful ones like buttercups, but old foul bad yellow things" (493).[46] And this wallpaper also has an insidious smell:

> It creeps all over the house. I find it hovering in the dining room, skulking in the parlor, hiding in the hall, lying in wait for me on the stairs. It gets into my hair. . . . Such a peculiar odor too! . . . It is not bad—at first, and very gentle, but quite the subtlest, most enduring odor I ever met. In this damp weather it is awful. I wake up in the night and find it hanging over me. . . . The only thing I can think of is that it is like the *color* of the paper! A yellow smell (493).

This too can be further explored according to Kristeva's analysis of the abject:

> It is as if dividing lines were built up between society and a certain nature, as well as within the social aggregate, on the simple logic of *excluding filth*, which, promoted to the ritual level of *defilement*, founded the "self and clean" of each social group if not of each subject.
> The purification rite appears then as that essential ridge, which, prohibiting the filthy object, extracts it from the secular order and lines it at once with a sacred facet. Because it is excluded as a possible object, asserted to be a non-object of desire, abominated as ab-ject, as abjection, filth becomes defilement, and founds on the henceforth released side of the "self and clean" the order that is thus only (and therefore, always already) sacred.

> Defilement is what is jettisoned from the *"symbolic
> system"* (65, original italics).

The wallpaper, then, can be understood as the very type of "filth,"
the abject, expelled, non-object of desire in opposition to the
approved clean self that finds itself in opposition to the excluded.
What happens in Gilman's story is that the self *identifies with* the
abject, the narrator finds herself in the figure she projects as trapped
within the pattern of the wallpaper, even merging with her as she
pulls it off the walls: "I pulled and she shook, I shook and she pulled,
and before morning we had peeled off yards of that paper" (495).
The abject *other* that the narrator recognizes is female, and inferentially, like herself a mother, maternal.[47] Among the several directions
taken by Kristeva's analysis of the abject is an insistence upon the
role of the maternal (pre-Symbolic) in abjection:

> But devotees of the abject, she as well as he, do not cease
> looking, within what flows from the other's "innermost
> being," for the desirable and terrifying, nourishing and mur-
> derous, fascinating and abject inside of the maternal body.
> For, in the misfire of identification with the mother as well
> as with the father, how else are they to be maintained in the
> Other? How, if not by incorporating a devouring mother,
> for want of having been able to introject her and joy in
> what manifests her, for want of being able to signify her:
> urine, blood, sperm, excrement. . . . Jouissance demands an
> abjection from which identity becomes absent (54).

Now the creeping old woman (or rather women, for they become
innumerable creeping figures outside), comes into clearer focus, as
the rejected and desired, loathed, feared, and identified with,
maternal body—at the same time, her own. If "she" gets out, she
must be tied up, as the narrator describes herself, securely fastened
by her well-hidden rope. As Annette Kolodny describes the narrator's situation of deprival (of reading and writing, or any opportunity for socially stimulating conversation) "—the wife's progressive
descent into madness provides a kind of commentary upon, indeed
is revealed in terms of, the sexual politics inherent in the manipula-
tion of those strategies."[48]

That well-hidden rope thus provides a satisfactory metaphor for Gilman's larger concerns, which are ultimately more social than psychological: the rope that ties up her protagonist is well-hidden by kindness and gender conventions, it is another version of the writhing bars of the wallpaper, the rings and bolts and nailed-down bed of the room, the bars at the window and the gate at the stairs, the forbidding of reading and writing, the overpowering knowingness of the male doctors (one of them her husband), the collusion of the well-meaning Jenny (his sister). One of the most cogent feminist critics of nineteenth century society, Gilman here demonstrates how the constraints for contemporary women may be well-hidden, and dismissed as fanciful, while remaining potentially fatal, a similar conclusion to Kate Chopin's, in *The Awakening* (1899).

In a slightly earlier ghost story, "The Great Wisteria" (1891), Gilman worked with another version of the same writhing, constricting metaphor, with the remains of a dead woman found in the tangled roots of the great vine, and a baby's bones in a well nearby.[49] The story involves a group of modern day visitors to a rented house, who amuse themselves with the fear of ghosts before dreaming of the house's past and subsequently discovering the grisly remains. Gilman provides an authorial account of the atrocious crime of a Puritan patriarch refusing to accept his daughter's illegitimate pregnancy, with fatal consequences.

Edith Wharton's ghost stories likewise draw upon an oppressed, buried, silenced, largely *female* domestic past. In her best tales—"All Souls," "The Looking Glass," "Bewitched," "Mr. Jones," "Miss Mary Pask,"—the ideas above regarding female abjection, its terror and the potential for identification with the abject, are realized. The possibly dead—but retrospectively it turns out, in fact still alive— Mary Pask engenders a horror of clinging femininity through her inappropriate "childish wiles" and "clumsy capering coquetry" or "pitiful low whimper" when rejected. The male narrator subsequently weeps over this ghost, of whom he thinks enough had survived her death "to cry out to me the unuttered loneliness of a lifetime, to express at last what the living woman had always had to keep dumb and hidden."[50] But his sentimental sympathy evaporates as soon as it is known that she was in fact at the time still alive.

As in "The Great Wisteria," the Gothic past survives as an echo or ripple in the fabric of the present. In "Mr. Jones," it is only the details of dates on gravestones that evoke the buried history of abuse of an imprisoned dumb wife by a servant after her husband's death. Another wife, in "Kerfol," wrongly convicted of murdering her brutal husband, has been shut up in the keep of her husband's avenging family's castle until she dies, "a harmless madwoman." But women too can be vengeful haunts, like the dead Rebecca-ish wife in "Pomegranate Seed," whose indecipherable letters continue to arrive at the house where a new bride cannot shake off her presence, which is felt even in the trace left by her removed portrait on the wall. Some victims, too, are male: sensitive younger men who suffer under the patriarchy, in "The Triumph of Night," or at the hands of an older sadist, like Culwin in "The Eyes," an aging homosexual whose mistreatment of young admirers ("he liked 'em juicy" as one observer puts it) results in his nightmares whenever he commits what he mistakenly thinks to be virtuous actions (such as proposing to a cousin he doesn't love, or flattering a handsome but untalented young man by telling him that he writes well). Culwin's horrific visions concern a pair of eyes—reminiscent of Gilman's wallpaper pattern—that he cannot recognize:

> There they hung in the darkness, their swollen lids drooped across the little watery bulbs loose in the orbits, and the sense of their tacit complicity, of a deep hidden understanding between us that was worse than the first shock of their strangeness.[51]

As he confronts his own image in a mirror with "a glare of slowly gathering hate" the reader is of course likely to think of "The Portrait of Dorian Gray," as well as the bulbous heads of the yellow wallpaper, and to understand such descriptions as making a repulsive connection between the eyes and male genitals (a connection Freud makes powerfully in "The Uncanny"). The image here suggests a profound disturbance occasioned by male homosexuality, a moment of surfacing of the Lacanian "piece of the real" disturbing the symbolic order; something that again fits perfectly with Kristeva's earlier quoted words on the abject:

. . . what is *abject*, on the contrary, the jettisoned object, is radically excluded and draws me towards the place where meaning collapses. . . . And yet, from its place of banishment, the abject does not cease challenging its master. Without a sign (for him), it beseeches a discharge, a convulsion, a crying out. . . . A massive and sudden emergence of uncanniness, which, familiar as it might have been in an opaque and forgotten life, now harries me as radically separate, loathsome. Not me, not that. But not nothing either. . . . A weight of meaninglessness, about which there is nothing insignificant, and which crushes me."[52]

Henry James, who was in some respects Edith Wharton's mentor, also explored the hallucinatory Gothic within modern life. The suppressed violence of the "real" in his work may be largely confined to metaphor, but in the flow and shocking manifestation of his metaphors the deeper inner lives of his characters are expressed. In *The Golden Bowl*, Maggie Verver abruptly comes to a consciousness of the deceptions of those closest to her, "the horror of finding evil seated, all at its ease, where she had only dreamed of good . . . like some bad-faced stranger surprised in one of the thick-carpeted corridors of quiet on a Sunday afternoon."[53] Finding herself in effect living in a Gothic novel, then, Maggie learns to turn the tables by an imaginative creativity beyond her tormenter's reach: "Marvellous the manner in which, under such imaginations, Maggie thus circled and lingered—quite as if she were, materially, following her unseen, counting every step she helplessly wasted, noting every hindrance that brought her to a pause." The hunted turned hunter, like James himself in his boyhood dream of turning on and pursuing some hideous creature down the endless corridors of the Louvre,[54] Maggie moves into the uncanny world of her own metaphor: "There were hours of intensity, for a week or two, when it was for all the world as if she had guardedly tracked her stepmother in the great house, from room to room, and from window to window, only to see her, here and there and everywhere, question her issue and her fate."

As all these instances suggest, domestic Gothic is intimately bound up with the idea of the house, gender, and the family, which becomes, through metaphor, a way of externalizing the inner life of fictional characters. As Gothic developed through the nineteenth century it increasingly came *inside*, following and fulfilling the direction that Poe had pointed to in his tales of deranged narrators and their houses as embodiments of their psyches. When Isabel Archer in *The Portrait of a Lady* (1881) perceives the nature of her psychic entrapment, the result of a dream of individual freedom, she immediately understands it in terms of the Gothic tradition: "When Isabel saw this rigid system closing about her, draped though it was in pictured tapestries, that sense of darkness and suffocation . . . took possession of her; she seemed to be shut up with an odour of mould and decay" (398).

In his greatest Gothic terror fiction *The Turn of the Screw* (1898), the house and family of domestic Gothic traps an innocent young vicar's daughter, who has read Gothic novels and interprets her strange circumstances in their terms. The angelic children she looks after as governess turn demonic in her eyes, the sunny, charming house becomes a dark mansion haunted by the far cry of a child in the night, and by the apparitions of her dead predecessors Miss Jessell and the manservant Peter Quint. Quint appears to the Governess, it seems, as a manifestation of repellent male sexuality; Miss Jessell as a model of (her own) female abjection; the thoroughly non-ghostly housekeeper, Mrs. Grose, as an inadequate mother figure. Inasmuch as this horror represents an irruption of the inadmissable "real" into the symbolic cognition of the Governess and her society, what the real strongly suggests here is an unacknowledged history of child abuse: at home, in the "family" constituted by the children and the servants, overseen at a distance by their remote, always absent, sexually attractive Uncle; and in the society that hypocritically overlooked such *domestic* abuse (although acknowledging the scandal of child prostitution and "white slavery").[55] The naiveté and religious upbringing of the seventeen-year-old Governess requires that she translate her experience of uncanny events or visions into the language of demonic possession instead of the possibility that the children are simply damaged rather than possessed, or, alternatively, that her own imagination is responsible for what she only *seems* to see. James plays on the boundary between Gothic as fantastic and Gothic as uncanny, and his tale has unleashed a hundred years of critical perplexity. He said himself that this tale was an *amusette* to catch those "not easily caught . . . the jaded, the disillu-sioned, the fastidious,"[56] a *jeu d'esprit* in which the reader must fill in the blanks, and so it has proved. Shoshana Felman, one of the best interpreters of *The Turn of the Screw*, points out that "the invitation to undertake a reading of the text is perforce an invitation to repeat the text, to enter into its labyrinth of mirrors," and "it is not so much the critic who comprehends the text, as the text which compre-hends the reader."[57]

As an example of the way the text works as a trap we might examine this description: "the little wretches denied it with all the added volume of their sociability and their tenderness, in just the crystal depths of which—like the flash of a fish in the stream—the mockery of their advantage peeped up."[58] It is only the Governess's perception through which we see that sinister "flash of a fish" in the crystal stream of the children's innocence; if we accept her version we are lost with her, but then if we refuse it we are lost in our own acts of interpretation. Toward the end of the story we are given this back, as in a mirror: ". . . if he *were* innocent," she asks about Miles, "what then on earth was *I?*" (83) Barely resisting seeing herself, as we may come to, eventually, as the Gothic villain, responsible in the end for Flora's hysterical illness and Miles's death—metatextually she is perhaps implying another recognition: *our own* complicity in enjoying this elegant and sadistic little fable.

James uses the tropes of the Gothic in *The Turn of the Screw* in a knowing second order of refinement. The house is partly ancient, with an old "machiolated" tower, crooked staircases, and obscure passageways, but still it is just a "big, ugly, antique but convenient house, embodying a few features of a building still older, half-displaced and half-utilised" (9); which would serve well as a descrip-tion of how James employs the half-displaced Gothic literary inheritance. We first encounter the house on a lovely afternoon: "I remember as a thoroughly pleasant impression the broad clear front, its open windows and fresh curtains and the pair of maids looking out, I remember the lawn and the bright flowers and the crunch of my wheels on the gravel and the clustered tree-tops over which the rooks circled and cawed in the golden sky" (7). How dif-ferent this is from a first encounter with, say, the House of Usher. But then, there are those ominous rooks. The guttering candle of

traditional Gothic is here too, but in a way that allows this jaded
motif new reaches of terror:

> . . . I knew in a moment after this that I had gone too far.
> The answer to my appeal was instantaneous, but it came in
> the form of an extraordinary blast and chill, a gust of frozen
> air and a shake of the room as great as if, in the high wild
> wind, the casement had crashed in. The boy gave a loud
> high shriek, which, lost in the rest of the shock of sound,
> might have seemed, indistinctly, though I was so close to
> him, a note either of jubilation or terror. I jumped to my
> feet again and was conscious of darkness. So for a moment
> we remained, while I stared about me and saw the drawn
> curtains unstirred and the window still tight. "Why, the can-
> dle's out!" I then cried.
> "It was I who blew it, dear!" said Miles (63).

Bly is an *English* country house, and the story concerns some of the
sinister implications of master-servant and class relations in English
society as seen by an anglicized American author who took British
citizenship at the outbreak of World War One. But James's sensibility was deeply American, and in fact his attitude to the uncanny and
the spiritual may have been shaped in part by his father's friendship
with Emerson.[59] James even wrote a book-length study of
Hawthorne, and many of his early tales are ghost stories, in
Hawthornean mode.

The ramifications of James's choice of a European life over
American possibilities were to generate another of his powerful
ghost stories, "The Jolly Corner," written in 1908 after a return visit
to the United States. The "Jolly Corner" of the deeply ironic title is
Spencer Brydon's pet name for his old family house in New York,
on the rental of which, together with income from another inherited house, he has lived an aesthetically fulfilling, if emotionally
shallow, life in Europe for thirty three years, before returning to
oversee the construction of a skyscraper on the site of the other
house. At night he finds himself haunting the house on the jolly corner, in which he feels some ghostly presence: the house is, he feels,

> . . . in the likeness of some great glass bowl, all precious
> concave crystal, set delicately humming by the play of a

moist finger round its edge. The concave crystal held, as it were, this mystical other world, and the indescribably faint murmur of its rim was the sigh there, the scarce audible pathetic wail, to his strained ear, of all the baffled forsworn possibilities.[60]

If "homosexual panic" was a commonplace response to the defining of homosexuality in the late nineteenth and early twentieth centuries,[61] "The Jolly Corner" might be considered as more or less its obverse, a "heterosexual panic," as Spencer Brydon encounters his ghostly alternative self—the self perhaps that he might have become had he stayed in America instead of adventuring abroad. To Alice Staverton, an old friend and admirer, he confesses that: ". . . I had then a strange *alter ego* deep down somewhere within me, as the full-blown flower is in the small tight bud, and that I just took the course, I just transferred him to the climate, that blighted him once and forever." Alice affirms his curious description: "I believe in the flower," she says, "I felt it would have been quite splendid, quite huge and monstrous." His reply is "Monstrous above all! . . . and I imagine by the same stroke, quite hideous and offensive." "You'd have had power," Alice responds.

Brydon stalks his supposed *alter ego* through the empty rooms and vistas of doorways in the old house at night, in a reprise of James's own terrifying childhood dream of being haunted in the Louvre in Paris:

> The lucidity, not to say the sublimity of the crisis, had consisted of the great thought that I, in my appalled state, was probably still more appalling than the awful agent, creature or presence, whatever he was . . . he sped for *his* life, while a great storm of thunder and lightning played through the deep embrasures of high windows.[62]

At last, finding a door closed that he was quite sure he had left open, Brydon escapes for the street in terror, but there in the hall of the house he encounters the presence that he fears, a figure in full evening dress and a monocle, with fingers missing from his hand, stands in the vestibule, on the "black and white squares of childhood." The meeting with the alternative self—this figure of the Law of the Father—completely unmans him:

> . . . the presence before him was a presence, the horror
> within him a horror, but . . . such an identity fitted his at *no*
> point, made its alternative monstrous. A thousand times,
> yes, as it came upon him nearer now—the face was the face
> of a stranger. It came upon him nearer now, quite as one of
> those expanding fantastic images projected by the magic
> lantern of childhood; for the stranger, whoever he might be,
> evil, odious, blatant, vulgar, had advanced as for aggression,
> and he knew himself give ground. Then harder pressed still,
> sick with the force of his shock, and falling back as under
> the hot breath and the roused passion of a life larger than
> his own, a rage of personality before which his own col-
> lapsed, he felt the whole vision turn to darkness, and his
> very feet give way. His head went round, he was going, he
> had gone.

When Brydon awakens he is cradled in Alice Staverton's lap, in her
"extraordinary softness and faintly refreshing fragrance . . . so grate-
fully, so abysmally passive" as to make the reader feel that he has
renounced his previous identity ("the experience of a man and the
freedom of a wanderer, overlaid by pleasure, by infidelity, by passages of life that were strange and dim to her" as Alice earlier put it)
and is now reborn as an infant heterosexual male.

   This story shows how the forms of the Gothic might become figurations of psychological crisis, however it does not so much simply
permit psychoanalytical interpretation as in effect thrust it upon us,
which might, of course, suggest the need of a certain diffidence in
making simple identifications, as much as *The Turn of the Screw*. The
powerful figure in the doorway is also pathetic. Alice has already
"seen" him: "He was no monster," she says, "I had accepted him." And,
she adds, pitied him, for his damaged hand, and poor ruined sight.
"He has a million a year [but] he isn't—no, he isn't—you."

   The clairvoyant figure of Alice provides several instances of how
James manages to evoke supernatural Gothic effects within a realist text. At one point she looks abstracted, "and things she didn't
utter, it was clear, came and went in her mind. She might even, for
the minute, off there in the fine room, have imagined some element
dimly gathering. Simplified like a death-mask of a handsome face,
it perhaps produced for her just then an effect akin to the stir of an

impression in the 'set' commemorative plaster." The same technique is used in *The Wings of the Dove* (1902), when heiress Milly Theale, as yet unaware of her own fatal illness, recognizes herself in a sixteenth-century Bronzino portrait showing:

> . . . the face of a young woman, all magnificently drawn, down to the hands, and magnificently dressed; a face almost livid in hue, yet handsome in sadness and crowned with a mass of hair rolled back and high, that must, before fading with time, have had a family resemblance to her own. The lady in question, at all events, with her slightly Michaelangeloesque squareness, her eyes of other days, her full lips, her long neck, her recorded jewels, her brocaded and wasted reds, was a very great personage—only unaccompanied by a joy. And she was dead, dead, dead.[63]

Others see the likeness, but Milly feels it most deeply: "Milly recognized her exactly in words that had nothing to do with her. 'I shall never be better than this.'" That, appropriately, the subject of the portrait, Lucrecia Panciatachi, was condemned to death for adultery, and that the chain around her neck in the picture bears the word "Amour" is not mentioned by James. Milly's exact recognition is "in words that had nothing to do with her," a semantic dislocation produced by the double, the double that according to Freud reminds us of our death. The speaking portrait of Gothic tradition is thus naturalized, and made realistic, while retaining all its force in speaking from the inner life, and, at the same time, encapsulating, as in *mise en abîme*, the *textual* inner life of the novel, its essential deeper meanings.

Ghosts and Monsters

In *American Gothic* (1982), Donald Ringe argues that the rise in spiritualism in the United States caused a decline in American Gothic fiction, and shows how the widespread popularity of fraudulent psychics encouraged a satirical treatment of their pretensions in novels such as James's *The Bostonians* (1886) or W. D. Howells' *The Undiscovered Country* (1880).[64] Henry James certainly disdained such scientific humbug (although he did once address the

Society for Psychical Research when his brother, the psychologist William James, was unable to deliver his planned lecture). His contemporaries, such as Arthur Conan Doyle and Howells (whose daughter Winifred died in 1889 during one of S. Weir Mitchell's rest cure treatments), were interested in seances in the hope of contact with departed spirits, but James had no time for trivial supposed "rappings" from the afterlife, or for *ordinary* ghosts, lacking agency and "washed clean of all clearness as by exposure to a flowing laboratory tap."[65] His interest was in how such appearances might appear *to* somebody, a part of his realist's interest in perception and narrative point of view. The ghosts in *The Turn of the Screw* depend upon the Governess's perception alone, and their meaning, in turn, on the readers' perception: ". . . make them think the evil, think it for themselves," said James, in filling in the "blanks" of the story.[66] In another of James's ghost stories, "The Beast in the Jungle," there is to be no supernatural destiny for John Marcher, despite his own lifelong conviction that he is destined for an exotic, wonderful, or possibly terrible fate. His fate in the end is dreadful enough: to have refused life on the basis of this delusion. The beast in the jungle is a metaphor, and seems again related to anxieties about male sexuality, but is as powerful as a "real" haunting for all that. When at the graveside of his loyal companion and would-have-been lover May Bartram he sees what he has truly been:

> He saw the jungle of his life and saw the lurking Beast; then, while he looked, perceived it, as by a stir of the air, rise, huge and hideous, for the leap that was to settle him. His eyes darkened—it was close; and, instinctively turning, in his hallucination, to avoid it, he flung himself, on his face, on the tomb.[67]

Darwinism and the Abhuman

Metaphor and psychological realism were the directions mostly taken by the predominantly realist modes of writing in this period of an increasingly secular and scientific culture, and they produced some of the greatest ghost stories. But other changes in cultural focus pointed in a different direction: toward a more directly monstrous and visceral horror in Gothic. In particular, the effects of

Darwinist thought registered within fantastic literature as a new conception of the connections between the human and the animal realms, present consciousness and archaic instincts. A range of texts explored these new concerns, and the consequent worries about deviations within the human, or the possibility of atavism. Bram Stoker's *Dracula* and Robert Louis Stevenson's *Dr. Jekyll and Mr. Hyde* were two such British fictions, and many others more or less explicitly displayed the same concerns: Bram Stoker's *The Lair of the Great White Worm*, Arthur Machen's *The Great God Pan*, Robert Jacob's "The Monkey's Paw," H. G. Wells's *The Island of Doctor Moreau.*

Darwinian ideas produced a crisis in familiar conceptions of the status of the human, intensifying anxiety about the body and about the role of genetic inheritance and unsuccessfully repressed instinctual behavior. Hysterical anxiety about the female body was displayed in such books as Stoker's *The Lair of the White Worm* and *Dracula*, in which the effect of vampire contamination renders the woman's body both erotic and horrific:

> [Lucy's] . . . breathing grew stertorous, the mouth opened, and the pale gums, drawn back, made the teeth look longer and sharper than ever. In a sort of sleep-waking, vague, unconscious way she opened her eyes, which were now dull and hard at once, and said in a soft voluptuous voice, such as I had never heard from her lips:—
> "Arthur! Oh, my love, I am so glad you have come! Kiss me!"[68]

The shades of Poe's "Berenice" and "Ligeia" hover in the bedroom here, but in the 1890s there was more than a female gender issue at work and the terror may be just as acutely experienced as regarding the *male* body out of control. Stevenson's *Jekyll and Hyde* has a perfunctory psychological motivation in that from an early age Jekyll has learned to conceal his mild misdemeanors and thus created an embryonic doubleness in personality. But when "Hyde" comes raging out he offers criminality of a different order and another, deeper concern about the human body is aroused:

> He thought of Hyde, for all his energy of life, as something not only hellish but inorganic. This was the shocking thing:

> that the slime of the pit seemed to utter cries and voices;
> that the amorphous dust gesticulated and sinned; that what
> was dead, and had no shape, should usurp the office of life.
> And this again, that that insurgent horror was knit closer to
> him than a wife, closer than an eye. . . . . [69]

This is not so much a question of aberrant human behavior; rather it is a dread that the assumed humanness may not exist at a deeper level: the Gothic past has become a primordial, *biological* past, offering a constant possibility of slippage back into the "slime of the pit." The horror is not of what Hyde *does* (which we are barely told), it is of what he *is*, a representative within the self of the archaic legacy that socialization struggles to conceal.

American writers of this period formulated such ideas theoretically in an offshoot of realism conventionally called Naturalism, a product of nineteenth-century insight into economics and social conventions, as well as biological science. The new scientism of the period undermined notions of free will, presenting human life as subject to larger forces than any within the consciousness, which at their extreme promoted cruelty, a drive for survival at all costs, and an inability to adhere to conventional morality if put to severe test. Stephen Crane, Theodore Dreiser, Jack London, and Frank Norris reduce their characters to pawns of great forces, clinging to the illusion of self-determination while acting under influences they can barely understand. Their moments of crisis are often expressed as Gothic tableaus, even in ostensibly realist texts, when the civilized self loses control to its own perverse, atavistic, or cruelly self-protective impulses. In Frank Norris's *McTeague* (1899), Trina's lottery win brings out her obsessive miserliness: although she has money she literally works her fingers to the bone (when poisoning from her labors eats the tips away), and her sexuality becomes bound up with her avarice, so that she rolls naked on her bed among her hoarded gold coins. McTeague the giant dentist is unable to control his drives when he works over Trina's unconscious body:

> There in that cheap and shabby "Dental Parlor" a dreaded
> struggle began. It was the old battle, old as the world, wide
> as the world—the sudden panther leap of the animal, lips
> drawn, fangs aflash, hideous, monstrous, not to be resisted,

and the simultaneous arousing of the other man, the better
self that cries, "Down, down," without knowing why; that
grips the monster; that fights to strangle it; to thrust it down
and back.[70]

This novel ends with the two male rivals for love and money hand-
cuffed together in the desert in a struggle to the death.

One of the more curious productions of this phase of American
Gothic is Norris's *Vandover and the Brute* (written at college in 1895
and published posthumously in 1914). A shipwreck scene in this
novel shows how Naturalist aesthetics might lead toward a Gothic
sensationalism that would not be out of place in de Sade's *Justine* or
Stoker's *Dracula*:

> One of them, close by Vandover's feet, he noticed particu-
> larly, had but a single garment to cover her. She was
> drenched through and through, her bare feet were blue
> with cold, her head was thrown back, her eyes closed. She
> was silent except when an unusual gust of wind whipped
> the rain and spray across her body like the long, fine lash of
> a whip. Then with every breath she moaned, drawing in her
> breath between her teeth with a little whistling gasp, too
> weak, too exhausted, too nearly unconscious to attempt to
> shield herself in any way (142).

The shipwreck provides an exemplary instance of the racist and
Darwinist assumptions underlying this kind of Gothic realism,
when a crewman beats off a man for whom there is no room in the
overfilled lifeboat:

> The engineer, exasperated, caught up the stump of one of
> the broken oars and beat on the Jew's hands where they
> were gripped whitely on the boat's rim, shouting, "Let go!
> let go!" But as soon as the Jew relaxed one hand he caught
> again with the other. He uttered no cry, but his face as it
> came and went over the gunwhale of the boat was white
> and writhing. When he was at length beaten from the boat
> he caught again at the oar; it was drawn in, and the engi-
> neer clubbed his head and arms till the water nearby grew
> red. The little Jew clung to the end of the oar like a cat,

writhing and grunting, his mouth open, his eyes fixed and staring. When his hands were gone, he tried to embrace the oar with his arms. He slid off in the hollow of a wave, his body turned over twice, and then he sank, his head thrown back, his eyes still open and staring, and a silver chain of bubbles escaping from his mouth (140).

In these instances, estrangement due to race and gender, together with an extreme voyeurism in representation, make it possible to read the realistic as Gothic, without any additional supernaturalism or conventional Gothic setting. Race and gender "disturb" the text, short-circuiting conventional reactions (of gentlemanly sympathy, humane concern for the other). Subsequently Vandover is divested of his privileged position as observer and forced to see himself as other when, like Jekyll, he discovers his own beast within:

For now at last it was huge, strong, insatiable, swollen and distorted out of all size, grown to be a monster, glutted yet still ravenous, some fearful bestial satyr, grovelling, perverse, horrible beyond words. . . . Little by little the brute had grown, and he, pleasureloving, adapting himself to every change of environment, luxurious, self-indulgent, shrinking with the shrinking of a sensuous artist-nature from all that was irksome and disagreeable, had shut his eyes to the voices that shouted warnings of the danger, and had allowed the brute to thrive and to grow, its abominable famine gorged from the store of that in him which he felt to be the purest, the cleanest, and the best, its bulk fattened upon the rot and decay of all that was good, growing larger day by day, noisome, swollen, poddy, a filthy inordinate ghoul, gorged and bloated by feeding on the good things that were dead (215).

Vandover's bizarre male "pregnancy" seen here originated in the horror he felt as a boy on discovering a profusely illustrated entry on "obstretics" in his father's encyclopedia, which is when "the first taint crept in, the innate vice stirred in him, the brute began to make itself felt, and a multitude of perverse and vicious ideas commenced to buzz about him like a swarm of nasty flies" (11). There is more than a hint of what Elizabeth Sedgewick calls "homosexual panic" when Vandover's full blown "lycanthropy-mathesis" finds him running naked around his room on sexually-suggestive all fours, while rowdy male college students parade around the town shouting "Rah-Rah-Rah." More sexual fears surface in his account of how the six-foot tall prostitute Flossie infects his (male) friend "Dolly" Haight with venereal disease through an uncalled-for kiss on his accidentally cut lips. Syphillis, Elaine Showalter points out, "became an obsessive public crisis at the precise moment when arguments over the future of marriage, discussions of the New Woman, and decadent homosexual culture were at their peak."[71] But it has to be admitted that however persuasive the diagnosis of social maladies as the anxiety-producing origins of such fictions may seem, their expression in lycanthropy is still a fully Gothic excess.

Like the other monstrous male birth fantasies of the period—*Jekyll and Hyde, The Island of Doctor Moreau,* and earlier, *Frankenstein*—*Vandover and the Brute* returns us to Julia Kristeva's concept of the abjected mother. In Vandover's case this could hardly be more explicit, given the inception of his pathological disturbance in gynecological illustrations. But in each case a different set of cultural anxieties seem to come to focus in abjection, which is to be expected if abjection—the casting out or tabooing of what is not acceptable—is itself the very mode of cultural creation in its origins, making culture possible by discriminations and prohibitions; of what may not be eaten or, as with incest, what may not be done. Where the "real"—in the sense of whatever is outside or beyond culture—comes into collision with the "symbolic"—in the sense of how things are agreed to be in culture and language—the outcome is horror.[72] Male "pregnancy," male "birth," would be an extreme example of such "collision," a destabilizing vortex of meanings under pressure in a particular period. In Shelley's *Frankenstein* such meanings would include scientific experimentation, Galvanism, issues of slave liberation, the rights of man. In Wells's *Island of Dr. Moreau,* Stevenson's *Jekyll and Hyde,* and Norris's *Vandover,* they cohere around Darwinism and eugenics, male sexual hysteria, and "decadence"—whether aesthetic or racial and nationalist.[73]

Among the sources of abhuman Gothic horror for many writers at this time were the urban squalor and misery of overcrowded cities in which poverty, ignorance, and crime among a polyglot immigrant population appalled middle-class observers. Books like Jacob Riis's *How the Other Half Lives* mapped the degradations suffered by inhabitants of the cities, and writers often drew on a Gothic vocabulary in attempting to describe such scenes. Stephen Crane, in *Maggie: A Girl of the Streets* (1900),[74] saw his ingénue growing up in oppressive New York City, yet somehow remaining pure, like a beset Gothic heroine. "The girl, Maggie, blossomed in a mud puddle. She grew up to be a most rare and wonderful production of a tenement district, a pretty girl. None of the dirt of Rum Alley seemed to be in her veins" (29). She ends in the river as a rejected prostitute, denied by all, even (and convulsively) by a benevolent clergyman: "At the foot of the tall buildings appeared the deathly black hue of the river. Some hidden factory sent up a yellow glare, that lit for a moment the waters lapping oilily against timbers. The varied sounds of life, made joyous by distance and seeming unapproachableness, came faintly and died away to a silence" (81). Urban Gothic offered salacious pleasures from the beginning, as Lippard's Philadelphia shows; here it is evident that a reformist impulse finds such language the most adequate to shock and dismay polite readers.

Some turned in revulsion against the alien "other" of the American urban scene. H. P. Lovecraft, a New Englander, invented in the 1920s a species of non-human monsters whose origin may ultimately have been in his own racial prejudice, stirred by visits to New York. David Punter observes, "The appalling feature of this aspect of Lovecraft's writing is that, reading through not only his fiction but also his letters, one realises that the terms which he applies to his invading non-human monstrosities are precisely the same as those in which he describes members of all American ethnic groups with the exception of the caste of East Coast 'Old Americans' to which he belonged."[75] In Lovecraft's peculiar stories, the small East Coast towns are threatened by monstrous creatures from outside, which like Robert W. Chambers's *The King in Yellow* (1893), have an explicit textual ancestry in Bierce's "Hali" and "Carcosa" (and behind both Chambers and Bierce, of course, is Poe, who wrote out of a not dissimilar sense of cultural dispossession). Lovecraft's Cthulthu also belongs to the same fictive realm as Algernon Blackwood's "Ancient Sorceries," or Stoker's *The Great White Worm* and Machen's *The Great God Pan*, in which racial stereotyping entwines with Naturalist psychology and sentimental archaic mysticism. His baroque, incantatory prose invokes an archaic language, which assaults the text and reader with an alternative realm of meaning:

> As the presence of the three men seemed to rouse the dying thing, it began to mumble without raising or turning its head. . . . At first the syllables defied all correlation with any speech of earth, but towards the last there came some disjointed fragments evidently taken from the *Necronomicon*, that monstrous blasphemy in quest of which the thing had perished. These fragments, as Armitage recalls them, ran something like "N'gai, n'gha' ghaa, bugg-shoggog, y'hah; Yog-Sothoth, Yog Sothoth. . . ." They tailed off into nothingness as the whippoorwills shrieked in rhythmical crescendoes of unholy anticipation.[76]

The lineage of this peculiar language might be found in the incomprehensible mutterings of the ghost crew in Poe's "MS Found in a Bottle," or the untranslatable hieroglyphics discovered in *Arthur Gordon Pym*; the difference being that one might suspect Poe of a sense of humor. But Lovecraft's inventions have found a cult following, and even this brief extract shows the legacy that was to be exploited in later twentieth-century horror fiction and film.

Gothic Modernism

Lovecraft invented his own consistent setting: an area of New England with its imaginary central town, Arkham.[77] So too did William Faulkner, in his fictional Yoknapatawpha County and its county town Jefferson—which might seem the only similarity between his writing and Lovecraft's. But Faulkner is another profoundly Gothic writer, also working out of a dispossessed region afflicted by loss of a grander history than its present condition. In Faulkner's southern Gothic the present can only be understood in terms of a working out of events from the past which emerge in uncanny interconnections and buried lineages, warped by the dark tangle of slavery and racial persecutions. A line from Lovecraft's "The Dunwich Horror" shows another unexpected consonance with

Faulkner's work: "You needn't ask how he called it out of the air. He didn't call it out. *It was his twin brother, but it looked more like the father than he did."* The vernacular of the New England locals, their ignorance and interrelationships, and the sense of family history shown here have "regional realist" parallels with Faulkner's ignorant but deeply embedded southerners, similarly represented by a sophisticated informed consciousness beyond their own reach.

Faulkner's haunted swamps, lost plantations, and defeated southern towns offer a Gothic landscape comparable to the ruins of feudalism in English Gothic; the impacted history of their denizens a rich source of Gothic interactions, violent and abrupt, but steeped in the implication of a lost "real." The ending of *Absalom! Absalom!* (1936) echoes the destruction of Poe's House of Usher, with even an implicit admission of literary stage-management:

> It loomed, bulked, square and enormous, with jagged half-toppled chimneys, its roofline sagging a little; for an instant, as they moved, hurried, toward it Quentin saw completely through it a ragged segment of sky with three hot stars in it as if the house were of one dimension, painted on a canvas curtain in which there was a tear; now, almost beneath it, the dead furnace-breath of air in which they moved seemed to reek in slow and protracted violence with a smell of desolation and decay as if the wood of which it were built were flesh (366).

As with Poe's grotesque house, and Hawthorne's later decrepit House of the Seven Gables, the ambitious design of Thomas Sutpen for a mansion and a family lineage is rotten from the start. In the foundations of Hawthorne's decaying mansion metaphorically lies a rotting corpse, a curse from a false accusation of witchcraft, and a missing Indian deed to the Pyncheon lands; and at the heart of the Sutpen dynasty is the destruction brought by race, the drop of black blood that makes Charles Bon a "nigger" and in the end brings down all Sutpen's grandiose plans.

The fictionality of Faulkner's world is rendered not only by such a Gothic awareness of the artificiality of the real, or, as is the case in *Absalom! Absalom!* explicitly, the attempt of its explicators to reimagine the past, but also in the often excessive figurations of the language, constantly trying to rephrase itself in search of an adequate expression of what language may be unable to describe. In Faulkner's descriptions time stops, or is slowed down to an unbearable intensity, his vision is cinematic—perhaps almost pornographic —in its obsessive recapitulations. In *Light in August* (1932) for example, mixed race victim-villain Joe Christmas beats his exhausted horse:

> But the horse slowed, sheering into the curb. Joe pulled at its head, beating it, but it slowed into the curb and stopped, shadowdappled, its head down trembling, its breathing almost like a human voice. Yet still the rider leaned forward in the arrested saddle, in the attitude of terrific speed, beating the horse across the rump with the stick. Save for the rise and fall of the stick and the groaning respirations of the animal, they might have been an equestrian statue strayed from its pedestal and come to rest in an attitude of ultimate exhaustion in a quiet and empty street splotched and dappled by moonshadow.[78]

In such iconic moments Faulkner reinvents the Gothic, focusing on its stylized intensity of violence and relation to the official past of memorial and statuary, within which the present becomes just another instance of the past, a repeated motif of condensed cruelty and inevitability that registers Joe Christmas's monstrous and unavailing struggle to escape his identity as both white and black. "The past isn't dead," says one of Faulkner's characters, "it isn't even past," which might serve as a motto for American Gothic itself as it explores the tensions between a culturally sanctioned progressive optimism and an actual dark legacy.

In Faulkner's modernism the labyrinth of the Gothic becomes the labyrinth of time and the street, the characteristic trope of the twentieth century:

> Looking, he can see the smoke low on the sky, beyond an imperceptible corner; he is entering it again, the street which ran for thirty years. It had been a paved street, where going should be fast. It had made a circle and he is still inside of it. Though during the last seven days he has had no paved street, yet he has travelled further than in all the

thirty years before. And yet he is still inside the circle. "And yet I have been further in these seven days than all the thirty years." He thinks. "But I have never got outside that circle. I have never broken out of the ring of what I have done and cannot ever undo," he thinks quietly, sitting on the seat, with planted on the dashboard before him the shoes, the black shoes smelling of negro: that mark on his ankles the gauge definite and ineradicable of the black tide creeping up his legs, moving from his feet upwards as death moves (*Light in August* 255).

The street, and time itself, is a labyrinth for mixed-race Joe Christmas because race is the spring of the American Gothic trap. Christmas becomes the lover of his employer, Joanna Burden, who is from a New England family of: "Yankees. Foreigners. Worse than foreigners: enemies. Carpetbaggers. . . . Stirring up the negroes to murder and rape, they called it" (187). In this love struggle he feels as "though he had fallen into a sewer" (192):

> Now and then she appointed trysts beneath certain shrubs about the grounds, where he would find her naked, or with her clothing half torn to ribbons upon her, in the wild throes of nymphomania, her body gleaming in the slow shifting from one to another of such formally erotic attitudes and gestures as a Beardsley of the time of Petronius might have drawn. She would be wild then, in the close, breathing halfdark without walls, with her wild hair, each strand of which would seem to come alive like octopus tentacles, and her wild hands and her breathing: "Negro! Negro! Negro!" (195)

Christmas kills her after she has offered to improve him through education and then, following his refusal, attempted to include him in a double suicide. Faulkner presents the event with a stylized sleepwalking fatality, as he does all of the events of the South; they are inevitable, they have somehow *already* happened, as though southern history is a sort of complex machine determined by its own inexorable pressures.

In Richard Wright's *Native Son* (1940), although set in Chicago, the same sense of inevitability is suggested in the murder of a young

white girl, Mary Dalton, again from a family well-disposed to black
people (although its wealth derives from the rents of their inadequate, exploitative housing). Bigger Thomas, taken on as chauffeur
to the Dalton family, is confused by the white liberalism of Mary
and her idealistic friends; when she gets drunk he carries her up to
her bedroom, hating her: "His fingers felt the soft curves of her body
and he was still, looking at her. This little bitch! He thought."[79] He
is excited as she lies on the bed and he feels her body. Then a white
ghost appears: "He turned and a hysterical horror seized him, as
though he were falling from a great height in a dream. A white blur
was standing by the door, silent, ghostlike. It filled his eyes and
gripped his body. It was Mrs. Dalton. He wanted to knock her out
of his way and bolt from the room" (125). When Mary mumbles he
is afraid the blind woman will come to the bed, so he silences the
girl with her pillow. "His eyes were filled with the white blur moving towards him in the shadows of the room . . . intimidated to the
core by the white blur moving towards him" he continues to press
down until Mrs. Dalton leaves (126). "Mary was dead and he had
killed her. He was a murderer, a negro Murderer" (127).

Bigger's terror of the "white blur" registers the inversion of conventional Gothic produced by the American racial situation. James
Baldwin once wrote a telling essay on the associations between
black and evil in the Christian inheritance, but in some respects for
the black American, from slave narratives through twentieth-
century writing, it seems the perspective is reversed and fulfills
Melville's insights into the whiteness of the whale. The white blur
is blind: like the white culture of Ralph Ellison's *Invisible Man*
(1952) it does not see the black truth. In this episode Wright plays
upon white fears of the black rapist, but it is those very fears that
cause Bigger to kill Mary Dalton, he feels that he must not be found
in her bedroom. The subsequent scene, in which with great difficulty Bigger cuts off Mary's head in order to feed her body into the
basement furnace, is another Gothic pastiche of white terrors, and
again Wright invokes a *white* wraith: "A noise made him whirl; two
green burning pools—pools of accusation and guilt—stared at him
from a white blur that sat perched on the edge of the trunk. It was
the white cat . . ." (132). The echo of Poe's "Black Cat" is unmistak-

able as Wright endorses yet reverses the terms of Gothic horror conventions. But what makes *Native Son* most Gothic, in these sequences, or Bigger's nightmare of carrying his own head in a bloody package, and his horrific murder of his black girlfriend Bessie with a brick after he realizes she will give him away, is its uncompromising *excess*. No quarter is given to liberal opinions: Bigger embraces his fate, determined as it may have been by poverty and ignorance and provocation; and finds his own full identity in *becoming* the horror that his situation has created. As his lawyer Max puts it, "after he murdered, he accepted the crime. . . . It was the first full act of his life; it was the most meaningful, exciting, and stirring thing that had ever happened to him. He accepted it because it made him free, gave him the possibility of choice, of action, the opportunity to act and to feel that his actions carried weight" (430). This is a rewriting of *Frankenstein*, with Bigger as the creature (and behind him, it is suggested in the lawyer's argument, twelve million American black people) made monstrous by the white hegemony rather than any experimenting scientist. Mary Shelley made the Creature's actions unforgivable because his situation was indefensible, unforgivable, and Wright does the same. The Gothic genius of the invention of Bigger is that he exceeds even the well-meaning excuses offered by his idealistic lawyer, whom he appalls in a final interview before death, shouting: "I didn't want to kill! . . . But what I killed for, I *am*! It must have been pretty deep in me in order to make me kill!" . . . "What I killed for must have been good!" "No; no; no. . . . Bigger, not that . . ." pleads his despairing defender (461).

Southern Gothic

The legacy of the South reaches up into the North in such fictions, but in the South there was a sense of history turning in upon itself as writers evoked a string of distorted figures trapped in structures that had lost their authority but not their power. Faulkner mapped out a conflict between the Old South and the so-called New South of modernizing but reductive tendencies from the turn of the century on; other writers articulated the same effects in an immediate and intense focus. In Lillian Hellman's *The Little Foxes* (1939);

Carson McCuller's *The Heart is a Lonely Hunter* (1940); Tennessee William's *Sweet Bird of Youth* (1959), *The Glass Menagerie* (1947), and *A Streetcar Named Desire* (1947); and Truman Capote's *Other Voices, Other Rooms* (1948) and *The Grass Harp* (1951), the neurotic, declining South is explored through the grotesques that it throws up. Eudora Welty, Robert Penn Warren, and Walker Percy add to the list of southern Gothicists after Faulkner, but the most powerful of them is Flannery O'Connor, who created grotesque people and situations born of—but in excess of—their southern context.

O'Connor is certainly a Gothic writer, although not in the conventional sense of working within a Gothic literary tradition; rather her Gothicism stems from the intensity and passion with which she works out the implications of what might be called a sort of fundamentalist, or even Puritan, Catholicism containing an inspiring terror of the possibility of grace and the fallenness of the world. Hazel Motes in *Wise Blood* (1952), for example, burns out his own eyes with quicklime in order to see better; another character in "Greenleaf," in *Everything That Rises Must Converge* (1956), finds his own grace through having a Christ tattooed on his back where only others can see it ("Parker's Back"), and a middle-aged woman rises to her epiphanic destiny when she is gored by a bull (it is probably enraged by the sun glittering on the car she leans on, which makes her death entirely incidental—in *this* world). The humor suggested here is characteristic in its bleakness as O'Connor moves from the tediously, brutally everyday world to the devastating possibility of a different sort of reckoning entirely. The Misfit, an escaped convict in "A Good Man is Hard to Find," commits his atrocities in lieu of proof of God's existence. He stops to investigate a family's crashed car, callously kills the children and their parents, and discusses life with the grandmother, whose idiot mistakes had caused the crash in the first place and whose folly in recognizing him from a news item seals their doom. After he kills her too, the Misfit reflects—"She might've been a good woman if on'y there'd been somebody there to shoot her ev'ry minute of the day" (*The Artificial Nigger* 1957). O'Connor's mordant wit—if it should be called humor at all—seems based on a view not all that far from "Sinners in the Hands of an Angry God": if religion *were* to be taken seriously, the consequences must be terrifying.

The Gothic Aesthetics of Absence

In *The Political Unconscious* (1981) Fredric Jameson traces the fate of "Magical Narratives" into the modernism of the twentieth century:

> Thus, in the first great period of bourgeois hegemony, the reinvention of romance finds its strategy in the substitution of new positivities (theology, psychology, the dramatic metaphor) for the older magical content. When at the end of the nineteenth century the search for secular equivalents seems exhausted, the characteristic indirection of a nascent modernism, from Kafka to Cortazar, circumscribes the place of the fantastic as a determinate, marked absence at the heart of the secular world. . . . [Jameson illustrates this with a quotation from Hofmannsthal, concerning an empty cityscape.] The unnatural neutrality of this vacant cityscape may stand as an emblem of *the contemporary fantastic in general, its expectant hush revealing an object world forever suspended on the brink of meaning, forever disposed to receive a revelation of evil or grace that never comes* (italics added).[80]

Jameson's point seems to be that the desacralization of the world caused by the explanatory powers of, for example, psychology, changes the possible epiphany of presence, or vision, to that of *absence*, or remembrance of what is no longer possible, an "unsentimental loyalty to those henceforth abandoned clearings across which higher and lower worlds once passed" (135). In Flannery O'Connor's work, perhaps, those worlds do still cross, with the shock of a thunderbolt, but for other writers Jameson's argument holds good. Thomas Pynchon, for example, often develops moments of almost-meaning, in which the merest suspicion of something going on is pursued into Jameson's "expectant hush revealing an object world forever suspended on the brink of meaning, forever disposed to receive a revelation of evil or grace that never comes." Pynchon's technique—which holds for many other recent Gothic

writers—is to bring into being through language some state that the
language simultaneously critiques and desires:

> Though she knew even less about radios than southern
> Californians, there were to both patterns a hieroglyphic
> sense of concealed meaning, of an intent to communicate.
> There'd seemed no limit to what the printed circuit could
> have told her (if she had tried to find out); so, in her first
> minute of San Narciso, a revelation also trembled just past
> the threshold of her understanding. Smog hung all round
> the horizon, the sun on the bright beige countryside was
> painful; she and the Chevy seemed parked at the centre of
> an odd, religious instant. As if on some other frequency, or
> out of the eye of some whirlwind rotating too slowly for her
> heated skin even to feel the coolness of, words were being
> spoken.[81]

The vocabulary ("beige, Chevy, parked, smog") and demotic syntax
("there'd seemed; to feel the centrifugal coolness of") undercuts and
thereby allows a numinous moment in a secular world; precisely
because it is an absence that is called up, a vision that doesn't come.
If science has demystified the magical world, it will be in science
that the mystical can be resurrected, the reductivism of the material world elegantly sidestepped. The same is true of Pynchon's representation of *history*, seen here in Oedipa's evocation of the
Trystero (a historical and also possibly contemporary organization)
as like a nightclub dancer:

> As if the breakaway gowns, net bras, jewelled garters and
> G-strings of historical figuration that would fall away . . .
> as if a plunge towards dawn indefinite black hours long
> would indeed be necessary before the Tristero could be
> revealed in its terrible nakedness. Would its smile, then, be
> coy, and would it flirt away harmlessly backstage, say good-
> night with a Bourbon Street bow, and leave her in peace?
> Or would it, instead, the dance ended, come back down the
> runway, its luminous stare locked to Oedipa's, smile gone
> malign and pitiless; bend to her alone among the desolate
> rows of seats and begin to speak words she never wanted to
> hear? (36)

Fears of science, contemporary paranoias about forces within history, and the vulnerability of the observer replace earlier belief structures in an uncanny new landscape, even more "unreal" than the stagy original Gothic, but equally representing "real" forces at play, real threats to the human, even if they are only to be seen off to the side. Where the poet offers imaginary gardens with real toads in them, Pynchon offers something like imaginary corporations with names like Yoyodyne, making real guidance systems for real rockets, whose elegant parabolas hang like doomsday traceries over the worlds of *V* and *Gravity's Rainbow*. William Gibson's *Neuromancer* takes the process another stage along, where the fantasy realm of magical romance becomes re-enabled by the development of cyber-technology and the original Gothic is possible again as a mental adventure that is not only within the mind.

Heritage Gothic

In his chapter "Magical Narratives" in *The Political Unconscious*, Fredric Jameson suggests that:

> now that the "experience" or the seme of evil can no longer be permanently assigned or attached to this or that human agent, it must find itself expelled from the realm of inter-personal or interworldly relations in a kind of Lacanian foreclusion and *thereby be projectively reconstituted into a free floating and disembodied element, a baleful optical illusion, in its own right:* that "realm" of sorcery and magical forces which constitutes the semic organization of the "world" of romance and henceforth determines the provisional invest-ment of its anthropomorphic bearers and its landscapes alike (119, italics added).

It follows, I think, that ideas of some *unspecified* evil or uncanniness can crop up anywhere in contemporary fiction and film; and also that there may be a sort of indifference to its logical coherence: the absurdity of Death say, taking a personal interest in the characters in *Meet Joe Black*, or the new Dracula suffering a broken heart through-out eternity in a film remake is not particularly problematic for a modern audience. What matters instead is the knowing homage to earlier versions of the story. If, as Jameson further argues (in *Postmodernism: The Cultural Logic of Late Capitalism*) the Past has become a museum, a repository of images that can be pillaged at will in the recreations of post-modern culture, then the *pastiche* that is a hallmark of postmodernism (that is, a "flat" referencing of something else, without satirical or critical intentions being apparent) may conjoin with the "counterfeit" aspect of the Gothic (as evident from the beginning) to offer a range of possible Gothic styles. There is a language of the Gothic, that may be employed in other genres (as in science fiction, *Blade Runner*; small town thriller, *Blue Velvet*; noir, *Angel Heart*; or war film, *Apocalypse Now*, to stay with film for the time being); a set of genre conventions that may inform a whole production (as in *Mary Shelley's Frankenstein*, the new *Dracula*, or *Sleepy Hollow*); or appear in subtle referencing as in the hints of "The Turn of the Screw" in *The Others*. The Gothic heritage becomes *Heritage Gothic*, a use of now conventional tropes that is legitimated simply through previous practice: *The Haunting of Hill House* becomes Robert Wise's *The Haunting*, becomes the *Haunting* remake in a progression of increasing distortion and arguably a loss of coherence and purpose; a *ghosting* of the original Gothic. But one advantage of this cultural revolving door is that the audience no longer needs persuasion of the authenticity of Gothic entertainments: absurdity or even incoherence are not problems, and the author or film maker is freed to play with the form; even to be straightforward in accepting its strangeness as if it were plausible. Anne Rice's *Vampire* series is exemplary of this, explaining how it *feels* to be a vampire, or a vampire doll-child, sexualized and adult but trapped forever in an infant body. Poppy Z. Brite's novels and stories similarly accept the possibility of vampirism while exploring the consequent angst of its practitioners. Such works seem to invite speculation about their relation to AIDS, teenage dislocation, homosexual alienations, just as the fantasies of the 1890s bear some reference to syphilis, or the notions of racial decline; but they do not ask to be read as allegories, in part because of the postmodern "emptying out" of significance and the substitution of mild free-floating "affect" for deep feeling. *Something* is evidently at stake, but it is difficult to say what that something is.

With such dispersions, attenuations, name-checking, and stylized imitations, does it any longer make sense to speak of the Gothic as a genre, or American Gothic as a distinct strand within it? Jameson proposes that all genre categories eventually become used up: "all generic categories, even the most time-hallowed and traditional, are ultimately to be understood (or 'estranged') as mere ad hoc, experimental constructs, devised for a specific textual occasion and abandoned like so much scaffolding when the analysis has done its work" ("Magical Narratives" 145). The death sentence may be tempting, but in fact the Gothic seems to be so recognizable, even when fragmented and circulating within other forms, that it stubbornly resists its own obsolescence, and invites us instead to recognize its continuing existence, through *hybridity*, as one of the most powerful genres, one which speaks of the depths as well as the surfaces of western culture.

Notes

1. *Charles Brockden Brown's Novels*, 1887 (McKay; facsimile reprint, New York: Kennikat Press, 1963); *Arthur Mervyn*, Kennikat ed., vol. II, p. 77.

2. Charles Brockden Brown, *Jane Talbot*, Kennikat ed., vol. V, p. 199.

3. Charles Brockden Brown, *Ormond*, Kennikat ed., vol.VI, p. 275.

4. *Ormond* (New York: Hafner Publishing Company, 1962) p. 235.

5. William Godwin, *Thoughts on Man* (reprint ed., New York: Augustus M. Kelley, 1969) p. 240.

6. *Ormond*, p. 209.

7. Such as that the overheard sounds cannot be identified as one of the main groups of languages.

8. Terence Martin, *The Instructed Vision: Scottish Common Sense Philosophy and the Origins of American Fiction* (Bloomington: Indiana University Press, 1961).

9. *Selected Writings of Edgar Allan Poe*, Edward Davidson, ed. (Boston: Houghton Mifflin, 1956) p. 194.

10. Letter to James Russell Lowell, July 2, 1844, in John Ostrom, ed., *The Letters of Edgar Allan Poe* (Cambridge, MA: Harvard University Press, 1948) vol. I, p. 137.

11. The will baffled Poe's rationalist contemporaries: it seemed a mysterious faculty, perhaps with some non-material or even divine input. Charles Upham's three-volume psychology text, *Elements of Philosophy* (Boston,

1831), has an entire volume on "The Will" but manages to establish virtually nothing about this strange power of volition. " . . . [I]t is in the will," Upham ventures, "that we find the point of union, the position of contact with the Divine Mind" (vol. III, p. 26). This is of course how the will is represented in "William Wilson."

12. In his 1850 review of Hawthorne's *Mosses From an Old Manse*.

13. "Introduction," *Selected Writings of Edgar Allan Poe*, Edward Davidson, ed. (Boston: Houghton Mifflin, 1956) p. xxvi.

14. *Selected Writings of Edgar Allan Poe*, Edward Davidson, ed. (Boston: Houghton Mifflin, 1956) p. 87.

15. Hawthorne preferred to stay in his garden with the children while his wife attended church.

16. Nathaniel Hawthorne, *The Scarlet Letter* (New York: Norton, 1961) p. 9. Hawthorne added the 'w' to his family name, perhaps to add to his distance from those oppressive ancestors.

17. Nathaniel Hawthorne, *Young Goodman Brown and Other Tales* (Oxford: Oxford University Press, 1987) p.123.

18. Eric Savoy also notes this in "The Rise of American Gothic," in Jerrold Hogle, ed., *Cambridge Companion to Gothic Fiction* (Cambridge, MA: Cambridge University Press, 2002) p. 186.

19. Ralph Waldo Emerson, "Nature," 1836, in *Selections from Ralph Waldo Emerson*, Stephen Whicher, ed., (Boston: Houghton Mifflin Co, 1960) p. 34.

20. "The Uncanny" (1919) in *Pelican Freud Library, 14*, trans. James Strachey (Harmondsworth, England: Penguin) pp. 335–376, p. 345.

21. David S. Reynolds, *Beneath the American Renaissance: The Subversive Imagination in the Age of Emerson and Melville* (Cambridge, MA: Harvard University Press, 1989) p. 246.

22. See Leslie Ginsberg, "Slavery and the Gothic Horror of Poe's 'The Black Cat,'" in *American Gothic: New Interventions in a National Narrative*, Robert Martin and Eric Savoy, eds., (Iowa City: University of Iowa Press, 1998).

23. See Nicholas Royle, *The Uncanny* (Manchester, England: Manchester University Press, 2003); and Allan Lloyd-Smith, *Uncanny American Fiction* (London: Macmillan, 1989).

24. The details differ, but the impulse is remarkably the same as that in Hawthorne's "Ethan Brand", the commission of the unpardonable sin.

25. In "Gothic Possibilities in Moby-Dick," Benjamin Franklin Fisher IV spells out some of the Gothic tropes Melville uses in this novel. See *Gothick Origins and Innovations*, Allan Lloyd Smith and Victor Sage, eds. (Amsterdam: Costerus-Rodopi, 1994) pp. 115–121. In the reading here I have attempted to move in some different but complementary directions.

26. See Leo Marx, *The Machine in the Garden: Technology and the Pastoral Ideal in America*, 1964 (Oxford: Oxford University Press, 2000).

27. *Arthur Gordon Pym*, (New York: Penguin, 1975) p. 239.

28. Harold Beaver notes: "As political satire, then, Pym's *Narrative* is even more unscrupulous, more offensive, more paranoiac than anything in *Gulliver's Travels*. The conscious political intent—of this there can be no doubt—was to forestall the degree zero, the South pole itself, of racial prejudice" (*Arthur Gordon Pym*, 25).

29. Stephen Whicher, ed., *Selections from Ralph Waldo Emerson* (Boston: Houghton Mifflin Co, 1960) p. 42.

30. But Emerson also could say, in "Experience": "but if I am the devil's child, I will live then from the devil."

31. *Frontier Gothic*, David Mogen, Scott P. Sanders, Joanne B. Karpinski, eds. (London and Toronto: Associated University Presses, 1993) p. 22.

32. D. H. Lawrence, *Studies in Classic American Literature*, 1923 (New York: Viking, 1964).

33. Leslie Fiedler, *The Return of the Vanishing American* (New York: Stein and Day, 1969).

34. Herman Melville, *Selected Tales and Poems* (New York: Holt, Rinehart and Winston, 1950) p. 88.

35. Kurtz's last words are reported by Marlowe as: "The horror! the horror!" Joseph Conrad, *Heart of Darkness* (London: Dent, 1946) p. 161.

36. Eric Sundquist, *To Wake the Nations: Race in the Making of American Literature* (Cambridge, MA and London: Harvard University Press, 1993).

37. H. L. Malchow, *Gothic Images of Race in Nineteenth Century Britain* (Stanford, CA: Stanford University Press, 1996).

38. In Charles L. Crow, ed., *American Gothic 1787–1916* (Oxford: Blackwell, 1999) pp. 7–19.

39. Ambrose Bierce, *Can Such Things Be?*, 1893 (London: Jonathan Cape, 1926) p. 12.

40. Mogen, *Frontier Gothic*, p. 20; quoting Peter N. Carroll, *Puritanism and the Wilderness* (New York and London: Columbia University Press, 1969) p. 11.

41. Sigmund Freud, "Das Unheimliche," 1919, in *Standard Edition of the Complete Psychological Works*, James Strachey, ed. and trans. (London: The Hogarth Press, 1953) p. 220.

42. After a month in his sanatorium she returned home, but would still "crawl into remote closets and under beds—to hide from the grinding pressure of that profound distress." *The Living of Charlotte Perkins Gilman, An Autobiography* (New York: Appleton-Century, 1935) quoted by Elaine Hedges in her Afterword "Postscript to Gilman" in *The Yellow Wallpaper*, Elaine Hedges, ed. (London: Virago, 1981) p. 119.

43. Charlotte Perkins Gilman, "The Yellow Wallpaper," manuscript version, in *Nineteenth-Century American Women Writers, An Anthology*, Karen L. Kilcup, ed. (Oxford and Cambridge, MA: Blackwell, 1997) pp. 486–495, 491. Quotations in the text are from this edition.

44. Sandra M. Gilbert and Susan Gubar, *The Madwoman in the Attic: The Woman Writer and the Nineteenth-Century Literary Imagination* (New Haven and London: Yale University Press, 1984) p. 91.

45. Julia Kristeva, *Powers of Horror: An Essay on Abjection*, Leon S. Roudiez, trans. (New York: Columbia University Press, 1982) pp. 1, 2.

46. These words appear only in the manuscript version.

47. The newborn child is only briefly referred to in the story, as being well taken care of by one "Mary"—a generic name for a nurse or servant.

48. Annette Kolodny, "A Map for Rereading," in *The New Feminist Criticism*, Elaine Showalter, ed. (London: Virago, 1986) p. 52.

49. Charles L. Crow, ed., *American Gothic 1787–1916* (Oxford: Blackwell, 1999) pp. 434–439.

50. In *The Ghost Stories of Edith Wharton* (London: Constable, 1975).

51. R. W. B. Lewis, ed., *The Collected Short Stories of Edith Wharton*, VII (New York: Scribners, 1968) p. 126.

52. Julia Kristeva, *Powers of Horror: An Essay on Abjection*, Leon S. Roudiez, trans. (New York: Columbia University Press, 1982) pp. 1, 2.

53. Henry James, *The Golden Bowl*, 1904 (Harmondsworth, England: Penguin Books, 1985).

54. Henry James, *A Small Boy and Others* (London: Macmillan, 1913), p. 363.

55. For details of the social background here, see my article "A Word Kept Back in *The Turn of the Screw*," *Victorian Literature and Culture*, 24 (1998).

56. Henry James, *The Art of the Novel: Critical Prefaces*, R. P. Blackmur, ed. (New York: Scribner's Sons, 1962) p. 172.

57. Shoshana Felman, "Turning the Screw of Interpretation," in *Literature and Psychoanalysis: The Question of Reading, Otherwise*, Shoshana Felman, ed. (Baltimore and London: Johns Hopkins University Press, 1982) pp. 101, 115. The point is valid, but on the other hand, if we consider the *frame* of the story: children at the mercy of servants in a remote house, exposed, in James's words to "the very worst action small victims so conditioned might be conceived as subject to," (*Preface*, 176) what else can it mean?

58. Henry James, *The Turn of the Screw*, Norton Critical Edition (New York and London: Norton & Company, 1999) p. 51.

59. Besides being a Transcendentalist, Henry James the elder was a Fourierist and a Swedenborgian, who wrote: "the natural inheritance of every one who is capable of a spiritual life, is an unsubdued forest where the wolf howls and every obscene bird of night chatters." *Substance and Shadow*, 1863, reprinted in F. O. Matthiessen, *The James Family* (New York: Knopf, 1961), p. 156. He had himself suffered from a horrifying spiritual-haunting experience, which he called the Vastation, in which some vile fetid beast seemed to squat in a corner of his room in Windsor.

60. In *The Ghostly Tales of Henry James,* Leon Edel, ed. (New Brunswick, NJ: Rutgers University Press, 1948).

61. See Eve Kosofsky Sedgewick, *Epistemology of the Closet* (London: Harvester Wheatsheaf, 1991) and Elaine Showalter *Sexual Anarchy* (London: Virago, 1992) on this point. Another relevant James story is "The Beast in the Jungle."

62. Henry James, *A Small Boy and Others,* (London: Macmillan, 1913) p. 363.

63. Henry James, *The Wings of the Dove* (Harmondsworth, England: Penguin Books, 1976). The portrait is of Lucrezia Panciatachi, 1541c, now in the Uffizi Gallery, Florence.

64. Donald Ringe, *American Gothic* (Lexington: University Press of Kentucky, 1982).

65. Henry James, *The Art of the Novel,* p. 172.

66. Henry James, *The Art of the Novel,* p. 176.

67. Henry James, *Selected Tales* (London: Dent, 1982) p. 283.

68. Bram Stoker, *Dracula* (New York: Airmont Publishing Co., 1965) pp. 167–8.

69. R. L. Stevenson, *The Strange Case of Dr. Jekyll and Mr. Hyde,* 1886.

70. Frank Norris, *McTeague: A Story of San Francisco* (New York: Holt, Rinehart and Winston, 1962) p. 22.

71. Elaine Showalter, *Sexual Anarchy* (London: Virago, 1992) p. 106. See also Kelly Hurley, *The Gothic Body: Sexuality, Materialism and Degeneration at the fin-de-siecle* (Cambridge, MA: Cambridge University Press, 1996).

72. This and related issues will be explored in the next chapter.

73. A thesis that had much influence at this time was Max Nordeau's *Degeneration,* 1892–1893, translated in 1895; see Showalter pp. 1–6.

74. Stephen Crane, *Maggie: A Girl of the Streets* (Greenwich, CT: Fawcett, 1960).

75. According to Punter, his biography by L. Sprague de Camp, *Lovecraft: A Biography* (New York: Doubleday, 1975): "contains page after page of out-pourings against the dangers of racial pollution, focusing on Jews, Mexicans, blacks and every variety of European." David Punter, *The Literature of Terror* (New York and London: Longman, 1996) Vol 2., p. 40.

76. H. G. Lovecraft, "The Dunwich Horror," in *Great Tales of Terror and the Supernatural,* Herbert A. Wise and Phyllis Fraser, eds. (London: Hammond, 1972), p. 815.

77. Enthusiasts adopted Arkham for the name of a Press to publish Lovecraft's work and their own continuations of it after his death. Punter, *The Literature of Terror,* Vol. 2, p. 41.

78. William Faulkner, *Light in August,* 1932 (Harmondsworth, England: Penguin, 1965) p. 158.

79. Richard Wright, *Native Son,* 1940 (Harmondsworth, England: Penguin, 1984) p. 123.

80. Fredric Jameson, *The Political Unconscious* (London: Methuen, 1981) pp. 134–135.
81. Thomas Pynchon, *The Crying of Lot 49*, 1967 (London: Picador, 1982) p. 15.

Chapter Six

Key Questions

Is Gothic a Genre?

What makes a piece of writing Gothic? There are a set of simple features which define the *early* Gothic clearly enough: extreme situations, anxiety, darkness, threat, paranoia; exaggerated villains and innocent victims; subterfuge and plots; ancient houses, castles, monasteries, dungeons, crypts and passages, wild scenery, craggy mountains or winding mazelike tracts; stage machinery, hidden trapdoors, secret passageways; speaking portraits, ghosts, doubles, and other supernatural-seeming beings; monstrous and grotesque creatures; pain, terror, horror, and sadism. Some underlying early Gothic issues included the subversion of rightful inheritance, feudal cruelties and persecution, hidden genealogies, Protestant opposition to Catholicism, the oppression of women by the patriarchy, difficulties in perception and understanding due to misleading appearances —all within a pleasurable cycle for the reader of *loss* followed by *restitution*.

This early Gothic could be at once both an *attack* on superstition and ignorance from an Enlightenment point of view, and at the same time an *endorsement* of the values and beauty of the past and tradition; a celebration of reason and daylight but one invoking a poetics of emotion and the night-side. The popular form could also be a vehicle of class criticism, an opportunity for disguised pornography, a satire, or an expression of Protestant religious intensity. Some Gothics, like Lewis's *The Monk*, might be all of these at once. But from almost the beginning, books that might be seen as Gothic fulfill these criteria only to a greater or lesser extent, so that William

Godwin's *Caleb Williams, or Things as They Are* (1794) for example, while it is a novel about persecution and the abuse of class privilege, is without castle spectres, and reflects his arguments on the rights of man in *An Enquiry Concerning Political Justice* (1793). And from an early stage in Gothic development the possibilities of this form for expressing what became called the deeper psychology became evident, as writers like Mary Shelley in *Frankenstein* (1818) pursued complex motivations in characters divided against themselves and, following Godwin, used the Gothic form to explore philosophical and social issues. Other works exploited some features of the Gothic without belonging entirely to the genre: *Wuthering Heights* (1847) or *Jane Eyre* (1847) would be good examples of partly Gothic texts. At what point then can we identify a fiction as Gothic, and is it reasonable to describe a brief episode in this way?

Horace Walpole's *Otranto* (1764) founded the genre and perhaps in its bizarre posturings it holds a key to this question. The Gothic, from the beginning, is *staged*, knowing, aware of itself as a particular sort of treatment of literary events, scenes, atmospheres. As Jerrold Hogle points out, Walpole's spectres are "ghosts of what is *already artificial* . . . they are not just counterfeits but ghosts of counterfeits," and this "use of the emptied past in ghosts of counterfeits has consequently allowed the *neo*-Gothic to be filled with antiquated repositories into which modern quandaries can be projected and abjected simultaneously."[1]

The "staging" may be more or less overt, it may include references to other Gothic texts, conventional features such as oppression, mystery, the imaginary Past; or it may simply be produced in the mode of treatment, an atmosphere or mood, a way of presenting the setting, a cultivation of certain responses in the reader—fear, anxiety, the voyeurism of pain, dread, morbidity. The problem is like that encountered, for example, in defining *film noir*, itself a variant of the Gothic dependent on certain sorts of plot, lighting, camera perspective, and character types. There are fully developed Gothic fictions, just as there are films that qualify entirely as *noir*, such as Jacques Tourneur's *Out of the Past*. But there are also many fictions and films containing some Gothic or *noir* episodes, or just brief scenes and images using these techniques. Such taxonomies in any case are mostly for convenience and can lead to an empty kind of formalism. The essential point is that when artists work with reference to a genre or mode, it is possible to discuss their work productively by reference to other examples within that tradition, exploring how for instance in Gilman's "The Yellow Wallpaper" the Gothic is a more productive comparison than would be, say, regional realism or the sentimental novel.[2] Deviations from the mode may also produce significance: a fear defused and mocked as "Gothic" may still retain the charge of the disparaged similarity. In Jane Austen's satire of the Gothic, *Northanger Abbey* (1818), her heroine is of course foolish to read her situation in storybook Gothic terms, and her supposed secret document turns out to be an old laundry list, but at the deeper level she is *right* in her fear of patriarchal oppression. The Gothic often provides a voice for silent or repressed concerns and disenfranchised groups, its distanced parallels with reality offering implicit critiques of accepted institutions and behaviors. Frankenstein's monster speaks for many in his complaint of inhuman treatment from his master and his master's society; he speaks for women and even for contemporary black slaves in ways that the text does not need to make overt.[3]

There is, however, a risk of offering too-inclusive definitions, when *everything* can start to be seen as Gothic, as Maurice Lévy complains. "During the last two decades, the word has shown a prodigious capacity for adaptation and an uncommon appetite for conquering new semantic space. There is indeed such a thing as cultural imperialism" (and, for that matter he adds, "semantic vacuousness").[4] What, in the modern world, is *not* Gothic? Fred Botting notes (although oddly missing out crime fiction): "Science fiction, the adventure novel, modernist literature, romantic fiction and popular horror writing often resonate with Gothic motifs that have been transformed and displaced by different cultural anxieties."[5] That is true, although each of these forms has its own idiom, so that, for example in a Patricia Cornwell novel, the horrors of the morgue examination table are not quite handled in a Gothic way—although that might be done, perhaps by Patrick McGrath.[6]

Is the Gothic Uncanny?

The Gothic depends for many of its effects on the production of a sense of the uncanny. In Tzvetan Todorov's formulation the uncanny describes a writing in which the Marvellous shades into the Real. In his view, then, a story that seems fantastic but is explained realistically should be called uncanny.[7] That view does not altogether seem to fit the usual understanding of the term uncanny, which may indeed include an element of realism but is concerned more with something that is not quite seen, off to the side; what Rosemary Jackson calls the "paraxial"; a certain persistent *strangeness* in the reality described.[8] Sigmund Freud offered a very perceptive understanding of the uncanny in his famous essay "Das Unheimliche" (1919) in which he looked at the significance of the double, repetition, and animism in producing the effect. As suggested earlier, his psychoanalytical interpretation has been very influential and it is particularly useful in literary criticism, in part because it is itself based on literary texts as much as his own experiences.

Freud begins his investigation with the German term for the uncanny, *das Unheimlich. Heimlich* means belonging to the house, familiar, tame, intimate—but paradoxically it can also mean concealed, kept from sight, withheld from others. The addition of the prefix *un* to this already ambiguous term gives a word for the eerie and frightening, and Freud endorses Schelling's definition of the term: *"Unheimlich" is the name for everything that ought to have remained . . . secret and hidden but has come to light.*[9] Another of Freud's starting points is Jentsch's "Zur Psychologie des Unheimlichen" which argues that dolls and automata produce an uncanny effect through an uncertainty as to whether they are human or not. Like Jentsch, Freud illustrates this idea by reference to the doll Olympia in E. T. A. Hoffman's story "The Sandman." This story enables Freud to make some further arguments about the uncanny regarding the Sandman himself, a bogy-man who supposedly tears out children's eyes. According to Freud anxiety about eyes and the fear of being blinded is "often enough" a substitute for the dread of being castrated, and as soon as we replace the Sandman "by the dreaded father at whose hands castration is expected" the story becomes intelligible.

Among perceptive readers who have explored Freud's ideas in "Das Unheimliche" are Hélène Cixous and Samuel Weber.[10] Both draw attention to the difficulties in Freud's selective attention to the story and, in Cixous's words, to the question: "What lies on the other side of castration?" She replies, an infinite game of substitutions "through which what constitutes the elusive moment of fear returns and eclipses itself again. . . . Even here, isn't everything a repercussion, a discontinuous spreading of the echo, but of the echo as displacement, and not in some way as a referent to some transcendental meaning?"[11] This identifies a particularly significant aspect of the uncanny, its echoing, reverberating emptiness, in which the search for stable meaning is continually frustrated, and it is easy to see how this aspect of the uncanny may arise within the uncertainties so often cultivated in the Gothic.

Freud identifies some other major themes involved in the uncanny which are also often found in Gothic fiction: the *double*, the *repetition compulsion*, and the idea of the *omnipotence of thought*. The double has been theorized extensively in psychoanalytical and literary theory, beginning with Otto Rank's famous work of 1914, *The Double*.[12] Within the category of the double come reflections in mirrors, shadows, beliefs in the soul, and fear of one's own death; for the double can be seen as originally a sort of insurance against the death of the ego, stemming from what Freud calls primary narcissism. Once that stage has been surmounted, Freud argues, the double reverses its function and becomes instead "the uncanny harbinger of death." Poe's "William Wilson" would be an appropriate example of that kind of doubling, but there is of course another kind of doubling to be considered, the doubling of the Other, as in "Ligeia" or Madeleine and Usher in "The Fall of the House of Usher." This highlights a certain "blindness" within Freud's own reading of Hoffman, in which he fails to see the importance of the doll Olympia's being a woman, and misreads a crucial scene in which Nathaniel, looking through a telescope, sees and is terrified by, not the Sandman as Freud supposes, but the eyes of his lover, Clara. Hélène Cixous comments: "And what if the doll became a woman? What if she *were* alive? What if, in looking at her, we animated her?" Cixous's critique points to a useful area of investigation in the uncanny, the extent to which its production is culturally associated with the female as Other in a masculinist culture: marked as amenable and subdued; but containing the potentiality for subversion, deviance, and masquerade, behind an amiable surface. Many Gothic tales and ghost stories work through precisely Cixous's question, and in American Gothic, at least, the woman-as-Medusa often may be feared as much by other women as by men.[13] Another substitution also arises in the specifically American context: that of race. As in "Benito Cereno," the assumed subservience of the black slave may be perceived as concealing a diabolic malevolence. Children too, as in *The Turn of the Screw*, can seem to produce such a terror of *disguised* mendacity and evil.

In more recent Gothic fictions the uncanny figure of the doll is rejuvenated through technology, producing the fears expressed in cyber-Gothic texts. Neuromancer in William Gibson's novel of that name (1984) is an Artificial Intelligence who (or which) at the end of the story merges with another A.I., Wintermute, to form a new entity of unlimited power, whose godlike interests may not be at all consonant with human needs and desires. The *Terminator* movie series similarly revitalizes the doll or automaton as an uncanny figure, shape-shifting like earlier demon figures, and with disturbingly changing allegiances. But whether or not such figures produce an uncanny effect seems to depend upon their literary or cinematic treatment: for example, "Robocop" is not an uncanny figure in the same way as Rachel in the film *Blade Runner*.

The double offers a way of expressing divisions and fragmentation within the self, as in Hogg's *Confessions of a Justified Sinner*, Poe's "William Wilson," or Stevenson's *Dr. Jekyll and Mr. Hyde*. But such overt doublings also point toward a subtler form, in which doubling may only be implied, often through repetitions. An example would be the way that the Governess in *The Turn of the Screw* finds the ghost of her predecessor, Miss Jessell, writing a letter at her desk just like herself; or she rushes outside to confront the ghost of Peter Quint, and instinctively repeats his action of peering in through the window (at Mrs. Grose, in this repetition, who is equally startled and herself repeats the Governess's actions. "With this," says the Governess, "I had the full repetition of what had already occurred"). These doublings in actions in turn point toward the importance of *repetition*, which as Freud argues, can itself produce an uncanny effect. In this episode from James it is possible to see how the act of repetition can imply some underlying pattern of connection, as Quint, the Governess, and Mrs. Grose exchange places, suggesting some psychic affinity that does indeed prove to be one of the hidden meanings of the story. Freud argues for a "compulsion to repeat" in the unconscious mind, powerful enough to overrule the pleasure principle and "lending to certain impulses of mind their daemonic character." The compulsion to repeat, if unconscious, may lead to a sense of being driven by some other force, another self—a double—or it may produce an uncanny sense of inevitability, as when Freud describes how he kept ending up in the same "street of painted women" in a small town, or notices the persistent appearance of the number 62 (his age at the time). Minor changes within a pattern of repetition, a slight failing in repetition, may produce a particularly uncanny effect, as in James's "The Jolly Corner" (where a door is found shut that should have been open). This, like doubling, needs to be considered as one of the literary determinants of uncanny reception in the reader since such an effect can be achieved by almost imperceptible textual patterns of reflection and repetition. In later Gothic this sometimes becomes apparent in repeated patterns of metaphor rather than the textual "actuality."

Freud finds another component of the uncanny in the idea of the omnipotence of thought. The primitive or childish belief in the animism of all things and narcissistic over-evaluation of the power of thought processes, while superseded by adult or "civilized" consciousness, may still be a thought process that can be suggested by events that seem to follow one another as though planned or controlled. In textual terms, of course, as Freud noted, such an experience of control, fate, or destiny is already implicit in the manipulations of the writer:

> . . . the story-teller has a peculiarly directive power over us; by means of the moods he can put us into, he is able to guide the current of our emotions, to dam it up in one direction and make it flow in another, and he often obtains a great variety of effects from the same material ("Das Unheimliche" 251).

Henry James used the same metaphor about his own writing when discussing *The Turn of the Screw:*

> Nothing is so easy as improvisation, the running on and on of invention; it is sadly compromised, however, from the moment its stream breaks bounds and gets into flood. Then the waters may spread indeed, gathering houses and herds and crops and cities into their arms and wrenching off, for our amusement, the whole face of the land—only violating by the same stroke our sense of the course and the channel. . . . To improvise with extreme freedom and yet at the same time without the possibility of a ravage, without the hint of a flood; to keep the stream, in a word, on something like ideal terms with itself: that was here my definite business.[14]

Fiction is here seen as an unruly force-field, controlled by its magician author, who himself feels the risks of his unnatural powers, and if this is true of all fictions, it is doubtless more true in the realm of the Gothic, in which the proprieties of familiar and realistic streams and rivers need not be observed.

The psychoanalytical perspectives opened by Freud have proved very useful in understanding the Gothic, not so much through their applications to the lives of authors (an example is Marie Bonaparte's study of Edgar Allan Poe), as in the interpretation of particular works, and in the tropes of Gothic more generally. That may be in part because Freud himself drew on Gothic texts in reaching his conclusions, for in many respects the Gothic seems to have prefigured and shaped his ideas about the unconscious, the role of paternal figures, automatic behaviors, and so on.[15]

What of Post-Freudian Psychoanalysis?

Lacan and the Symbolic, the Real, and the Uncanny

Post-Freudian psychoanalytical theorists have provided further concepts that are illuminating for literary criticism in this genre. The most widely known of these is the French theorist Jacques Lacan, whose work, while difficult to understand, and remaining much contested, may yet prove to be as productive as Freud's. Two examples will show how his ideas might apply to the categories of the uncanny and horror.

Like Freud, Lacan argues for a tripartite division of mental experience, but rather than Freud's Id, Ego, and Superego, Lacan offers the three "orders" of the Imaginary, the Symbolic, and the Real, which are complexly interrelated. Of these three, the most stress falls on the Symbolic, because Lacan argues that it is language—understood in its largest sense as comprising all symbolic systems—that determines the human experience. The *pre*-Symbolic he calls the Imaginary, and what is *outside* the Symbolic—and thus unknowable in its terms, he calls the Real. The unconscious in this view is not simply "structured 'like a language,' for it has no existence outside language and no structure other than the one that language affords."[16] Lacan's famous "mirror stage" is a way of representing the subject's passage from the Imaginary into the Symbolic order through recognition of the self in its reflections by the other, which is a version of the fall into language and the cultural meanings that it entails. The *Imaginary*, as Malcolm Bowie describes Lacan's formulation,

> . . . is the order of mirror-images, identifications and reciprocities. It is the dimension of experience in which the individual seeks not simply to placate the Other but to dissolve his otherness by becoming his counterpart. By way of the Imaginary, the original identificatory procedures which brought the ego into being are repeated and reinforced by the individual in his relationship with the external world of people and things. The Imaginary is the scene of a desperate delusional attempt to be and to remain "what one is" by gathering to oneself ever more instances of sameness, resemblance and self-replication; it is the birthplace of the narcissistic "ideal ego" (Bowie 92).

The *Symbolic* order "is the realm of language, the unconscious and an otherness that remains other. . . . the symbolic is inveterately intersubjective and social" (Bowie 92–93). The third order, the *Real*, is what remains outside of these two, and "a permanent agent of disharmony between them. The gravitational pull exerted by the Real upon the Symbolic and the Imaginary is such that their relationship can never be other than skewed and unstable" (Bowie 94).

The Real "is that which lies outside the symbolic process, and it is to be found in the mental as well as the material world: a trauma, for example, is as intractable and unsymbolizable as objects in their materiality" (94). It is, in Lacan's words, "a noise in which everything can be heard, and ready to submerge in its outbursts what the 'reality principle' constructs within it under the name of the external world" (quoted in Bowie 95).

This may seem a long way from American Gothic, but the implications of Lacan's ideas are helpful in understanding the emergence of the uncanny and the irruption of horror in literature or film. Like Freud's, Lacan's language is *already* Gothic, perhaps suggesting the extent to which this kind of thinking inflects that of anyone seeking to bring to light the more complex elements of mind. Lacan speaks of the "phantasmatic activity" revealed by the analytic experience (Bowie 100); and of the "statue in which man projects himself, with the phantoms which dominate him, or with the automaton in which, in an ambiguous relation, the world of his own fabrication tends to find completion." As Malcolm Bowie notes of this choice of expression, Lacan speaks here in tones reminiscent of the Gothic tale, ". . . terms that Dr. Frankenstein would have found familiar. From spare parts, an armoured mechanical creature is being produced within the human subject, and developing unwholesome habits and destructive appetites of its own" (26). Even more spectacularly, Lacan offers us:

> Hieroglyphics of hysteria, blazons of phobias, labyrinths of *Zwangsneurose* [obsessional neurosis]—charms of impotence, enigmas of inhibition, oracles of anxiety—armorial bearings of character, seals of self-punishment, disguises of perversion—these are the hermetic element that our exegesis resolves. . . . (quoted in Bowie 60).

But how such Gothic language might be brought to bear on the genre that is evidently its rhetorical genesis is a further question.

One of the liveliest and most accessible commentators on Lacan's ideas as they might inform a view of the Gothic is Slavoj Žižek, who in *Looking Awry: An Introduction to Jacques Lacan through Popular Culture* (1991) explains some of Lacan's more recondite ideas and shows how they help us to rethink what is going on in popular fictions and plays (and especially in Hitchcock's films). The suggestion of misalignment between the Symbolic and the Real, for example, can produce a strong sense of the uncanny:

> In *Foreign Correspondent*, there is a short scene that exemplifies what might be called the elementary cell, the basic matrix of the Hitchcockian procedure. In pursuit of the kidnappers of a diplomat, the hero finds himself in an idyllic Dutch countryside with fields of tulips and windmills. All of a sudden he notices that one of the mills rotates against the direction of the wind. Here we have the effect of what Lacan calls the *point de capiton* (the quilting point[17]) in its purest: a perfectly natural and "familiar" situation is denatured, becomes "uncanny," loaded with horror and threatening possibilities, as soon as we add to it a small supplementary feature, a detail that "does not belong," that sticks out, is "out of place," does not make any sense within the frame of the idyllic scene. This "pure" signifier without signified stirs the germination of a supplementary, metaphorical meaning for all other elements: the same situations, the same events that, till then, have been perceived as perfectly ordinary acquire an air of strangeness. Suddenly we enter the realm of double meaning, everything seems to contain some hidden meaning that is to be interpreted by the Hitchcockian hero, "the man who knows too much." The horror is thus internalized, it reposes on the *gaze* of him "who knows too much" (Žižek 88).

The uncanny is here created at the point of intersection between the real and the world of the signified, in the supplementary feature that "sticks out," what we might call a "piece of the real."[18]

In American Gothic a good example of this intrusion of a piece of the real into the symbolic order could be the lightly sensed contradictions in "reality" perceived by the American Captain Delano in Melville's "Benito Cereno." Following the shaving scene and a sullen lunch with Cereno under Babo's watchful presence:

> Upon gaining the deck Captain Delano started at the unexpected figure of Atufal, monumentally fixed at the threshold, like one of the sculptured porters of black marble guarding the porches of Egyptian tombs.

> But this time the start was, perhaps, purely physical.
> Atufal's presence, singularly attesting docility even in sul-
> lenness, was contrasted with that of the hatchet-polishers,
> who in patience evinced their industry; while both specta-
> cles showed, that lax as Don Benito's authority might be,
> still, whenever he chose to exert it, no man so savage or
> colossal but must, more or less, bow (59).

Atufal is "out of place" and it takes all the cleverest efforts of
Delano's stupidity to close up the fissure that threatens to appear,
bringing with it thoughts of ancient mysteries and prohibitions, and
the occult—Egyptology provides a kind of shorthand at this time for
the indecipherable and magical[19]—only insecurely warded off by its
instant relegation as art (the "sculptured"), and servility ("porters").
"Guarding" is *exactly* what Atufal *is* doing, and "tombs" brings in a
suggestion of the ship's cabin, and the ship itself, as a sarcophagus—
which indeed it is—and forebodes Delano's own likely future. To
avert such catastrophic realization Delano ingeniously turns the
fearsome Ashanti axe-polishers into exemplars of useful industry,
and both these protruberances from the expected surface of things
into supporting instances of Cereno's indomitable authority. But the
reader is instructed in effect, by the careful insertions of pauses and
the use of "perhaps," to be less reassured.

What is the Place of Horror in the Gothic?

If the uncanny and terror, then, are produced by the *intimation* of
the Real, and the disturbance or distortion thus produced in the
ensuing reorientation of the Symbolic order, horror comparably, is
occasioned by the *incursion* of the Real. In this scene from Faulkner's novel *Sanctuary* (1931), Temple Drake is raped in a barn by a
vicious psychopath, Popeye, and we are shown not the rape—the
impotent Popeye using a corncob—but Temple's efforts to resist this
incursion of the Real by a frantic attempt to reassert her Symbolic
order, "I told you it was!"

> Moving, he made no sound at all; the released door yawned
> and clapped against the jamb, but it made no sound either;
> it was as though sound and silence had become inverted.
> She could hear silence in a thick rustling as he moved

towards her through it, thrusting it aside, and she began to say something is going to happen to me. She was saying it to the old man with yellow clots for eyes. "Something is happening to me!" she screamed at him, sitting in his chair in the sunlight, his hands crossed on the top of his stick. "I told you it was!" she screamed, voiding the words like hot silent bubbles into the bright silence about them until he turned his head and the two phlegm-clots above her where she lay tossing and thrashing on the rough sunny boards. "I told you! I told you all the time!"[20]

Temple had believed that Popeye was safely locked out of the barn, but he was *already inside*, a model of the way that the real is always already there but inaccessible; and she sees not *his* eyes, which have been described earlier as like "two knobs of soft black rubber" but the yellow eyes ("phlegm-clots") of the old blind man, a father-figure she hoped might protect her. This collapsing of two moments can be seen as an episode of *nachträglichkeit*, delayed psychic action, in which something *fully* happens only when something resembling it happens again. Temple is calling out not only to this blind surrogate father, but perhaps to her own father, in some earlier and not shown time. Confirming this, at the end of the novel Temple is seen in Paris with her father, "his hands crossed on the head of his stick" (253).

In Žižek's account of Hitchcock's film *The Birds*, he points out that the flocking, attacking birds "are not 'symbols,' they play a direct part in the story as something inexplicable, as something outside the rational chain of events, as a *lawless* impossible real. The diegetic action of the film is so influenced by the birds that their massive presence completely overshadows the domestic drama: the drama—literally—*loses its significance*" (105). This is exactly right: there *is* a symbolic chain in which the birds are related to the lovebirds bought by Melanie as a gift for Mitch and thereby related to his mother's pathetic over-dominance of her son and resistance to his new love, but that chain is completely overwhelmed by the incursion of the Real when the birds behave outside all such possible ascriptions of significance. That in my view produces the arrival of *horror*: as Žižek says, instead of supporting the plot of the domestic triangle, the birds "*block, mask*, by their massive presence, the film's 'signification'" (106). Similarly we know that Temple Drake's instinctive reliance on the old man father-figure, and behind that her own father, will not protect her from the "lawless impossible real" of Popeye's brutal rape. In these ways, then, Lacan's formulation of the orders of the Real and the Symbolic can be productive in unveiling the roots of both the uncanny and horror in Gothic fiction.

Many of Lacan's ideas will be found suggestive in working with Gothic texts: the *points de capiton*, quilting points or "attachment points between the signifier and the signified, which are necessary for a human being to be called normal, and which, when they break, produce the psychotic" (Lacan quoted in Bowie 74); the *objet à* (*autre*, or other, with a lower-case 'a'); the intimation of mortality inscribed in all speech, and also the object of desire (Bowie 165–166), which may be useful in looking at certain Gothic elements such as the textual nodes of meaning when the Real collides, as it were, with the Symbolic order that guarantees the subject's existence, as in "Benito Cereno" above; or the unassuageable desire, the Quest, search for meaning that underpins Gothic plots; or the presence in these fictions of particular "magical" objects as a form of fetishism. The difficulty in working with such concepts, however, is compounded by Lacan's having composed many of his complex descriptions provocatively, in a "spirit of carnival" as Bowie terms it—such as "woman does not exist," or "the sexual relation is impossible" and so on—and the way that some, like the *objet à*, develop more than one usage over time in the development of his theories. Here interpreters such as Slavoj Žižek and Malcolm Bowie are indispensable.

What is "The Phantom"?

Other post-Freudian analysts also suggest ideas of great interest to us in understanding the Gothic, in particular Nicolas Abraham and Maria Torok's work on family secrets and "the Phantom." Abraham and Torok held that traumatic events or secrets could be passed on without coming to conscious attention, being transmitted directly from the unconscious of the mother for example to that of the child, and that the "kernel" of such an unacknowledged trauma could act like a phantom in provoking symptomatic behaviors. The maternal unconscious, they argue, communicated without having been spoken, "resides as a silent presence within the newly formed unconscious of the child. As the child matures, it will add its own repressions—produced by its own lived experiences—to this central core."[21] Their scheme avoids some of the weaknesses of other psychoanalytical models: there is no preprogrammed sequence of drives and repressions as in Freud's formulation of oral, anal, and genital developmental stages, and no single and privileged drive and repression, such as is represented by the "phallus" in Lacan's formulation. But in their view, since every mother is herself the child of another mother there is a "genealogical inheritance" of the unconscious. "We are all the products of our infinitely regressive family histories" (Rashkin 35).

Abraham and Torok as practicing psychoanalysts inevitably focused most closely on family dynamics, but we might stress the potential openness of their model to including *cultural* determinants as well as strictly personal ones: the child absorbs a cultural inheritance incorporating certain secrets, absences or silences. The "Phantom" is Abraham and Torok's term for this unknowing awareness of another's secret, introducing, "via the concept of 'transgenerational haunting,' a novel perspective on the potential configurations of psychic history and on their role in pathogenic processes and symptom formation" (Rashkin 37). It will be noted that this process also describes very well the inscriptions of family trauma within the Gothic, in which an inherited secret very often determines the plot.[22] An American example would be Brown's *Wieland*, discussed earlier, in which Carwin's ventriloquism triggers Theodore Wieland's madness, itself no doubt handed on from his father and involving the father's mysterious death, and somehow connected with Wieland's incestuous feelings about his sister Clara, leading him to attempt to kill her after murdering his own wife and children. In fact Abraham uses exactly this analogy of *ventriloquism* in describing the operation of the phantom:

> The phantom is a formation of the unconscious that has never been conscious—for good reason. It passes . . . from the parent's unconscious into the child's. Clearly, the phantom has a function different from dynamic repression. The phantom's periodic and compulsive return lies beyond the scope of symptom-formation in the sense of a return of the repressed; it works like a ventriloquist, like a stranger within the subject's own mental topography.[23]

Hawthorne's *The House of the Seven Gables* is another novel that might be reconsidered in the light of Abraham and Torok's ideas. The family dynasty of the Pycheons is founded on an unadmitted, unconscious secret—the persecution of Thomas Maule by the original Colonel Pyncheon. The present Judge Pyncheon is described in terms of a house, carrying both the meanings of an actual house and the lineage of the House of Pyncheon, in which, in a hidden basement, there is a rotting corpse. " . . . [I]n some low and obscure nook—some narrow closet on the ground floor, shut, locked and bolted, and the key flung away . . . a corpse, half decayed, and still decaying, and diffusing its death scent all through the palace!" But visitors "smell only the rich odors which the master sedulously scatters. . . ."[24] In due course, the Judge himself becomes that festering corpse.[25]

The bizarre behavior of the present-day Pyncheons, the evil Judge, but also the eccentric, tic-ridden, and half-demented Clifford and Hepzibah, is occasioned by an ancient wrong, when Thomas Maule was falsely accused of witchcraft and thus killed, in order to obtain the land for the house. But if we follow the implications of the buried secret in the chamber more connections emerge, not only to the young man Holgrave, the descendant of Thomas Maule who seems (through his Mesmerism and photography) to share some of Maule's occult powers, but also to an "actual" secret chamber within the house, which is revealed at the end of the novel. Within this recess are hidden the missing land deeds that have been the spur behind the present-day evil. And these land deeds, supposedly representing a great fortune for the Pyncheons, are signed by Indian sagamores. They are now worthless in financial terms, being so long out of date, but that does not reduce their emblematic significance. The wrong in the House of Pyncheon is then in the first place a class wrong, the dispossession of a poor man for his land; but in the second place it is the larger wrong of the dispossession of the Native Americans. Here some extension of the Abraham and Torok theory seems invited: The phantom "holds the individual within a group dynamic constituted by a specific familial (and sometimes extrafamilial) topology that prevents the individual from living life as her or his own" (Rashkin 40, italics added). That phrase "and sometimes extrafamilial" suggests we might consider the unspeakable, or at any rate unspoken, secret or secrets in a larger cultural sense; everything that is denied within the culture, and yet remains the truth; as in Schelling's definition of the uncanny: "everything that ought to have remained . . . secret and hidden but has come to light."[26] One of the wrongs that "ought to have remained hidden" in the American culture was the scandal or atrocity of Native American dispossession; a theme that also engages Cooper in several novels, especially *The Pioneers* (1823), in which he, like Hawthorne, makes desperate recourse to the clichéd plot device of marriage between competing ancestral claims to allow a positive novelistic reconciliation.

Another of Hawthorne's Gothic novels provides material for an analysis of this kind, *The Marble Faun* (1860). In his novel about expatriate American artists in Italy, Hawthorne develops another plot based upon a family secret: Miriam has some strange connection with a sinister artists' model, a hooded figure encountered in the catacombs, and eventually under Miriam's wordless prompting her lover Donatello kills him. Hawthorne's narrator admits in his Postscript that he didn't himself know what the enigma of the book really meant, it was "clear as a London fog"; but we may be sure it has something to do with another and more famous family secret, that of Beatrice Cenci—whose story was made familiar by Percy Shelley in *The Cenci* (1819). Beatrice, along with her brother, was supposed to have killed their cruel and incestuous father; she was condemned to death; whereupon she became the subject of a famous portrait, and later pardoned. In Hawthorne's story Miriam is associated with Beatrice, and it seems, the Model with her brother, the mysterious partner in an unspeakable—although perhaps justifiable—crime. Miriam's family secret is also in a sense made a cultural secret, related to the endless crimes of Rome, that city Hawthorne's narrator envisions as built over an abyss or lake of blood; and also to culturally-founding prohibitions such as the taboos against incest and patricide, the institution and observance of which was seen by the Romantics as a founding act of civilization.

In this most fully Gothic of Hawthorne's novels portraits and sculptures come alive. Donatello exactly resembles, and even has the ears of a famous sculpture, the "Faun" of Praxitiles, Miriam is the inspiration for a sculpture of Cleopatra ("fierce, voluptuous, tender, wicked, terrible, and full of rapturous and poisonous enchantment" [IV 16]); her friend Hilda the model for a sculptural fragment, a marble hand; and in a scene late in the novel an ancient sculpture is excavated. The effect of replacing the head on the statue "was magical. It immediately lighted up and vivified the whole figure, endowing it with personality, soul, and intelligence" (IV 424). In these tropes Hawthorne reprises the Gothic figure of the speaking or prophetic portrait or statue; and perhaps nowhere more so than in the description of the picture of "Beatrice Cenci" by Guido Reni, much brooded over by Hilda, who faithfully copies it, and which is given deep emotional expression by the nineteenth-century Romantic aesthetic that Hawthorne espoused:

> The figure represented simply a human head; a very youthful, girlish, perfectly beautiful face, enveloped in white drapery, from beneath which strayed a lock or two of what seemed a rich, though hidden luxuriance of auburn hair. The eyes were large and brown, and met those of the spectator, but evidently with a strange, ineffectual effort to escape. There was a little redness about the eyelids, very slightly indicated, so that you would question whether or not the girl had been weeping. The whole face was quiet; there was no distortion or disturbance of any single feature; nor was it easy to see why the expression was not cheerful, or why a single touch of the artist's pencil should not brighten it into joyousness. But, in fact, it was the very saddest painting ever painted or conceived; it involved an unfathomable depth of sorrow, the sense of which came to the observer by a sort of intuition. It was sorrow that removed this beautiful girl out of the sphere of humanity, and set her in a far-off region, the remoteness of which— while her face is yet so close before us—makes us shiver as at a spectre (IV 64).

This surely is "the Phantom" itself, the ultimate family secret, operating disturbingly on the observer and distorting the book that attempts to organize itself around her. It represents both a personal and a more general, cultural, family secret; the secret of the Cencis, of Miriam and the Model, but also of Romantic aesthetics and philosophy, grounded as it was in extreme subjectivity and a consequent but suppressed valorization of the incestuous; in that the inward-looking, intuitive "deeper" self can only, in a way, most fully commune with itself.

Guido Reni's "Beatrice Cenci" portrait blinded Herman Melville too. In *Pierre* (1852) he also imagined a family secret and chose Beatrice metaphorically as its representative. Discovering that his idolized dead father had an illegitimate French daughter, Isabel, Pierre decides to marry her in order to give her recognition and protection. The narrator comments that the "latent germ" of this extraordinary choice, "—namely the nominal conversion of a sister into a wife—might have been found in the previous conversational conversion of a mother into a sister." And so the Cenci portrait by Guido Reni takes on profound significance in this novel too (while being seen quite differently than it is by Hawthorne):

> . . . that sweetest, most touching, but most awful of feminine heads—the Cenci of Guido. The wonderfulness of which head consists chiefly, perhaps, in a striking, suggested contrast, half-identical with and half-analogous to, that almost supernatural one—sometimes visible in the maidens of tropical nations—namely, soft and light blue eyes, with an extremely fair complexion, veiled by funereally jetty hair. But with blue eyes and fair complexion, the Cenci's hair is golden—physically, therefore, all is in strict, natural keeping; which, nevertheless, still the more intensifies the suggested fanciful anomaly of so sweetly and seraphically blonde a being, being double-hooded, as it were, by the black crape of the two most horrible crimes (of one of which she is the object, and of the other the agent) possible to civilized humanity—incest and parricide. [27]

If Beatrice is the new model for the Romantic Gothic heroine she is now a more equivocal innocent, the bearer of a family secret for which she is both "the object" and "the agent," in Melville's words, and her secret, which like Isabel in *Pierre*, she may not properly know herself, will have unpredictable effects in the worlds that she enters.

Abraham notes that the "phantom" will produce havoc, as is the case in both *The Marble Faun* and *Pierre*—an almost complete destruction of stability. "A surprising fact gradually emerges," he elaborates:

> . . . the phantom coincides in every respect with Freud's
> death instinct. First of all, it has no energy of its own; it
> cannot be "abreacted", merely designated. Second, it pur-
> sues in silence its work of disarray. Let us add that the phan-
> tom is sustained by secreted words, invisible gnomes whose
> aim is to wreak havoc, from within the unconscious, in
> the coherence of logical progression. Finally it gives rise to
> endless repetition and, more often than not, eludes ration-
> alization (291).

It is possible to argue that certain peculiarities and disjunctions even
in the textual surface can be seen as markers, symptoms, of such
strains. An example might be Donatello's absurd furry faun's ears in
The Marble Faun. Undoubtedly an aesthetic misstep of huge proportions for Hawthorne, such a strange and insistent textual anom-
aly perhaps points toward some underlying disturbance. Here a
signifying chain is suggested: the faun's ears refer back to the
Golden Age, when all were innocent and unconstrained, before the
civilization that has led to the terrible history Rome represents. In
the "Golden Age" (to which the novel often refers) all is permitted;
but to be civilized, to grow, as Hawthorne sees it here and elsewhere,[28] into full humanity, the self must submit to constraints—the
divisions and taboos of society and language. Of these foundational
taboos, incest and parricide are among the greatest and it is these
that are transgressed in the Cenci story, and thus by inference in
Miriam's family secret. Donatello's recognition of those taboos, and
acceptance of punishment for his own crime of murder (which was
implicitly in this case an attempted "correction" of incest and parricide), allows Donatello to grow to become more fully human; it is
the "fortunate fall" that is almost endorsed at the end of the novel.
Hawthorne's preoccupation with the incest motif has been often
noted—by Frederick Crews, for example, in *The Sins of the Fathers*
—and an incest scandal had in fact been a long kept secret within
his own family. Hawthorne did not discover until his adulthood
investigation of archives that two members of his family had been
convicted of incest and made to wear the letter "I" in public as punishment. The Scarlet Letter inevitably takes on some added implications in the light of this information, and the subterranean

presence of the theme in *The Marble Faun* seems to indicate ongoing disturbances from those "invisible gnomes" of the phantom.

As with Freud's "talking cure" and Lacan's understanding of the unconscious as language, Abraham and Torok's work depended upon both systematic and imaginative linguistic analysis, a sort of detective process, working like Poe's Dupin back up the chain of signification to its possible origins. This provides interesting ways to uncover the sort of hidden logics that may underlie Gothic treatments of repetitive themes. There is, for example, a hidden connection between the names of Chilling*worth* in *The Scarlet Letter* (1850) and Hol*grave* in *The House of the Seven Gables* (1851), although that connection does not properly emerge until retrospectively (in 1852), in the naming of Hol*lingsworth* in *The Blithedale Romance*. Chillingworth, Hester's estranged husband and the blight of her life, is a cold, but magnetic, resourceful alchemist and herbalist who exercises almost magical powers over the characters of *The Scarlet Letter*. Hollingsworth is similarly a cold, magnetic, resourceful, and dominating reformer (a nineteenth-century equivalent), who plans to bend the utopian experiment of the Blithedale colony to his own monomaniacal plans for prison reform. Holgrave, the middle link between these two, subterraneously connected to Chillingworth through the "Hol" of Hol-lingsworth, is the secret descendant of the original "wizard" Thomas Maule, and his son Matthew Maule. Matthew, according to Holgrave's story, exercised an evil magnetic power over Alice Pyncheon, whom he led to an early (hollow?) *grave* in revenge for the wrong done to his family. Holgrave is an enthusiastic reformer like Hollingsworth, and also possesses the mesmeric powers of his supposed wizard ancestors. At an important juncture of *The House of the Seven Gables* he repeats the occult entrancement of Alice in his effect on her descendant, Phoebe Pyncheon, but at the critical moment of repetition, Holgrave chooses to repudiate his uncanny power and releases Phoebe from the old Maule/Alice spell. The reformer in him triumphs over the atavistic wizardry, in much the way that his occupation as photographer rephrases Gothic notions of magicians as soul-stealers. The hollow (unquiet) grave that is perpetually threatening to erupt in his name is exorcised; in the terms of Abraham and Torok we might argue that the "crypt" is exhumed and the phantom placated by this gesture, which then permits a restitutive unification through marriage between the houses of Pyncheon and Maule.

The resolution of *The House of the Seven Gables*, in which the reformer cheerfully abandons his radicalism to accept with Phoebe the inheritance of houses and a shower of (undeniably corrupt) gold from the estate of Judge Pyncheon, seems unconvincing to many readers and, of course, this phantom that is dimly visible behind its creaking plot is *not* placated. Through the Chilling-worth, Holgrave, Hollings-worth semantic chain, "worth" carries the trace of "grave"—an association made manifest in *The Blithedale Romance* (1852), when the drowned Zenobia is fished from the lake, mutilated in the breast with a boathook during Hollingsworth's recovery of her stiff body. Her death has been a direct consequence of Hollingsworth's magnetic self-serving exploitativeness, disguised as idealism for prison reform. Somewhere between Hawthorne and his fictional texts the phantom of a buried secret seems to hover, as it continues to do in *The Marble Faun* and the last romances.

Hawthorne's staging of repetitions is undoubtedly in some respects a formal literary practice that organizes his books. The Scaffold scenes of *The Scarlet Letter* are paralleled in *Blithedale* by the scenes at Eliot's Pulpit, a rock in the forest associated with the famous "Apostle to the Indians," where Hollingsworth both wins Zenobia's love and then rejects her in favor of her (secret) sister Priscilla when he discovers *she* is not after all going to be wealthy, but her sister is. In these repetitive scenes, as in the Pyncheon-Maule repetitions of *The House of the Seven Gables*, it seems that Hawthorne is working toward some version of *nachträglichkeit*, or deferred action, in which the later recapitulation gives meaning to the former and, in a sense, allows it to fully "happen," or shows what it really meant. The repetitions produce a sense of what Chillingworth in *The Scarlet Letter* calls "dark necessity" ("Let the black flower blossom as it may," the hallmark of the Gothic as well as Calvinism); but the variations offer a sense of the possibility of a "working through," or traversing of the fantasy.

While Nicolas Abraham's ideas of the "Phantom," or Freud's repetition and *nachträglichkeit* can be productive in looking at

Hawthorne, they are quite as much so in relation to Edgar Allan Poe. Abraham's description: ". . . the phantom coincides in every respect with Freud's death instinct. . . . it pursues in silence its work of disarray. . . . the phantom is sustained by secreted words, invisible gnomes whose aim is to wreak havoc, from within the unconscious, in the coherence of logical progression. . . . it gives rise to endless repetition and, more often than not, eludes rationalization" (291) seems exactly applicable to Poe's tales and poems.

"Ligeia" stages an uncanny repetition in which the spirit of his dead wife Ligeia seems to the narrator to animate the dying body of his second wife, Rowena. Viewed as deferred action, the second moment repeats an earlier deathbed scene, the death of Ligeia, when she shrieked and leapt to her feet protesting, but then, "as if exhausted with emotion, she suffered her white arms to fall, and returned solemnly to her bed of death," still murmuring her favorite lines, supposedly from Glanvill *"—Man doth not yield himself to the angels, nor unto death utterly, save only through the weakness of his feeble will"* (87). In the second deathbed scene, the narrator "saw, or dreamed that I saw, fall within the goblet, as if from some invisible spring in the atmosphere of the room, three or four large drops of a brilliant and ruby colored fluid" (91). Because the scene is staged as traumatic repetition we as readers are forced to re-confront the much lamented death of Ligeia and the narrator's rather odd protestations, "that she loved me I should not have doubted" (85); or

> How poignant, then, must have been the grief with which, after some years, I beheld my well-grounded expectations take wings to themselves and fly away! Without Ligeia I was but as a child groping benighted. . . . I saw that she must die—and I struggled desperately in spirit with the grim Azrael. And the struggles of my passionate wife were, to my astonishment, even more energetic than my own. There had been much in her stern nature to impress me with the belief that, to her, death would have come without its terrors; but not so (85).

Reading the second deathbed scene in terms of *nachträglichkeit*, of course, would lead us to a different view of the first death.

"The Dead Mother"?

Leaving aside the tempting question of the narrator's possible murderous agency in "Ligeia," what is it that this double deathbed might
represent or repeat? Clearly enough, the death of the *mother*, without whom he is "but as a child groping benighted." Ligeia's "gigantic," "astounding" knowledge, her "infinite supremacy," has led him
to resign himself "with a child-like confidence, to her guidance" in
his but "little sought" and "less known" studies in metaphysics,
toward that "delicious vista by slow degrees expanding before me,
down whose long, gorgeous, and all untrodden path, I might at
length press onward to the goal of a wisdom too divinely precious
not to be forbidden" (85). The mother will not die, her "tumultuous
vultures of stern passion" (84) bring her back even from the dead.
But rather than dismiss this simply as an oedipality so extreme as to
be embarrassing (although it certainly is that), it might be usefully
aligned with Ambrose Bierce's "The Death of Halpin Frayser" (discussed in Chapter Five), and Alfred Hitchcock's *Psycho*, as embodying features of the "Dead Mother" syndrome described by André
Green.

"The dead mother" is the title of a paper Green wrote in 1983,
in which he developed "a paradigm of the child's response to a
traumatic disruption of maternal relatedness in infancy and early
childhood" and its "subsequent pathology."[29] The mother in question may be *emotionally* rather than physically dead (although, of
course, Poe's own mother did die in his infancy). Green's concept
refers to:

> an *imago* which has been constituted in the child's mind,
> following maternal depression, brutally transforming a liv-
> ing object, which was a source of vitality for the child, into
> a distant figure, toneless, practically inanimate, deeply im-
> pregnating the cathexis of certain patients . . . and weigh-
> ing on the destiny of their object libidinal and narcissistic
> future . . . [The] dead mother . . . is a mother who remains
> alive but who is, so to speak, psychically dead in the eyes of
> the young child in her care.[30]

Gregorio Kohon elucidates this notion of "blank anxiety" as among
a series of concepts created by Green on the effects of the "dead

mother" including "negative hallucination, blank psychosis, blank mourning," all of which are connected to "the problem of emptiness, or of the negative . . ." (Kohon 3). For Green this "blankness" is "the result of one of the components of primary repression: massive decathexis of the maternal primary object, which leaves traces in the unconscious in the form of 'psychic holes.'" The sudden loss of love causes a psychical catastrophe and is "followed by loss of meaning; for the child nothing makes sense any more" (3). One consequence may be an incapacity for love:

> The subject's trajectory evokes a hunt in quest of an introjectable object, without the possibility of renouncing it or losing it, and indeed, the possibility of accepting its introjection into the ego, which is cathected by the dead mother. In all, the subject's objects remain constantly at the limit of the ego, not wholly within, and not quite without. And with good reason, for the place is occupied, in its centre, by the dead mother.[31]

There is, then, no room for anyone else. But "behind the dead mother complex, behind the blank mourning for the mother, one catches a glimpse of the mad passion of which she is, and remains, the object, that renders mourning for her an impossible experience" (Kohon 4). How well such a formulation might describe Edgar Allan Poe, the man, is a question for his biographers; how well it describes his literary work, on the other hand, will interest students of the Gothic.

A test for the applicability of psychoanalytical structures in literature might be to ask whether they enhance understanding of the text or seek to impose on it, bending it to fit a preconceived formulation of psychic reality. Ordinary mothers are not much in evidence in the Gothic,[32] although there are numerous "bad" mother figures in the service of villains. In a strongly patriarchal culture it may be that the motherless child is peculiarly exposed, both emotionally and physically, in ways that more or less inevitably generate a Gothic affect. Poe's personal experience is in fact particularly suggestive in these respects: he was an orphan, adopted but later rejected by the wealthy John Allan (for gambling debts, and also very possibly, for an improper fixation on his stepmother), who married his very young cousin, thirteen-year-old Virginia Clemm, whose mother Mrs. Clemm was able to fill a mothering role for Edgar. But biography may easily lead to a false insistence that the work directly follows from the life, and so it is worth remembering that the Gothic itself played some formative part in the imaginative development of psychoanalysis, as we have seen in the case of Freud's "Das Unheimliche." There is a risk that we will not escape from the circle thus created, in which Gothic inspires certain psychoanalytical schemes, which we then reapply to the Gothic.

How Does Abjection Inform the Female Gothic?

Julia Kristeva's theorising of the abject in *Powers of Horror,* introduced in Chapter Five, also illuminates Poe's work in relation to women, and particularly this missing mother.

> . . . devotees of the abject, she as well as he, do not cease looking, within what flows from the other's "innermost being," for the desirable and terrifying, nourishing and murderous, fascinating and abject inside of the maternal body. For, in the misfire of identification with the mother as well as with the father, how else are they to be maintained in the Other? How, if not by incorporating a devouring mother, for want of having been able to introject her and joy in what manifests her. . . . Jouissance demands an abjection from which identity becomes absent (54).

Ligeia seems, exactly, the devouring mother, desirable and terrifying, nourishing and murderous. But it is worth speculating beyond Poe's psychic particulars, and toward some sense of the role of the woman, especially the mother, in ante-bellum American culture. The figure of the woman at this time is of one displaced, with few political or economic rights; and assumed to exercise such rights only indirectly (as in voting) through her husband. Women were expected to be reticent in order to be decent (Hawthorne, for example, forbade his wife from publishing her memoir of her youthful visit to Cuba), and yet at the same time women in this society were given very significant roles as custodians of morality and culture, and expected to be figures of sexual attraction as well as idols of domestic gentleness in the highly esteemed role of mother. The combination of respect and abjection inevitably gives rise to implications of masquerade (since masquerade was thus required in social terms), which in turn enhances the idea of the desirable yet terrifying female, the Romantic *belle dame sans merci*, the dark lady of romance; the blank mask of feminine grace behind which may lurk unspeakable motives.

Women authors, as much or even more than men, used this figure as a type in domestic Gothic. A fine British example is George Eliot's "The Lifted Veil," and an American instance is Louisa May Alcott's disturbing "Behind a Mask: or, A Woman's Power" (1866).[33] In this novella a seemingly elegant and talented young governess wins the affections of an aristocratic family by her graceful charm and skills. She sets two brothers against each other as rivals, before seducing and marrying the family patriarch and thus making herself proof against their unveiling of her machinations. The extraordinary insight and skill with which she plays on their good and bad qualities is seen as almost supernatural; she is indeed a witch, as they jokingly suggest. The reader is given inside knowledge of her reality:

> Still sitting on the floor she unbound and removed the long abundant braids from her head, wiped the pink from her face, took out several pearly teeth, and slipping off her dress appeared herself indeed, a haggard, worn, and moody woman of thirty at least. The metamorphosis was wonderful, but the disguise was more in the expression she assumed than in any art of costume or false adornment. Now she was alone, and her mobile features settled into their natural expression, weary, hard, bitter (142).

The story is a model of *masquerade*, in which the reader is invited halfway behind the curtain of this former actress's calculated machinations. The moment when she sets the two brothers against each other with a well-judged glance is an example of the subtlety with which Alcott measures her governess's coquettish skills:

> "I wish to remain, but—" She paused and looked up. Her eyes went from one face to the other, and she added, decidedly, "Yes, I must go, it is not wise to stay even when you are gone."

> Neither of the young men could have explained why that hurried glance affected them as it did, but each felt conscious of a willful impulse to oppose the other (154).

Alcott carefully balances the implied reader's sympathy, admiration, and disquiet, until the revelation of the Governess's letters to her dissolute accomplice show her as vicious and grasping. But the contrast between her hard life and the unearned indolence of the spoiled Coventry family lingers on after this unmasking.

In Eliot's "The Lifted Veil" Latimer finds himself the unfortunate possessor of the gift of insight into his wife's mind— and finds her a monster:

> . . . Bertha was entering with a candle in her hand—Bertha, my wife—with cruel eyes, with green jewels and green leaves on her white ball-dress; every hateful thought within her present to me . . . "Madman, idiot! Why don't you kill yourself then?" It was a moment of hell. I saw into her pitiless soul—saw its barren worldliness, its scorching hate—and felt it clothe me round like an air I was obliged to breathe.[34]

The ending of the story supplies objective proof of his intuitions on her deathbed, when his wife's servant tells of her murder plot.

Femininity as performance and masquerade, then, seems to be one of the issues raised by the opaque combination of abjection and hyper-valuation of the female in Victorian society on both sides of the Atlantic. At a more sophisticated level the same traumatic representation of the abject but scheming, relentless, and remorseless female appears in Madame Merle in Henry James's *Portrait of a Lady*, or Kate Croy in *The Wings of the Dove*. These are the avatars of the femmes fatales of thirties thrillers and the *films noir* of the forties. Even more ambivalent versions also reappear in twentieth-century Gothic, in, for example, Molly of William Gibson's *Neuromancer*, whose fingernails snick out razor-sharp knives with a discreet click. The other side of abjection, it appears, may be a "jouissance" that men—and sometimes other women too—find murderous.

Notes

1. Jerrold Hogle, *The Cambridge Companion to Gothic Fiction* (Cambridge, MA: Cambridge University Press, 2002) pp. 15, 16.

2. Which is not to say, of course, that seeing Gilman's story in those terms will not also produce worthwhile insights.

3. See Allan Lloyd-Smith, "This Thing of Darkness: Race in Mary Shelley's *Frankenstein,*" forthcoming in *Gothic Studies* (2004).

4. In *Gothick Origins and Innovations,* Allan Lloyd-Smith & Victor Sage, eds. (Amsterdam: Rodopi, 1994) pp. 9, 10.

5. Fred Botting, *Gothic* (London: Routledge, 1996) p. 13.

6. In his novel *Martha Peake* (2002), McGrath almost does this.

7. Tzvetan Todorov, *The Fantastic* (Ithaca, NY: Cornell University Press, 1975).

8. Rosemary Jackson, *Fantasy: The Literature of Subversion* (London: Methuen, 1981).

9. Sigmund Freud, "The Uncanny," 1919, in *Pelican Freud Library, 14,* James Strachey, trans. (Harmondsworth, England: Penguin) pp. 335–376.

10. Samuel Weber, "The Sideshow, or: Remarks on a Canny Moment," *Modern Language Notes* 88 (1973) pp. 1102–1133.

11. Hélène Cixous, "Fiction and Its Phantoms," *New Literary History* 7 (1975) pp. 525–548.

12. Otto Rank, *The Double: A Psychoanalytic Study* 1914 (Chapel Hill: University of North Carolina Press, 1921).

13. See Allan Lloyd-Smith, *Uncanny American Fiction* (London: Macmillan, 1989) Chapter Seven, "Women and the Uncanny."

14. Henry James, *The Art of the Novel,* pp. 171, 172.

15. See, for example, Jerrold Hogle, *Cambridge Companion to Gothic Fiction:* "In some way the Gothic is usually about some 'son' wanting to kill and striving to be the 'father' and thus feeling fearful and guilty about what he most desires, all of which applies as well to Gothic *heroines* who seek both to appease and to free themselves from the excesses of male and patriarchal dominance . . ." (4).

16. Malcolm Bowie, *Lacan* (London: Fontana, 1991) p. 71.

17. *Point de capiton:* the quilting point in upholstery, where the fabrics are held together, the point of connection between the two realms.

18. But what "sticks out" is of course still part of a signifying system, even though it suggests an alternative real.

19. See John T. Irwin, *American Hieroglyphics* (New Haven, CT: Yale University Press, 1980).

20. William Faulkner, *Sanctuary*, 1931 (Harmondsworth, England: Penguin, 1965) p. 82.

21. Esther Rashkin "Tools for a New Psychoanalytic Literary Criticism," *Diacritics* 18:4 (1988) pp. 31–52, p. 34.

22. Although, once again, the Gothic itself seems to have generated the terms of this way of thinking about neurosis.

23. Nicolas Abraham, "Notes on the Phantom: A Complement to Freud's Metapsychology," Nicholas Rand, trans., *Critical Enquiry* 13.2 (Winter 1987) pp. 287–292.

24. Nathaniel Hawthorne, *The House of the Seven Gables* (Columbus: Ohio University Press, Centenary edition, 1974) Vol. II, pp. 229–230.

25. See Ringe, p. 171.

26. Quoted by Freud in "The Uncanny" ("Das Unheimlich"), 1919, p. 225.

27. Herman Melville, *Pierre: or, The Ambiguities*, 1852 (New York: New American Library, 1964) p. 393. Hawthorne saw Beatrice's hair in the same portrait as "auburn," not blonde, and saw her as in white drapery, not the "black crepe" of Melville's metaphorically intensified rendition.

28. In, for example, "The Maypole of Merry Mount" and *The Scarlet Letter.*

29. Arnold H. Modell, "The dead mother syndrome and the reconstruction of trauma," in *The Dead Mother*, Gregorio Kohon, ed. (London: Routledge, 1999) p. 78.

30. André Green, "The dead mother," in Kohon, p. 2.

31. Green, in Kohon, p. 4.

32. Claire Kahan, "The Gothic Mirror," in *The (M)other Tongue: Essays in Feminist Psychoanalytical Interpretation*, Shirley Nelson Garner, Claire Kahan, and Madelon Sprengnether, eds. (Ithaca, NY: Cornell University Press, 1986).

33. In *American Gothic*, Charles Crow, ed., pp. 136–196.

34. (Penguin, 1996, 25).

Chapter Seven

American Gothic Criticism

Botting, Fred, *Gothic* (London and New York: Routledge, 1996). Botting provides a very accessible yet thorough introduction to the field of Gothic studies. His brief account of American Gothic focuses on Brown, Hawthorne, and Poe but there is reference to Southern Gothic and discussion of American films including *Angel Heart, Blue Velvet,* and *Twin Peaks.*

Byron, Glennis; Punter, David, eds., *Spectral Readings: Towards a Gothic Geography.* (New York and London: St. Martin's Macmillan, 1999). Among other essays, this collection includes Eric Savoy's "Spectres of Abjection: The Queer Subject of James's 'The Jolly Corner.'"

Chase, Richard, *The American Novel and its Tradition* (New York: Anchor Books, 1957). Chase argues that the American novel has been more characterized by romance than realism in setting, character, and plot. This view is in keeping with those of D. H. Lawrence and Leslie Fiedler, and was very influential in shaping the assumptions of American criticism in the fifties and sixties. Like Harry Levin's *The Power of Darkness* it is, however, open to the objection that in itself it is part of a particular process of canon formation that favored those qualities over others, as Jane Tompkins points out in *Sensational Designs,* and Russell Reising also indicates in his review of American criticism, *An Unusable Past.*

Davis, Rupert Con, and Schleifer, Ronald, eds., *Contemporary Literary Criticism* (New York and London: Longman, 1989). Useful in understanding many different areas of recent criticism, this collection of seminal essays also contains Jacques Lacan's seminar on "The Purloined Letter," and Barbara Johnson's response both to that and to Jacques Derrida's critique of Lacan's arguments.

Docherty, Brian, ed., *American Horror Fiction From Brockden Brown to Stephen King* (Basingstoke, England: Macmillan, 1990). Essays on Poe, Brown, Lovecraft, Faulkner, Bloch's *Psycho*, Patricia Highsmith and Shirley Jackson, Stephen King and S. M. Charnas. Interesting collection of work by British scholars in the field.

Fiedler, Leslie, *Love and Death in the American Novel,* 1960 (New York: Delta, 1966). Fiedler's comprehensive survey of the American novel argues for its essential Gothicism and is still the most lively and engaging opening up of the field. His observations on race and on male bonding and homosociality have had enormous influence and remain apposite. He further pursued some of these themes in his subsequent study of Native Americans in literature, *The Return of the Vanishing American* (New York: Stein and Day, 1969).

Freud, Sigmund, "Das Unheimliche," 1919, in *Standard Edition of the Complete Psychological Works*, edited and translated by James Strachey (London: The Hogarth Press, 1953). Also in the *Pelican Freud Library, 14* (Harmondsworth, England: Penguin, 1985). Freud's groundbreaking essay on the Uncanny remains essential reading for discussions of Gothic and has generated some extremely interesting commentaries, among them Hélène Cixous's "Fiction and its Phantoms," *New Literary History*, 7 (1975) pp. 525–548, and Samuel Weber's "The Sideshow, or: Remarks on a Canny Moment," *Modern Language Notes* 88 (1973) pp. 1102–1133.

Gilbert, Sandra M. and Susan Gubar, *The Madwoman in the Attic: The Woman Writer and the Nineteenth-Century Literary Imagination* (New Haven, CT and London: Yale University Press, 1984). This study helped to shape the new feminist criticism and contains useful material on, for example, Charlotte Perkins Gilman.

Gothic Studies, The (refereed) journal of Gothic Studies began in 1999. It is edited by William Hughes for the International Gothic Association http://www.wlu.ca/~wwwgac/

Hoeveler, Diane Long, *Gothic Feminism: The Professionalization of Gender from Charlotte Smith to the Brontës* (University Park: Pennsylvania State University Press, 1998). Between Smith and the Brontës Hoeveler gives two chapters to Ann Radcliffe, and has another on Austen and Mary Shelley. "Hoeveler's phrase 'Gothic feminism' might sound like an oxymoron, but she uses it to define the way that women writers created fictional worlds which in some way addressed the problem of their physical and social vulnerability" (Deborah Kennedy, *Romantic Circles* review).

Hogle, Jerrold, *The Cambridge Companion to Gothic Fiction* (Cambridge, MA: Cambridge University Press, 2002). A fine collection of essays on the Gothic, including an excellent brief commentary on themes in American Gothic by Eric Savoy.

Hurley, Kelly, *The Gothic Body: Sexuality, Materialism and Degeneration at the fin-de-siècle* (Cambridge, MA: Cambridge University Press, 1996).

International Gothic Association, http://www.wlu.ca/~wwwgac/ Scholarly association which runs biannual conferences; thus far held in Norwich, England; Stirling, Scotland; Strawberry Hill, England; Halifax, Nova Scotia; Vancouver, British Columbia; and Liverpool, England. Includes links to Gothic resources.

Irwin, John T., *American Hieroglyphics* (New Haven, CT: Yale University Press, 1980). Irwin offers fascinating insights into the craze for Egyptian hieroglyphics in the nineteenth century, and how this reads into American texts by writers such as Poe and Melville.

Jackson, Rosemary, *Fantasy: The Literature of Subversion* (London: Methuen, 1981). An excellent and very readable survey of texts and critical theory concerning the fantastic.

Kerr, Howard, John W. Crowley, and Charles Crow, eds., *The Haunted Dusk: American Supernatural Fiction, 1820–1920* (Athens: The University of Georgia Press, 1983). Contains fine essays by eminent Gothicists on Irving, Poe, Hawthorne and Melville, Spofford, Twain, James and Howells, London and Bierce.

Kristeva, Julia, *Powers of Horror: An Essay on Abjection,* translated by Leon S. Roudiez (New York: Columbia University Press, 1982). Although this is not directly concerned with American writing it opens profoundly important interpretative possibilities for study of the Gothic, and has become the foundation for many studies of the body, feminism, and abjection in fiction.

Lawrence, D. H., *Studies in Classic American Literature,* 1923 (New York: Viking, 1964). Much the most important early work in this area. Lawrence's eccentric readings of famous American writers like Poe, Melville, and Whitman set up an influential Gothic resonance. Lawrence comments, for example, that Walt Whitman, wrote "great, fat, rank graveyard poems of death"; the American soul is "hard, isolate, stoic; a killer," and so on.

Levin, Harry, *The Power of Blackness* (New York: Vintage, 1958). In company with Fiedler and Chase, and before them, Lawrence, Levin explores the thematics of light and dark, good and evil, and Manicheanism in the American novel. This readable and trenchant study set the agenda for early American Gothic criticism.

Literary Gothic, The, http://www.litGothic.com/LitGothic/general.html. Useful web pages on the Gothic generally, and reviews of relevant texts. Includes links to other internet resources.

Lloyd-Smith, Allan and Victor Sage, eds., *Gothick: Origins and Innovations* (Amsterdam: Editions Costerus-Rodopi, 1994). Contains articles on American Gothic including Benjamin Franklin Fisher IV on *Moby-Dick*, William Veeder and Allan Lloyd-Smith on Irving's "Rip Van Winkle," Charles Crow on Jack London's *Sea-Wolf,* and Francesca Orestano on John Neal. Essays from the first International Gothic Association Conference.

Lloyd-Smith, Allan, *Uncanny American Fiction* (London: Macmillan, 1989). The uncanny and the Gothic are closely inter-related. This study uses a range of theoretical approaches to discuss significant uncanny Gothic texts from Brown to Pynchon and Atwood.

Malchow, H. L., *Gothic Images of Race in Nineteenth-Century Britain* (Stanford, CA: Stanford University Press, 1996). Valuable account of racial inflexions in British culture, with some relevance to American nineteenth-century texts. Not always concerned with the Gothic itself.

Martin, Robert K. and Eric Savoy, eds., *American Gothic: New Interventions in a National Narrative* (Iowa City: University of Iowa Press, 1998). Includes, for example, Leslie Ginsberg's essay on racial issues implied in Poe's "The Black Cat."

Martin, Terence, *The Instructed Vision: Scottish Common Sense Philosophy and the Origins of American Fiction* (Bloomington: Indiana University Press, 1961). Much more relevant than its title might suggest: essential reading for an understanding of the intellectual environment of the early American Gothicists.

Mogen, David, Scott P. Sanders, and Joanne B. Karpinski, eds., *Frontier Gothic: Terror and Wonder at the Frontier in American Literature* (London and Toronto: Associated University Presses, 1993). Sometimes a rather quirky choice of topics but contains some important essays on this particularly American aspect of the Gothic.

Morrison, Toni, *Playing in the Dark: Whiteness and the Literary Imagination* (Cambridge, MA: Harvard University Press, 1992). A brief but important intervention by novelist Toni Morrison, who argues that blackness is ever present in the literature of historically racialist America: "Explicit or implicit, the Africanist presence informs in compelling and inescapable ways the texture of American literature" even, significantly, when that literature does not seem to refer to race, because it is implicit in the constructions of whiteness.

Mulvey-Roberts, Marie, ed., *The Handbook to Gothic Literature* (Basingstoke, England: Macmillan Press, 1998). Offering a good introduction to Gothic issues, with "engaging, surprising, and provocative entries" (Glennis Byron in *Romanticism on the Net*) explaining Female Gothic, American, English-Canadian, and Australian Gothic; individual writers; and "Gothic Specialisms" like the Döppelganger, Gothic Science Fiction, Illuminati Novels, The Grotesque, Lycanthropy, The Phantom, and many others.

Punter, David, *The Literature of Terror* (London: Longman 1980) and Volume 2, *The Modern Gothic* (London: Longman, 1996). On first appearance in 1980 *The Literature of Terror* (which became Volume 1 of this later edition) redrew the map of Gothic studies: "releasing the study of terror-fiction from the stranglehold of hobbyists into something more like the clear light of twentieth-century critical sanity" (Chris Baldick in *Romanticism on the Net*); and it remains the most persuasive wide-ranging exploration of the genre.

Punter, David, ed., *A Companion to the Gothic* (Oxford and Malden, MA: Blackwell, 2000). Essays on: Gothic Film, Contemporary Women's Vampire Fictions, Comic Gothic, American Gothic, "Stephen King's Queer Gothic"; the Counterfeit and Abjection; Magical Realism in Contemporary Gothic. The collection might better be called a Companion to Gothic Criticism, says Douglass H. Thompson in his *Romanticism on the Net* review. There is centrally a challenging article by Chris Baldick and Robert Mighall, which attacks recent criticism of Gothic on the grounds that it has "abandoned any credible historical grasp upon its object, which it has tended to reinvent in the image of its own projected intellectual goals of psychological 'depth' and political 'subversion.'" This new Gothic criticism "is condemned to repeat what it has failed to understand . . . .," reproducing in its own discourse the trope of "Gothicizing" the past, and casting the nineteenth-century bourgeoisie in the terms Radcliffe or Lewis reserved for the Spanish Inquisition, thus congratulating itself "upon its liberation from the dungeons of Victorian sexual repression or social hierarchy." Most contributors to the volume would be among those assailed here. In the splendid phrase of the editor, this is an ongoing, "exemplarily ruinous" debate.

Reynolds, David S., *Beneath the American Renaissance: The Subversive Imagination in the Age of Emerson and Whitman* (Cambridge, MA: Harvard University Press, 1989). Offers a fascinating and well documented understanding of the cultural practices underlying the dominant traditions of nineteenth century American writing, and especially useful for its accounts of the erotic imagination, the traditions of dark reform literature, women's rights agitation, and the sensational press. Frequently offering surprising new perspectives on the underworld of the polite imagination.

Ringe, Donald, *American Gothic: Imagination & Reason in Nineteenth-Century Fiction* (Lexington: University Press of Kentucky, 1982). The most thorough and thoroughly well informed account of American Gothic from its origins up to the end of the nineteenth century. Ringe's survey is particularly acute on the influence of European Gothic writers on American Gothicists.

Romanticism on the Net, http://www.ron.umontreal.ca/ Articles and reviews often of relevance to the Gothic.

Royle, Nicholas, *The Uncanny* (Manchester, England: Manchester University Press, 2003). Sometimes profound, sometimes eccentric, essays, musings, and fiction about the uncanny, not referring directly to American works but suggesting ideas that might be applied to American fictions.

Sage, Victor and Allan Lloyd-Smith, eds., *Modern Gothic: A Reader* (Manchester, England: Manchester University Press, 1996). "This new collection of essays . . . sets itself a truly Gothic task in tracing the survival of the Gothic in post-war culture, specifically in fiction and film. For the most part, the essays succeed, with the best opening up the Gothic mode to significant scrutiny far beyond the author or work under discussion. The best also explicitly retain their grounding in the earlier manifestations of the mode, resisting the current tendency to see the Gothic in every shadow, which renders the term meaningless. The collection opens with one of the best definitions of Gothic recently offered, first nodding to the venerable practice of offering a laundry list of conventions as a substitute for definition:

Evidently, the Gothic is not merely a literary convention or a set of motifs: it is a language, often an anti-historicising language, which provides writers with the critical means of transferring an idea of the otherness of the past into the present.

Though the essays move readily between literature and film, the focus is on the language of allusion, a rich language that confers the 'paradoxical ability to flaunt and camouflage itself,' through which the Gothic survives." (Quoted from a review by Rebecca E. Martin in *Romanticism on the Net*).

The collection includes Laura Mulvey on *Blue Velvet*, David Punter on Stephen King, Judie Newman on Postcolonial Gothic. Other essays concern Iain Banks and John Banville, Feminist Criticism, Postmodernism and the Gothic, Isak Dinesen, Horror Film, *The Body Snatchers*, John Ramsay Campbell, Toni Morrison's *Beloved*.

Savoy, Eric, "The Rise of American Gothic," in *Cambridge Companion to Gothic Fiction*, Jerrold Hogle, ed. (Cambridge, MA: Cambridge University Press, 2002) pp. 167–188. A very strong introductory essay focusing on Brown, Hawthorne, and Poe.

Sedgwick, Eve Kosofsky, *The Coherence of Gothic Conventions* (New York: Methuen, 1986). Important study redefining the importance of those elements often dismissed as merely surface features of the Gothic.

Senior, John, *The Way Down and Out: Occultism in Symbolist Literature* (Ithaca, NY: Cornell University Press, 1959). Not addressing the Gothic as such, but providing a wealth of information on the buried occultist or hermetic traditions within European culture.

Showalter, Elaine, *Sexual Anarchy* (London: Virago, 1992). Compares the 1890s with the 1990s in fascinating parallels. Useful, for example, in thinking about the likeness between reactions to AIDS and nineteenth-century fears of syphilis.

Smith, Andrew, Diane Mason, and William Hughes, eds., *Fictions of Unease: The Gothic from Otranto to The X-Files* (Bath, England: Sulis Press, 2002). This collection covers the ground from the early Gothic of Walpole to the diffuse Postmodern Gothicisms of the Black Lace series, contemporary feminist Gothic, and the suspicions of the American government in *The X-Files*. Along the way come a series of illuminating glimpses into wildly different academic terrain. These papers largely stem from the third International Gothic Association conference, held at Strawberry Hill, England, under the title *Legacies of Walpole*.

Sundquist, Eric, *To Wake the Nations: Race in the Making of American Literature* (Cambridge, MA and London: Harvard University Press, 1993). Essential reading for its detailed and subtle analyses of race in American writing, and especially strong in the extended reading of Melville's Gothic novella "Benito Cereno."

Thompson, G. R., *Poe's Fiction: Romantic Irony in the Gothic Tales* (Madison: University of Wisconsin Press, 1973). Provides an interpretative framework for Poe's ironic stance, grounded in the practices of early Romanticism.

Todorov, Tzvetan, *The Fantastic* (Ithaca, NY: Cornell University Press, 1975). An influential formalist and structuralist account of the fantastic founded on the notion of uncertainty or hesitation as a central requirement in deciding between the fantastic, the marvellous, and the uncanny.

Tomkins, Jane, *Sensational Designs: The Cultural Work of American Fiction 1790–1860* (New York: Oxford University Press, 1985). Tomkins provides acute readings of *Wieland* and *Uncle Tom's Cabin* in readdressing the canonical assumptions of American criticism, and shows the cultural importance of the popular sentimental novel in the period.

Wilczynski, Marek, *The Phantom and the Abyss: The Gothic Fiction in America and Aesthetics of the Sublime 1798–1856* (Frankfurt and New York: Peter Lang, 1999). A very intriguing use of Abraham and Torok's theory of "the phantom" in examining early American Gothicists.

Wolstenholme, Susan, *Gothic (Re)Visions: Writing Women as Readers* (New York: State University of New York Press, 1993). Some fine material on *Uncle Tom's Cabin* and significant arguments on the "staging" of scenes involving women in Gothic fictions.

Chapter Eight

Glossary

Alchemy   The precursor of chemistry, using unscientific methods including magic and sometimes ritual in the search for such ideals as the elixir of life which would bestow immortality, and the philosopher's stone, which would turn base metals into gold.

Cabbalism   (Cabalism) Jewish occult studies from the Cabbala; an oral tradition connected to a secret written tradition and influencing alchemists, Freemasons, and other occultists. The story of the Golem is the most famous version of the power of the rabbis and can be seen as related to Mary Shelley's *Frankenstein.*

Common Sense Philosophy   The dominant intellectual position in America during the late eighteenth and early nineteenth centuries, chiefly based on the work of the Scottish Common Sense philosophers who argued that Berkeleyan Idealism was misguided and that the material world could be experienced directly through the senses and the mind's reflection in a simple and direct way. They added that an innate moral sense prevented the danger of religious and moral skepticism as seen in the work of Hume. Poe's spirit of the perverse is a challenge to that assurance.

Döppelganger   The double or alter ego, an alternative self usually representing some duality within the self, as in Poe's "William Wilson" in which the double is a manifestation of Wilson's conscience. Other powerful examples are Stevenson's *Jekyll and Hyde,* or Wilde's *The Picture of Dorian Gray.* To a greater or lesser extent the motif is familiar in American Gothic in, for example, Henry James's "The Jolly Corner" where the double is quite explicitly a psychological projection of the protagonist's inner divisions.

The Enlightenment   A development of new ideas in the late eighteenth and early nineteenth centuries regarding the role of reason in all things, which led to free thinking in religion, feminism, and utopianism in political freedoms, a belief in the superiority of reason over emotion and the cultivation of proper sentiments. Much Gothic writing oscillates between this set of ideas and a countercurrent that became the Romantic movement, privileging intuition, feeling, and the supposed Higher Reason which offered deeper truth than mere calculation.

Faculty Psychology   The belief that the mind operated by means of "faculties" such as the reason, the emotions, and the will, and that human behavior could be systematically explained by reference to such faculties (and their malfunctioning). See also Phrenology.

The Fantastic   According to Tzvetan Todorov's influential definition, the fantastic in literature is a mode of "hesitation" in which uncertainty is maintained in the reader as to whether the events are marvellous and possibly supernatural, or have some natural and realistic explanation, in which case they may be seen as uncanny.

Golem   The Golem is a mighty creature in human form made of clay, conjured up in Jewish lore by the occultist tradition known to the rabbis and associated with alchemical ideas. A Golem was supposed to have been created to protect the Jews of Prague from a Christian pogrom.

The Grotesque   Elements of incongruity and disproportion, deriving from the discovery of monstrous figures in Roman dwellings or grottoes. This frequently appears in the Gothic, especially in descriptions of people with freakish features or behaviors. Frankenstein's monster is a grotesque figure, but so also is Stephen Crane's burn victim in "The Monster." There is a close connection to be made here with horror, the encountering of disturbing and ugly material or experiences that cannot be seen as sublime.

The Illuminati   A secret society founded in Ingolstadt in 1776 with the aim of reforming society (and religion) along rational lines. The society is related to the Freemasons, and, like the **Rosicrucians**, inspires fear of its potential for subversion, as we see in Brown's novel *Ormond*. A similar society appears in the memoirs of *Carwin the Biloquist*, appended to *Wieland*.

Necromancy   Attaining power and knowledge by raising the spirits of the dead. An element of this can be seen in, for example, Poe's "Ligeia."

The Phantom   A metaphor used by recent French psychoanalysts Nicolas Abraham and Maria Torok to suggest the disturbing effects of an untold family event upon those who do not know it but experience its presence as an encrypted (another metaphor) secret. Another name for their set of arguments is thus "**cryptonomy.**"

Phrenology   A popular pseudo-science based on the idea that the shape of the head indicates the strength or weakness of the various faculties of mind, in which models of the head are marked to show the different areas of mental ability and character.

The Picturesque   In some respects a companion to the sublime: an appreciation of humanized landscapes or architecture with a humble or comforting charm. A pleasant prospect with a ruined cottage or mill to bring out its human scale while suggesting a desirable pastness, rustic folk engaging in their innocent pursuits and melodies, and nature in its benign and unthreatening modes are often found as a counterpoint to the terror and horror of Gothic events or expectations.

Puritanism   A set of fundamentalist Christian beliefs based on the teachings of John Calvin in particular, requiring scrupulous conduct and self scrutiny in the effort to be saved, in an awareness that life is predestined and that all are sinners (due to original sin), and that grace and salvation depend upon the will not of man but of God. Thus even the "elected" or supposed saints on earth, cannot be sure of their salvation.

Romanticism   Not to be confused with romance. The Romantic movement privileged intuition, feeling, and the Higher Reason which offered deeper truth than conventional thought. These ideas derived ultimately from Kant's philosophy, which argues for the necessary preexistence of such categories as time and space, and thus could be popularized as offering the possibility of reaching profound intuitions through opening the mind to its inner knowledge. Some influence was evident in America at the beginning of the nineteenth century, but it is most noticeable in the work of Emerson and his fellow **Transcendentalists** (so called after Kant's transcendent reason).

Spirit Rapping   Manifestations of the spirits of departed relatives and loved ones, called up in seances in the vogue of spiritualism in the nineteenth century. The Fox sisters were instrumental in popularizing this practice when the spirits they claimed to contact made their presence known by mysterious rappings on the table.

The Sublime   An important element in the origins of both Gothic and Romantic literature. Edmund Burke's *Philosophical Inquiry into the Origin of our Ideas of the Sublime and Beautiful* (1756) helped to redirect attention to the aesthetic power of the "Sublime," showing how even the emotion of terror might be pleasurable in the right context. What had been seen previously as barbaric, monstrous, or terrifying could alternatively be experienced as sublimely affecting through its production of powerful emotional reactions in the observer. The aesthetic of the Gothic is clearly related to this new respect for the overpowering, the primitive, and the fear-inducing, just as the Gothic fashion in architecture depended upon admiration for the complex vistas and visual mystifications of ancient buildings and churches in particular. Settings, buildings, and landscapes in the Gothic are often properly described as sublime, with endless passages or rugged crags threatening the belittled observer.

The Uncanny   An effect incapable of precise definition, but well explored by Sigmund Freud in his essay "Das Unheimliche" in which he noted that the effect could be produced by a sense of the strange in the familiar; by what should have been hidden but nevertheless comes to light, as in "the return of the repressed"; and by atavistic feelings about death, against which the double was once a defence; coincidence; repetitions, and so on.

Urban Gothic   A form in which the windings of the labyrinthine city substitute for the castle dungeons or monastery crypts of earlier Gothic, as in Poe's detective stories and "The Man of the Crowd," or George Lippard's *The Quaker City*. This has become a dominant form of Gothic in recent work, through *noir* thrillers to *Blade Runner*, and is frequently the origin of a subtle Gothicism in otherwise more realistic fiction. Another American variant is the use of a wild landscape in which characters are lost and subject to strange delusions, as in Hawthorne's "Young Goodman Brown" or Ambrose Bierce's "The Death of Halpin Frayser."

Chapter Nine

Suggestions for Further Reading

A critical reading list and list of further reading in the field including other works by main proponents of American Gothic, and works which are related to American Gothic, but do not fall strictly within the definitions of the term.

Some American Gothic and Related Texts

Allston, Washington, *Lectures on Art, and Monaldi,* 1850, R. H. Dana, ed., (Gainsville, FL: Scholars Facsimiles and Reprints, 1967).

Bierce, Ambrose, *Can Such Things Be?* 1893 (London: Jonathan Cape, 1926).

Brown, Charles Brockden, *Arthur Mervyn, Charles Brockden Brown's Novels,* 1887 (McKay; facsimile reprint, New York: Kennikat Press, 1963) Vol. II.

———, *Edgar Huntly; or, Memoirs of a Sleepwalker,* 1799 (Kent, OH: Kent State University Press, Bicentennial Edition, 1984).

———, *Jane Talbot, Charles Brockden Brown's Novels,* 1801 (McKay; facsimile reprint, New York: Kennikat Press, 1963) Vol. V.

———, *Ormond, Charles Brockden Brown's Novels,* 1799 (McKay; facsimile reprint, New York: Kennikat Press, 1963) Vol. VI.

———, *Wieland, or, The Transformation,* 1798 (New York: Harcourt Brace and World, undated facsimile of 1926 edition).

Conrad, Joseph, *Heart of Darkness,* 1902 (London: Dent, 1946).

Crane, Stephen, *Maggie: A Girl of the Streets*, 1893 (Greenwich, CT: Fawcett, 1960).

Edel, Leon, ed., *The Ghostly Tales of Henry James* (New Brunswick, NJ: Rutgers University Press, 1948).

Emerson, Ralph Waldo, *Selections from Ralph Waldo Emerson*, Stephen Whicher, ed. (Boston: Houghton Mifflin Co., 1960).

Faulkner, William, *Light in August*, 1932 (Harmondsworth, England: Penguin 1965).

———, *Sanctuary*, 1931 (Harmondsworth, England: Penguin, 1965).

Gilman, Charlotte Perkins, "The Yellow Wallpaper," 1892, manuscript version, in *Nineteenth-Century American Women Writers, An Anthology*, Karen L. Kilcup, ed. (Oxford and Cambridge, MA: Blackwell, 1997) pp. 486–495.

———, *The Living of Charlotte Perkins Gilman, An Autobiography* (New York: Appleton-Century, 1935).

Hawthorne, Nathaniel, *The House of the Seven Gables*, 1851 (Columbus: Ohio University Press, centenary edition, 1974).

———, *The Scarlet Letter*, 1850 (New York: Norton, 1961).

———, *Young Goodman Brown and Other Tales* (Oxford: Oxford University Press, 1987).

———, *The Marble Faun*, 1860 (Columbus: Ohio University Press, 1974).

James, Henry, *A Small Boy and Others*, (London: Macmillan, 1913).

———, *Selected Tales* (London: Dent 1982).

———, *The Art of the Novel: Critical Prefaces*, R. P. Blackmur, ed. (New York: Scribner's Sons, 1962).

———, *The Golden Bowl*, 1904 (Harmondsworth, England: Penguin Books, 1985).

———, *The Portrait of A Lady*, 1881 (New York: New American Library, 1963).

————, *The Wings of the Dove*, 1902 (Harmondsworth, England: Penguin Books, 1976).

————, *The Turn of the Screw*, 1898, Norton Critical Edition (New York and London: Norton & Company, 1999).

Lovecraft, Herbert P. "The Dunwich Horror" in *Great Tales of Terror and the Supernatural*, Herbert A. Wise and Phyllis Fraser eds. (London: Hammond, 1972).

McGrath, Patrick, *Martha Peake* (2002).

Melville, Herman, *Pierre; or, The Ambiguities*, 1852 (New York: New American Library, 1964).

————, *Selected Tales and Poems* (New York: Holt, Rinehart and Winston, 1950).

Norris, Frank, *McTeague: A Story of San Francisco*, 1899 (New York: Holt, Rinehart and Winston, 1962).

Poe, Edgar Allan, *Arthur Gordon Pym*, 1838 (Harmondsworth, England: Penguin Books, 1975).

————, *Selected Writings of Edgar Allan Poe*, Edward H. Davidson, ed. (Boston: Houghton Mifflin Company, 1956).

Pynchon, Thomas, *The Crying of Lot 49*, 1967 (London: Picador, 1982).

Stevenson, R. L., *The Strange Case of Dr. Jekyll and Mr. Hyde*, 1886 (New York: Norton and Co., 2002).

Stoker, Bram, *Dracula*, 1897 (New York: Airmont Publishing Co., 1965).

Stowe, Harriet Beecher, *Uncle Tom's Cabin*, 1852 (New York: Norton, 1994).

Wharton, Edith, *The Ghost Stories of Edith Wharton* (London: Constable, 1975).

Wright, Richard, *Native Son*, 1940 (Harmondsworth, England: Penguin, 1984).

Relevant Critical Readings

Abraham, Nicolas, "Notes on the Phantom: A Complement to Freud's Metapsychology," Nicholas Rand, trans., *Critical Enquiry* 13.2 (Winter 1987) pp. 287–292.

Allen, Michael, *Poe and the British Magazine Tradition* (New York: Oxford University Press, 1969).

Armitt, Lucie, *Theorising the Fantastic* (London: Arnold, 1996).

Auerbach, Nina, *Our Vampires, Ourselves* (Chicago: University of Chicago Press, 1995).

Austin, Elliot and Lawrence Austin, *Ghosts of the Gothic* (Princeton, NJ: Princeton University Press, 1980).

Badley, Linda, *Writing Horror and the Body: The Fiction of Stephen King, Clive Barker, and Anne Rice* (Westport, CT: Greenwood Publishing Co.,1996).

Baldick, Chris, *In Frankenstein's Shadow: Myth, Monstrosity, and Nineteenth-Century Writing* (Oxford: Clarenden Press, 1987).

Becker, Suzanne, *Gothic Forms of Feminine Fictions* (Manchester, England: Manchester University Press, 1996).

Bayer-Berenbaum, Linda, *The Gothic Imagination: Expansion in Gothic Literature and Art* (Rutherford, NJ: Fairleigh Dickinson University Press, 1982).

Birkhead, Edith, *The Tale of Terror: A Study of the Gothic Romance* (London: Constable, 1921).

Bloom, Clive, ed., *Gothic Horror: A Reader's Guide from Poe to King and Beyond* (New York: St. Martin's, 1998).

Botting, Fred, *Gothic* (London and New York: Routledge, 1996).

———, *Making Monstrous: 'Frankenstein', Criticism, Theory* (Manchester, England: Manchester University Press, 1991).

Botting, Fred, ed., *The Gothic* (Cambridge, MA: Cambridge University Press, 2001).

Bronfen, Elizabeth, *Over Her Dead Body: Death, Femininity and the Aesthetic* (Manchester, England: Manchester University Press, 1992).

Brooks, Peter, *The Melodramatic Imagination: Balzac, James, Melodrama and the Mode of Excess* (New York: Columbia University Press, 1985).

Bruhm, Stephen, *Gothic Bodies: The Politics of Pain in Romantic Fiction* (Philadelphia: University of Pennsylvania Press, 1994).

Butler, Judith, *Bodies That Matter: On the Discursive Limits of "Sex"* (New York: Routledge, 1993).

Byron, Glennis and David Punter, eds., *Spectral Readings: Towards a Gothic Geography* (New York and London: St. Martin's and Macmillan, 1999).

Carpenter, Lynette and Wendy K. Kolmar, eds., *Haunting the House of Fiction: Feminist Perspectives on Ghost Stories by American Women* (Knoxville: University of Tennessee Press, 1991).

Carroll, Peter N., *Puritanism and the Wilderness* (New York and London: Columbia University Press, 1969).

Cassuto, Leonard, *The Inhuman Race: The Racial Grotesque in American Literature and Culture* (New York: Columbia University Press, 1997).

Castle, Terry, *The Female Thermometer: Eighteenth-Century Culture and the Invention of the Uncanny* (Oxford: Oxford University Press, 1995).

Castricano, Jodey, *Cryptomimesis: The Gothic and Jacques Derrida's Ghost Writing* (Montreal: McGill-Queen's University Press, 2001).

Cavaliero, Glen, *The Supernatural and English Fiction* (Oxford: Oxford University Press, 1995).

Chase, Richard, *The American Novel and its Tradition* (New York: Anchor Books, 1957).

Christophersen, Bill, *The Apparition in the Glass: Charles Brockden Brown's American Gothic* (Athens: University of Georgia Press, 1993).

Cixous, Hélène, "Fiction and Its Phantoms," *New Literary History*, 7 (1975) pp. 525–548.

Clemens, Valdine, *The Return of the Repressed: Gothic Horror from the Castle of Otranto to Alien* (Albany: State University of New York Press, 1999).

Clery, E. J., *The Rise of Supernatural Fiction, 1762–1800* (Cambridge, MA: Cambridge University Press, 1995).

Cohen, Jeffrey Jerome, ed., *Monster Theory* (Minneapolis, MN: University of Minnesota Press, 1996). (Includes "Vampire Culture" on Anne Rice, by Frank Grady.)

Cornwell, Neil, *The Literary Fantastic: From Gothic to Postmodern* (London: Harvester Wheatsheaf, 1990).

Cornwell, Neil and Maggie Malone, eds., *The Turn of the Screw and What Maisie Knew: Henry James, Contemporary Critical Essays* (New York: Palgrave Macmillan, 1998).

Crow, Charles L., ed., *American Gothic: An Anthology 1787–1916* (Oxford: Blackwell, 1999).

Davis, Rupert Con and Ronald Schleifer, eds., *Contemporary Literary Criticism* (New York and London: Longman, 1989). Contains Lacan's famous essay on "The Purloined Letter," and Barbara Johnson's response.

Day, William Patrick, *In the Circles of Fear and Desire: A Study of Gothic Fantasy* (Chicago and London: University of Chicago Press, 1985).

Delamotte, Eugenia, *Perils of the Night: A Feminist Study of Nineteenth-Century Gothic* (New York: Oxford University Press, 1989).

Docherty, Brian, ed., *American Horror Fiction: From Brockden Brown to Stephen King* (New York: St. Martin's Press, 1990).

Donaldson, Susan V., "Making a Spectacle: Welty, Faulkner, and Southern Gothic," *Mississippi Quarterly: The Journal of Southern*

Culture (Mississippi State University) 50:4 (Fall 1997) pp. 567–583.

Edmundson, Mark, *Nightmare on Main Street: Angels, Sadomasochism, and the Culture of Gothic* (Cambridge, MA: Harvard University Press, 1997).

Edwards, Justin D., *Gothic Passages: Racial Ambiguity and the American Gothic* (Iowa City: University of Iowa Press 2003).

Ellis, Kate Ferguson, *The Contested Castle: Gothic Novels and the Subversion of Domestic Ideology* (Chicago: University of Illinois Press, 1989).

Felman, Shoshana, ed., *Literature and Psychoanalysis: The Question of Reading, Otherwise* (Baltimore and London: Johns Hopkins University Press, 1982).

Fiedler, Leslie, *Love and Death in the American Novel,* 1960 (New York: Delta, 1966).

———, *The Return of the Vanishing American* (New York: Stein and Day, 1969).

Fisher, Benjamin Franklin, IV, *The Gothic's Gothic: Study Aids to the Tradition of the Tale of Terror* (London: Garland, 1988).

———, "Gothic Possibilities in *Moby-Dick,*" *Gothick Origins and Innovations,* Allan Lloyd-Smith and Victor Sage, eds. (Amsterdam: Rodopi, 1994).

Fleenor, Juliann E., ed., *Female Gothic* (Montreal: Eden Press, 1983).

Frank, Frederick S., *The First Gothics: A Critical Guide to the English Gothic Novel* (London: Garland, 1987).

———, *Gothic Fiction: A Master List of Twentieth-Century Criticism and Research* (London: Meckler, 1988).

Freud, Sigmund, "Das Unheimliche," 1919, *Standard Edition of the Complete Psychological Works,* James Strachey, ed. and trans. (London: The Hogarth Press, 1953). Also available in the *Pelican Freud Library* 14 (Harmondsworth, England: Penguin, 1985).

Gamer, Michael, *Romanticism and the Gothic: Genre, Reception and Canon Formation* (Cambridge, MA: Cambridge University Press, 2000).

Gardner, Jared, *Master Plots: Race and the Founding of an American Literature* (Baltimore: Johns Hopkins University Press, 1998).

Geary, Robert F., *The Supernatural in Gothic Fiction: Horror, Belief, and Literary Change* (Lewiston, NY: The Edwin Mellon Press, 1992).

Gelder, Ken, *Reading the Vampire* (London: Routledge, 1994).

Gilbert, Sandra M. and Susan Gubar, *The Madwoman in the Attic: The Woman Writer and the Nineteenth-Century Literary Imagination* (New Haven, CT and London: Yale University Press, 1984).

Ginsberg, Leslie, "Slavery and the Gothic Horror of Poe's 'The Black Cat,'" in *American Gothic: New Interventions in a National Narrative*, Robert Martin and Eric Savoy, eds. (Iowa City: University of Iowa Press, 1998).

Goddu, Teresa A., *Gothic America: Narrative, History and Nation* (New York: Columbia University Press, 1997).

Graham, Kenneth W., *Gothic Fictions: Prohibition/Transgression* (New York: AMS Press, 1989).

Green, André, "The dead mother," in *The Dead Mother*, Gregorio Kohon, ed. (London: Routledge, 1999).

Grixti, Joseph, *Terrors of Uncertainty: The Cultural Contexts of Horror Fiction* (London: Routledge, 1989).

Gross, Louis R., *Redefining the American Gothic: From Wieland to Day of the Dead* (Ann Arbor, MI and London: U.M.I. Research Press, 1989).

Haggerty, George F., *Gothic Fiction/Gothic Form* (London: University of Pennsylvania Press, 1989).

Halttunen, Karen, "Gothic Imagination and Social Reform: The Haunted House of Lyman Beecher, Henry Ward Beecher, and Harriet Beecher," in *New Essays on Uncle Tom's Cabin*, Eric J.

Sundquist, ed. (Cambridge, MA: Cambridge University Press, 1986).

Halttunen, Karen, *Murder Most Foul: The Killer and the American Gothic Imagination* (Cambridge, MA: Harvard University Press, 1998).

Heller, Terry, *The Delights of Terror: An Aesthetics of the Tale of Terror* (Urbana: University of Illinois Press, 1987).

Hemenway, Robert, "Gothic Sociology: Charles Chesnutt and the Gothic Mode" *Studies in the Literary Imagination* 7:1 (1974) pp. 101–119.

Hoeveler, Diane Long, *Gothic Feminism: The Professionalization of Gender from Charlotte Smith to the Brontës* (State College: Pennsylvania State University Press, 1998).

Hogle, Jerrold, *The Cambridge Companion to Gothic Fiction* (Cambridge, MA: Cambridge University Press, 2002).

Hoppenstand, Gary and Ray B. Browne, eds., *The Gothic World of Anne Rice* (Bowling Green, OH: Popular, 1996).

Howard, Jacqueline, *Reading Gothic Fiction: A Bakhtinian Approach* (Oxford: Clarendon Press, 1994).

Howells, Coral Ann, *Love, Mystery and Misery: Feeling in Gothic Fiction* (London: Athlone Press, 1978).

Hughes, William, *Bram Stoker, A Bibliography* (Brisbane: University of Queensland, 1997).

Hume, Robert D., "Gothic Versus Romantic: A Reevaluation of the Gothic Form." *PMLA* 84 (1969) pp. 282–290.

Hurley, Kelly, *The Gothic Body: Sexuality, Materialism and Degeneration at the fin-de-siècle* (Cambridge, MA: Cambridge University Press, 1996).

Irwin, John T., *American Hieroglyphics* (New Haven, CT: Yale University Press, 1980).

Jackson, Rosemary, *Fantasy: The Literature of Subversion* (London: Methuen, 1981).

Jaffe, Nora and Patricia L. Skarda, eds., *The Evil image: Two Centuries of Gothic Short Fiction and Poetry* (New York: New American Library, 1981).

Jameson, Fredric, *The Political Unconscious* (London: Methuen, 1981).

Kahane, Claire, "The Gothic Mirror," in *The (M)other Tongue: Essays in Feminist Psychoanalytical Interpretation*, Shirley Nelson Garner, Claire Kahan, and Madelon Sprengnether, eds. (Ithaca, NY: Cornell University Press, 1985).

Kerr, Howard, John W. Crowley, and Charles Crow, eds., *The Haunted Dusk: American Supernatural Fiction, 1820–1920* (Athens: The University of Georgia Press, 1983).

Kilgour, Maggie, *The Rise of the Gothic Novel* (London: Routledge, 1995).

King, Nicola, *Memory, Narrative, Identity: Remembering The Self* (Edinburgh: Edinburgh University Press, 2000).

Kolodny, Annette, "A Map for Rereading," in *The New Feminist Criticism*, Elaine Showalter, ed. (London: Virago, 1986).

Kovacs, Lee, *The Haunted Screen: Ghosts in Literature and Film* (Jefferson, NC: McFarland, 1999).

Kristeva, Julia, *Powers of Horror: An Essay on Abjection*, Leon S. Roudiez, trans. (New York: Columbia University Press, 1982).

Lawrence, D. H., *Studies in Classic American Literature*, 1923 (New York: Viking, 1964).

Levin, Harry, *The Power of Blackness* (New York: Vintage, 1958).

Lévy, Maurice, "Gothic and the Critical Idiom," in *Gothick: Origins and Innovations*, Allan Lloyd-Smith and Victor Sage, eds. (Amsterdam: Editions Costerus-Rodopi, 1994).

Lloyd-Smith, Allan, "Hawthorne's Gothic Tales," in *Critical Essays on Hawthorne's Short Stories*, Albert J. von Frank, ed. (Boston: Hall and Co, 1991).

———, "The Phantoms of *Drood* and *Rebecca*: The Uncanny Reencountered through Abraham and Torok's 'Cryptonomy'," *Poetics Today* 13:2 (Summer 1992).

————, "This Thing of Darkness: Race in Mary Shelley's *Frankenstein*," (*Gothic Studies* forthcoming 2004).

————, *Uncanny American Fiction: Medusa's Face* (Basingstoke, England: Macmillan, 1989).

————, "A Word Kept Back in *The Turn of the Screw*," *Victorian Literature and Culture* 24 (1998).

Lloyd-Smith, Allan and Victor Sage, eds. *Gothick: Origins and Innovations* (Amsterdam: Editions Costerus-Rodopi, 1994).

Lovecraft. H. P., *Supernatural Horror in Literature* (New York: Dover, 1973).

MacAndrew, Elizabeth, *The Gothic Tradition in Fiction* (New York: Columbia University Press, 1979).

Magistrale, Tony, *Landscape of Fear: Stephen King's American Gothic* (Bowling Green, OH: Popular, 1988).

Magistrale, Tony and Sidney Poger, *Poe's Children: Connections between Tales of Terror and Detection* (New York: Peter Lang, 1999).

Malchow, H. L. *Gothic Images of Race in Nineteenth Century Britain* (Stanford, CA: Stanford University Press, 1996).

————, "The Half-Breed as Gothic Unnatural" in *The Victorians and Race*, Shearer West, ed. (Aldershot, England: Scolar Press, 1996).

Malin, Irving, *New American Gothic* (Carbondale, IL: Southern Illinois University Press, 1962).

Martin, Robert K. and Eric Savoy, eds., *American Gothic: New Interventions in a National Narrative* (Iowa City: University of Iowa Press, 1998).

Martin, Terence, *The Instructed Vision: Scottish Common Sense Philosophy and the Origins of American Fiction* (Bloomington: Indiana University Press, 1961).

Massé, Michelle A., *In the Name of Love: Women, Masochism and the Gothic* (Ithaca, NY: Cornell University Press, 1992).

Meindl, Dieter, *American Fiction and the Metaphysics of the Grotesque* (Columbia: University of Missouri Press, 1996).

Messent, Peter B., ed., *Literature of the Occult; A Collection of Critical Essays* (Englewood Cliffs, NJ: Prentice-Hall, 1981).

Mighal, Robert, *A Geography of Victorian Gothic Fiction: Mapping History's Nightmares* (Oxford: Oxford University Press, 1999).

Milbank, Alison, *Daughters of the House: Modes of the Gothic in Victorian Fiction* (Basingstoke, England: Macmillan, 1992).

Miles, Robert, "'Tranced Griefs': Melville's *Pierre* and the Origins of the Gothic," *ELH* 66:1 (Spring 1999) pp.157–177.

Miles, Robert, *Gothic Writing 1750–1820: A Genealogy* (London: Routledge, 1993).

Mogen, David, Scott P. Sanders, and Joanne B. Karpinski, eds., *Frontier Gothic: Terror and Wonder at the Frontier in American Literature* (London and Toronto: Associated University Presses, 1993).

Morretti, Franco, *Signs Taken for Wonders* (London: Verso, 1983).

Morrison, Toni, *Playing in the Dark: Whiteness and the Literary Imagination* (Cambridge, MA: Harvard University Press, 1992).

Mulvey-Roberts, Marie, ed., *The Handbook to Gothic Literature* (Basingstoke, England: Macmillan, 1998).

Mussell, Kay, *Women's Gothic and Romantic Fiction: A Reference Guide* (Westport, CT: Greenwood Press, 1981).

Napier, Elizabeth R., *The Failure of Gothic: Problems of Disjunction in an Eighteenth-Century Literary Form* (Oxford: Clarendon Press, 1987).

Palmer, Paulina, *Lesbian Gothic: Transgressive Fictions* (London: Cassell, 1999).

Penzoldt, Peter, *The Supernatural in Fiction* (London: Peter Nevill, 1952).

Punter, David, *Gothic Pathologies: The Text, The Body, and the Law* (Basingstoke, England: Macmillan, 1998).

————, *The Literature of Terror: A History of Gothic Fictions from 1765 to the Present Day* (London: Longman, 1980) and Volume 2, *The Modern Gothic* (London: Longman, 1996).

Punter, David, ed., *A Companion to the Gothic* (Oxford and Malden, MA: Blackwell, 2000).

Punter, David and Glennis Byron, *The Gothic* (Oxford: Blackwells, 2004).

Putzel, Max, "What Is Gothic About *Absalom! Absalom!*" *Southern Literary Journal* 4:1 (1971) pp. 3–19.

Radcliffe, Elsa J., *Gothic Novels of the Twentieth Century: an Annotated Bibliography* (Metuchen, NJ: Scarecrow Press, 1979).

Railo, Eino, *The Haunted Castle: A Study of the Elements of English Romanticism* (London: George Routledge and Sons, 1927).

Rank, Otto, *The Double: A Psychoanalytic Study,* 1914, Harry Tucker, Jr., trans. (Chapel Hill: University of North Carolina Press, 1971).

Rashkin, Esther, "Tools for a New Psychoanalytic Literary Criticism" *Diacritics* 18:4 (1988) pp. 31–52.

Reynolds, David S., *Beneath the American Renaissance: The Subversive Imagination in the Age of Emerson and Whitman* (Cambridge, MA: Harvard University Press, 1989).

Ringe, Donald, *American Gothic: Imagination & Reason in Nineteenth-Century Fiction* (Lexington: University Press of Kentucky, 1982).

Ringel, Faye, *New England's Gothic: History and Folklore of the Supernatural from the Seventeenth through the Twentieth Centuries* (Lewiston, NY: E. Mellen Press, 1995).

Royle, Nicholas, *Telepathy and Literature: Essays on the Reading Mind* (Oxford: Blackwell, 1991).

———, *The Uncanny* (Manchester, England: Manchester University Press, 2003).

Sage, Victor, *Horror Fiction in the Protestant Tradition* (London: Macmillan, 1988).

Sage, Victor, ed., *The Gothic Novel: A Casebook* (London: Macmillan, 1990).

Sage, Victor and Allan Lloyd-Smith, eds., *Modern Gothic: A Reader* (Manchester, England: Manchester University Press, 1996).

Savoy, Eric, "The Rise of American Gothic," in *Cambridge Companion to Gothic Fiction*, Jerrold Hogle, ed. (Cambridge, MA: Cambridge University Press, 2002).

————, "Spectres of Abjection: The Queer Subject of James's 'The Jolly Corner,'" in *Spectral Readings: Towards a Gothic Geography*, Glennis Byron and David Punter, eds. (London: Macmillan, 1999).

Scarborough, Dorothy, *The Supernatural in Modern Fiction* (New York: Putnam, 1917).

Schmitt, Cannon, *Alien Nation: Nineteenth-Century Gothic Fictions and English Nationality* (Philadelphia: University of Pennsylvania Press, 1997).

Sedgwick, Eve Kosovsky, *The Coherence of Gothic Conventions*, 1980 (London: Methuen, 1986).

————, *Epistemology of the Closet* (London: Harvester Wheatsheaf, 1991).

Senior, John, *The Way Down and Out: Occultism in Symbolist Literature* (Ithaca, NY: Cornell University Press, 1959).

Shetty, Nalini V., "Melville's Use of the Gothic Tradition," in *Studies in American Literature: Essays in Honour of William Mulder*, Jagdish Chander and Narindar S. Pradhan, eds. (Delhi: Oxford University Press, 1976) pp. 144–153.

Showalter, Elaine, *Sexual Anarchy* (London: Virago, 1992).

Smith, Andrew, Diane Mason, and William Hughes, eds., *Fictions of Unease: The Gothic from Otranto to The X-Files* (Bath, England: Sulis Press, 2002).

Stein, William B., "Bierce's 'The Death of Halpin Frayser': The Poetics of Gothic Consciousness," *ESQ: A Journal of the American Renaissance* 67 (1972).

Sundquist, Eric, *To Wake the Nations: Race in the Making of American Literature* (Cambridge, MA and London: Harvard University Press, 1993).

Thompson, G. R., *Poe's Fiction: Romantic Irony in the Gothic Tales* (Madison, WI: University of Wisconsin Press, 1973)

Thompson, G. R., ed., *Romantic Gothic Tales, 1790–1840* (New York: Harper and Row, 1979).

Todorov, Tzvetan, *The Fantastic* (Ithaca, NY: Cornell University Press, 1975).

Tomkins, Jane, *Sensational Designs: The Cultural Work of American Fiction 1790–1860* (New York: Oxford University Press, 1985).

Varma, Devendra, *The Gothic Flame* (London: A. Barker, 1957).

Veeder, William, *Mary Shelley and Frankenstein: The Fate of Androgeny* (London and Chicago: University of Chicago Press, 1986).

Velie, Alan R., "Gerald Vizenor's Indian Gothic," *MELUS: The Journal of the Society for the Study of the Multi-Ethnic Literature of the United States* 17:1 (Spring 1991–1992) pp. 75–85.

Vinson, James, ed., *Twentieth-century Romance and Gothic Writers* (Detroit, MI: Gale Research, 1982).

Voller, Jack, *The Supernatural Sublime: The Metaphysics of Terror in Anglo-American Romanticism* (DeKalb: Northern Illinois University Press, 1994).

Walker, Ian, "The 'Legitimate Sources' of Terror in 'The Fall of the House of Usher'," *Modern Language Review* 61 (October 1966) pp. 585–592.

Wardrop, Daneen, *Emily Dickinson's Gothic: Goblin with a Gauge* (Iowa City: University of Iowa Press, 1996).

Watt, James, *Contesting the Gothic: Fiction, Genre and Cultural Conflict 1764–1832* (Cambridge, MA: Cambridge University Press, 1999).

Weber, Samuel, "The Sideshow, or: Remarks on a Canny Moment," *Modern Language Notes* 88 (1973) pp. 1102–1133.

Weinstock, Jeffrey Andrew, ed., *Special America: Phantoms and the National Imagination* (Madison: University of Wisconsin Press, 2004).

Weissberg, Liliane, "Gothic Spaces: The Political Aesthetics of Toni Morrison's *Beloved*," in *Modern Gothic: A Reader*, Victor Sage and Allan Lloyd-Smith, eds. (Manchester, England: Manchester University Press, 1996).

Wilczynski, Marek, *The Phantom and the Abyss: The Gothic Fiction in America and Aesthetics of the Sublime 1798–1856* (Frankfurt and New York: Peter Lang, 1999).

Williams, Anne, *Art of Darkness: A Poetics of Gothic* (Chicago: University of Chicago Press, 1999).

Winter, Kari J., *Subjects of Slavery, Agents of Change: Women and Power in Gothic Novels and Slave Narratives, 1790–1865* (Athens: University of Georgia Press, 1992).

Wolfreys, Julian, *Victorian Hauntings: Spectrality, Gothic, The Uncanny and Literature* (Basingstoke, England and New York: Palgrave, 2002).

Wolstenholme, Susan, *Gothic (Re)Visions: Writing Women as Readers* (Albany: State University of New York Press, 1993).

Žižek, Slavoj, *Looking Awry: An Introduction to Jacques Lacan through Popular Culture 1991* (Cambridge, MA: MIT Press, 2002).

Index

green
press
INITIATIVE

Continuum Publishing is committed to preserving ancient forests and natural resources. We have elected to print this title on 30% postconsumer waste recycled paper. As a result, this book has saved:

3.5 trees

164 lbs of solid waste

1,489 gallons of water

2.5 kw hours of electricity

323 lbs of air pollution

Continuum is a member of Green Press Initiative, a nonprofit program dedicated to supporting publishers in their efforts to reduce their use of fiber obtained from endangered forests. For more information, go to www.greenpressinitiative.org.